THE MARRIAGE CHECKUP

THE MARRIAGE CHECKUP

A Scientific Program for Sustaining and Strengthening Marital Health

JAMES V. CÓRDOVA

JASON ARONSON
Lanham • Boulder • New York • Toronto • Plymouth, UK

Published in the United States of America
by Jason Aronson
An imprint of Rowman & Littlefield Publishers, Inc.

A wholly owned subsidiary of
The Rowman & Littlefield Publishing Group, Inc.
4501 Forbes Boulevard, Suite 200, Lanham, Maryland 20706
www.rowmanlittlefield.com

Estover Road
Plymouth PL6 7PY
United Kingdom

British Library Cataloguing in Publication Information Available

Library of Congress Cataloging-in-Publication Data

Córdova, James V., 1966–
The marriage checkup : a scientific program for sustaining and strengthening marital health / James V. Córdova.
p. cm.
Includes bibliographical references and index.
ISBN 978-0-7657-0639-3 (cloth : alk. paper) — ISBN: 978-0-7657-0639-3 (electronic : alk. paper)
1. Marriage. I. Title.
HQ734.C86513 2009
646.7'8—dc22 2008048285

Printed in the United States of America

∞™ The paper used in this publication meets the minimum requirements of American National Standard for Information Sciences—Permanence of Paper for Printed Library Materials, ANSI/NISO Z39.48-1992.

For Cindy, Ariana, and Sammy

CONTENTS

INTRODUCTION ix

1 INTIMACY: STRENGTH IN VULNERABILITY 1

2 EMOTION SKILLS IN MARRIAGE: PRACTICING EMOTIONAL GRACE 23

3 COMMUNICATION: HEALTHY MISCOMMUNICATION 45

4 MINDFULNESS: LEARNING TO LOVE IN THE MOMENT 73

5 ACCEPTANCE: GOD GRANT ME THE SERENITY 93

6 FORGIVENESS AND REPAIR: GRACE, GENEROSITY, AND COMPASSION 111

7 TEAM SPIRIT: MARRIAGE AS A SPIRITUAL JOURNEY 135

8 SEXUAL AUTHENTICITY: SHARING THE SACRED 149

9 MONEY: SPENDERS, SAVERS, AND THE DELICATE BALANCE 183

10 COPARENTING: COMRADES IN ARMS 201

11 AND THE COURAGE TO CHANGE: PROBLEM SOLVING AND CHANGE 227

12 ATTACHMENT STYLES: ESTABLISHING A SECURE BASE 245

BIBLIOGRAPHY 265

INDEX 271

ABOUT THE AUTHOR 273

INTRODUCTION

Marital Health, Physical Health, and Happiness

The point of this book is to help us all regularly attend to strengthening and maintaining the health of our marriages. Very few of us think of our marital relationship in terms of its "health," in the same way that we think of our physical health. We hear a lot about how to maintain and improve our physical health, but relatively little about how to maintain and improve our marital health. We usually think of our relationships, if we think of them at all, in terms of happiness and satisfaction, rather than in the much more serious and substantial terms of health and well-being. We easily recognize the central importance of our health as the foundation upon which all the other aspects of our lives are built. However we usually think of marriage in terms of "happiness," which we tend to regard as a state which is nice when you can achieve it, but not central to the quality of every other aspect of our lives. In other words, we see physical health as vitally important to all aspects of our lives, and marital happiness as maybe just a romantic ideal. However, scientific research over the course of the last several decades has found that the health and strength of our marriages is at least as important, if not more important than our physical health in terms of its impact on all the other aspects of our lives. This is an important point and the central point of this book; so let me make it again. Substantial scientific research has found that marital health is inextricably connected to all the other areas of your life including your physical health, mental health, the health of your children, the quality of your work life, and your satisfaction with life in general.

Your marital relationship, just like your physical body, can be healthy and resilient or sickly and vulnerable. Studies have shown that exactly like your physical health, your marriage needs proper care and attention to be healthy and that the right type of care and attention can make your marriage even healthier, more vibrant, and more resilient to "the slings and arrows of outrageous fortune." Like a strong, healthy body, a strong healthy marriage grants us greater happiness, a greater sense of security, a clearer mind, and allows us to meet all of life's challenges more effectively and with a greater sense of well-being. Also exactly like our own physical health, if we neglect our marital health, and fail to provide it with proper care and feeding, or actively harm it, then our marital relationship will become weak, painful, and susceptible to injury and illness.

Not only can we think of marital health as directly akin to physical health in its need for proper care and its ability to be greatly strengthened, but a great deal of scientific evidence has shown us that our marital health actually directly affects our physical health and our mental health (or our capacity to be happy, smart, and creative). For example, studies have shown that people in healthy marriages are significantly more physically healthy and less likely to get sick than people in unhappy marriages. In fact, research has shown that when we have taken proper care of our marriages to make and keep them healthy, we are not only less likely to catch common ailments such as the common cold and the flu, but are also less likely to suffer from serious illnesses such as heart disease. Some of the most interesting scientific work done in the field of relationship science has shown that people in healthier marriages have stronger, more powerfully responsive immune systems that respond more quickly and effectively to the viruses and bacteria that can make us sick.

Scientific research has also shown us that the healthiness of our marriages strongly affects our general mental health. People in healthy marriages are up to ten times less likely to experience depression (often thought of as the common cold of mental health), than people in less healthy marriages. People in healthy marriages are also less likely to suffer from alcoholism, anxiety, and worry than people in unhealthy marriages. So, health begets health. The healthier and stronger we can make our marital relationships, the healthier and stronger we are ourselves, both physically and mentally.

Even more importantly, perhaps, the healthier and stronger we make our marriages, the healthier and stronger our children grow. Again, hundreds of scientific studies have shown the powerful influence of marital health on children's health. Children whose parents have a healthy marriage are much less likely to become physically ill from both common and serious illnesses. The children of healthy marriages are also psychologically stronger and more resilient to the challenges of childhood and adolescence. They are less likely to become depressed, to act out destructively, to drink and use drugs, and to act out sexually. Scientific studies have also shown that the children of healthy marriages are generally, simply more successful than the children of unhealthy marriages. Children of healthy marriages do better in school, stay in school longer, and are generally more healthy and successful as adults. Again, health begets health. The healthier we can make our marriages, the healthier both our children and we ourselves are, both in the short run and the long run.

The purpose of this book is to help us all take better advantage of the fact that health begets health. Decades of relationship science have taught us what factors are most important to pay attention to when examining the health of our marriages, as well as which practices are the most effective in terms of sustaining and strengthening the health of our marriages. This book is intended to help you perform a thorough self-examination of the health of your marriage and to determine what you can do to stay healthy and get even healthier. Because I am both a relationship scientist and a marital therapist, this book will address both the art and science of healthy marriage. My hope for this book is that it will help us all take advantage of what the broad area of relationship science has discovered to help us improve the health of our marriages and families and, further, that it will convince us all to regularly attend to our marital health and to regularly engage in those practices that are the "eat right and get plenty of exercise" equivalent for healthy marriages. My belief is that regular attention to our marital health is as important as regular attention to our physical health, and that by responsibly attending to our own marital health, we will all live healthier and happier lives.

1

INTIMACY: STRENGTH IN VULNERABILITY

ASSESSING YOUR RELATIONSHIP HEALTH IN TERMS OF CLOSENESS AND INTIMACY

Although there are several places we might start a thorough relationship checkup, I have chosen closeness and intimacy because I believe that this is (a) the best general indicator of the strength of your relationship, (b) the best early warning indicator (the canary in the coal mine) of deteriorating relationship health, and (c) the essential foundation of strong and resilient marital health.

The following questionnaire (Table 1.1) will help you assess the strength of your own intimate relationship.

The questionnaires in this book are designed to be easy to interpret. Since you are making your own determination about whether each of these items is a strength or weakness in your relationship, simply completing the questionnaire helps you determine which parts of your intimate relationship you can celebrate and which parts you might consider as areas for improvement.

People reporting mostly strengths on these items obviously have the healthiest intimate relationships, those with a moderate number of strengths have fairly healthy intimate relationship, but may be beginning to suffer from neglectful or damaging practices, and those with

Table 1.1. The Intimate Safety Questionnaire

Definitely Something We Need to Improve 1	*Could Use Some Improvement* 2	*Neither a Strength nor Area for Improvement* 3	*Something of a Strength* 4	*Definitely a Strength* 5

_____ 1. When I am with my partner I feel relaxed, like I'm safe and accepted.
_____ 2. I feel comfortable telling my partner things I would not tell anyone else.
_____ 3. I enjoy sharing my successes with my partner.
_____ 4. When I'm upset I can talk to my partner.
_____ 5. I feel secure in our relationship even when my partner tells me I have done something to upset him/her.
_____ 6. I feel comfortable consoling my partner when he/she is upset.
_____ 7. I feel comfortable when my partner initiates sex with me.
_____ 8. I feel comfortable talking to my partner while we are making love.
_____ 10. I feel close to my partner during and after lovemaking.
_____ 11. I enjoy having my partner with me when I am out with friends.

few strengths have intimate relationships in poor health and in need of immediate attention. No matter how you score, there are things you can do to improve and maintain the health of your intimate relationship. The first step toward further strengthening your intimate relationship is to understand how intimacy works.

WHY IS INTIMACY IMPORTANT TO MARITAL HEALTH?

Susan and Bill came to see me because they were afraid. They were afraid that the yawning distance between them was insurmountable and that despite how much they loved and needed each other, their relationship would shatter from the sheer fragility of its being. Although they clung to each other, they were lonely, unknown, and unfulfilled. Their youngest child had been away at college now for just over a year and they quickly discovered that with her went the very basis of their lives together. They were wonderful, in some ways phenomenal, parents together. When they talked about parenting and their shared love for their children, they simply glowed with joy, pride, and affection. This shared journey had been their deepest connection and now it was gone. In its place, despite their love and longing, they found only bits and scraps of shared connection. Although they were proud of each other and loved each other deeply, they were suffering from a profound absence of intimacy.

I introduce Susan and Bill here to begin to tell the story of intimacy. We'll return to their particular story throughout this chapter, but first let's look more closely at intimacy itself. Closeness and intimacy are the best indicators of the strength of your relationship because manifest in your feelings of closeness and intimacy is your sense that you are part of something greater than yourself, that you are whole, acceptable, and made strong through partnership. This sense that we are fully embraced, that we are safe being ourselves, and that we are safe being vulnerable is the linchpin in the secure base that helps us to move confidently and effectively in the world. A healthy sense of intimacy makes us strong, happy, and resilient; a weak sense of intimacy makes us brittle, unnerved, and numb.

WHAT IS INTIMACY?

Although it has been described in many ways, we recognize intimacy most thoroughly as a sense that our vulnerabilities are held safely, accepted, and conscientiously protected by our intimate partner. To the degree that we feel safe being vulnerable, we feel loved, nurtured, and strengthened. This feeling of intimate safety has many positive effects. First, it helps us feel genuinely happy and content, more satisfied with life, and better able to cope with the slings and arrows of fate. Beyond simply feeling better, however, having a sincere intimate partner helps us to *be* stronger and more effective in the world. We are more centered, clearer minded, more creative, harder and smarter working, more resistant to being derailed by adversity, and much better able to recover from the occasional stumble when we have that safe, intimate base to operate from.

Scientific research suggests that those with a greater sense of intimacy are more deeply satisfied with their relationships and more satisfied with their lives in general, having a more pervasive sense that their lives are fulfilling and meaningful. People with a greater sense of intimacy in their relationship also have a greater sense of personal well-being in terms of feelings of self-worth and self-esteem; they feel more connected and less lonely, as couples they tend to argue less frequently and less intensely, they tend to think more positively and fondly of their partners and to be quicker to both forgive and seek forgiveness, they tend to be more sexually satisfied, more resistant to illness and generally healthier.

HOW DOES INTIMACY DEVELOP?

Being Open

Intimacy is created out of two mutually dependent practices. The first practice involves our openness to being unguarded, our willingness to be ourselves unmasked and vulnerable with our partner. In order to feel deeply accepted and safe being vulnerable, we must make ourselves available to being known. We must actively show our partners who we are in all our ongoing complexity, including both what we are comfortable with and what we are uncomfortable with. Sometimes we make ourselves available to being known by simply living our lives in close relation to another caring human being, and by doing so, reveal in unspoken ways who we are, what we care about, what we fear, and how we are both perfect and broken.

We also often make ourselves available to being known by what we say about ourselves and how we talk about our lives. We talk about our day-to-day triumphs and disappointments, we talk about the minor annoyances and the ordinary joys, we talk about our deepest fears and greatest aspirations, we share our hopes and dreams, our fantasies and our nightmares, our sense of shame, loneliness and despair, as well as, our sense of peace, happiness, and love, our experience of both the soul-crushing and the sacred. This first ingredient, this opening of the self, is the emotionally courageous and essential first ingredient of genuine intimacy.

Susan and Bill connected like this around their children, but with their children out of the house, they discovered that they actually shared very little of themselves with each other. They were married straight out of high school, in a very real sense rescuing each other from very emotionally dysfunctional homes. They clung to each other like life rafts and shared a determination to be for their children what their parents never were for them. However, we discovered in working together that they needed each other so desperately that neither of them could risk being themselves with the other. Their deepest fear was that they would lose each other and because of that fear they could not risk the first essential practice of intimacy, being open.

EMBRACING VULNERABILITY

The second, and equally important, practice is our attentive, accepting, warm and embracing response to our partner's vulnerability. As our partners make themselves vulnerable to us and open themselves unprotected from us, we must in turn be wholly available, attentive, and affectionately accepting of that trusting gesture. A necessary quality for nurturing intimacy is kindness. As our partners allow themselves to be vulnerable to us, we must in turn provide a consistently kind and nurturing environment for that vulnerability. While it is true that few of us consistently make a point of being conscientiously kind to our partners across all circumstances, it nevertheless remains a basic truism that our partners will only feel safe being vulnerable with us (the most important sign of true intimacy) to the degree that we make ourselves genuinely safe to be vulnerable around. The most basic ingredient of that safe space is an enduring commitment to kindness. Other ingredients include fondness, compassion, loving-kindness, flexibility, responsiveness, and a pervasive sense that "we are in this together."

In combination, then, intimacy grows out of our courageous willingness to make ourselves unguarded and vulnerable and our compassionate attentiveness and caring for the unguarded vulnerability of the other. If and when this process gets started, it often gathers momentum very quickly. Intimacy develops especially quickly and powerfully at the beginning of our relationships. We reveal bits of our vulnerable selves and respond in warm and caring ways to each other, setting in motion a compelling process by which we are drawn out, making ourselves more and more open and gaining a deep and potent feeling of acceptance and intimacy. This is often a heady and joyous time in a relationship during which we often have a strong sense of literally *falling* in love. The more we risk being open and find that our partner accepts us for that, the more willing and able we are to be open and vulnerable with our partner in the future. This process of intimacy gains a great deal of momentum during the early phase of a relationship leading to ever greater degrees of openness and vulnerability, and an ever greater sense of being accepted, understood, and embraced for who we really are. The ultimate payoff is creation of that secure base where we feel safe being vulnerable and from which we can more courageously and effectively move out into the world.

For Bill and Susan, now that their children were out of the house and they were each beginning to grow in new directions as individuals, they found that that growth scared the hell out of them. They were each desperately afraid that the other one would grow in such a way that he or she simply wouldn't need the other anymore. They were both afraid that growth would mean abandonment. Because of that fear, neither of them could really show up to be compassionately attentive to the other's vulnerability. When either of them revealed in any small way the new person they were becoming, the other would panic or shut down. Intimacy couldn't grow because they had become timid and skittish, but only because they were afraid of disappointing or losing each other.

THERE IS A PRICE OF ADMISSION INTO INTIMACY

Achieving intimacy sounds like it should be easy, doesn't it? However, most of us know that it isn't. There is a price to be paid for admission into a genuinely intimate relationship and that price is openness to being hurt. Because the process of developing intimacy leads us to expose more and more of our vulnerability, we end up standing unguarded before our partner, particularly susceptible to hurt. As is sometimes said, the closer you are to someone, the easier it is to hurt each other. This is an existential truth about intimacy, albeit one that we rarely acknowledge. Around most people, we remain guarded and protect our vulnerable selves with the armor of anonymity, of being unknown and unexposed. However, with our intimate partners, this becomes no longer the case as our desire to be known and accepted leads us to shed our protective inscrutability. As a result, we create a situation in which we consciously lay down our usual protection and make ourselves irreversibly open to being hurt by this one other person. The real price of intimacy is vulnerability and vulnerability makes emotional hurt unavoidable.

Because we are so much more vulnerable with our intimate partners, we are open to being hurt by even the little things our partner does that bump us the wrong way. When our partner is grouchy or distracted or stressed or suffering, he or she may do or say things that hurt us unintentionally, and may even hurt deeply. Not only are we more open to being hurt accidentally, but we are also, necessarily more open to being hurt intentionally. That we are moving around in close emotional proximity to another complicated human being, guarantees that we will accidentally step on each other's emotional toes. On top of that, we all regularly become hurt by, frustrated with, angry with, disappointed in, and made anxious by our intimate partner and respond to those occasions in sometimes deliberately hurtful ways. Although this is common, and perhaps inevitable, the result is particularly painful because we act to intentionally hurt the person that has made themselves most vulnerable to our attacks.

Susan and Bill were growing in different ways and each found the other's growth threatening because of the risk that the other would change so much that the marriage would be left behind. Bill was growing spiritually. He was actively pursuing increasingly profound spiritual experiences and would come home bursting to tell Susan all about them. In response, Susan would panic and shut down, unable to stay engaged and curious in response to Bill's vulnerable expression of spiritual growth. Bill would in turn feel pushed away and abandoned. He would become angry and lash out at her for being "shallow" and for not caring about the things that were most deeply meaningful to him. He would also vent his panic that if she couldn't keep up with his spiritual growth, their relationship would blow away.

Susan, for her part, was beginning to seriously come into her own at work. She had achieved greater and greater responsibility at work and was reveling in her sense of mastery and accomplishment. In turn, she would want to share the joys and struggles with Bill and they would repeat exactly the same pattern, with Bill panicking and urging Susan to take better care of her health (rather than listening openly) and Susan dismissing Bill and settling into a great huff.

YOU ONLY HURT THE ONES YOU LOVE

Many of us tend to believe that as we become more comfortable with our partners we should be able to be more open and free with our anger and that somehow the person who is closest to us should be best able to withstand and cope with our snappishness, irritability, dismissiveness, sarcasm, pettiness, childishness, irrationality, and angry tantrums. In a way, the intimacy process necessarily leads us to believe that this should be true, because the process makes us feel settled, attached, and safe. We often find ourselves believing that since we are comfortable with each other, we shouldn't have to be as careful as we might be with others. However, just the opposite is true. Because our intimate partners are the people who are most openly vulnerable to being hurt by us, we need to be most careful, most kind, most diplomatic, most tender, and most caring with them, particularly when we are upset, whether that upset is about them, or not. In a sense, by consciously and willfully entering into an intimate relationship, we accept adult-level responsibility for caring for and protecting the emotional well-being of this other open and vulnerable human being. If we are not willing or able to accept that responsibility, then in some real sense, we have no business pursuing genuine intimacy. It is akin to desperately wanting a baby and yet not being willing to vigilantly protect that baby from harm. This is another part of the price of admission to intimacy, recognizing and accepting our own personal responsibility to gently hold and protect from harm the vulnerability so graciously and lovingly offered to us by this, our beloved other.

WE ARE ONLY HURT BY THE ONES WE LOVE

The remaining price of intimacy comes in the form of being challenged to accept that we will be occasionally hurt by our intimate partner, usually unintentionally, but sometimes quite on purpose (usually as a reaction to their own hurt). The challenge given this inevitability is to remain open and vulnerable *despite* the occasional hurt. If we can remain open, then intimacy will thrive. If we cannot, then intimacy will wither on the vine. This challenge necessitates that we find ways to gracefully cope with those times when we are hurt such that we (a) do not react aggressively, emotionally harming our partners, ourselves, and our relationship, but instead practice the principle of "first do no harm;" (b) do not withdraw and cut off the roots of intimacy, but instead remain open and in genuine contact with our partners; and (c) communicate our experience effectively with our partners so that hurt might be acknowledged and repaired and so that injuries do not fester and rot.

OCCASIONAL HURT FEELINGS ARE NORMAL

At the same time that we are taking delicate care of our partners' vulnerability, we must also wisely and courageously care for our own vulnerability in order to maintain intimacy over the long run. First, we must recognize that feeling hurt occasionally in an intimate relationship is normal and a sign, in some sense, that we are indeed actively engaged in the process of intimacy. That our partner hurts our feelings from time to time (accidentally or through lashing out in pain or confusion) does not mean that he or she is a bad or hurtful person, malicious, worthy of punishment, deserving of vengeance, or flawed in a way that warrants contempt, but simply means that loving an emotionally complicated human being is unavoidably emotionally challenging. It, further, does not mean that there is anything wrong or broken about the relationship itself. As long as those hurts are managed well and openly communicated in a spirit of generosity so that reassurance and repair can occur, then occasional hurt is the natural price of courageous vulnerability.

When hurt and anger become the most frequent emotions experienced in the relationship, however, far outpacing love, affection, fondness, admiration, and endearment, then it should be clear that the relationship is not well and may need help (more about this later). However, occasional hurts, the odd rough patch, are a normal part of loving and the goal is to respond to such hurts in an open and compassionate way (compassionate to both your partner and yourself).

FIRST DO NO HARM

In addition to recognizing that our suffering the occasional hurt is a normal aspect of intimacy, we must also resolve not to attack or withdraw in reaction to the pain. Many of us respond to being hurt by becoming vengeful and retaliatory ("I'll hurt you back to show you how it feels"), and many of us react to hurt by withdrawing behind protective emotional barriers ("I'll never let you hurt me like that again"). Both of these reactions are powerfully corrosive to a loving relationship. Retaliation essentially cuts off our nose to spite our face. We hurt the one person in the world most easily hurt by us and we hurt ourselves not only by damaging this precious relationship that we have been granted stewardship of, but by coarsening our own character through the willful practice of spite, rather than the healthy practices of compassion and loving-kindness.

REMAIN OPEN

As corrosive as retaliation is, withdrawal may be even more corrosive to a strong marriage. If we think of intimacy as a living organism, then open connection and kind, compassionate understanding, are the essential nutrients, the food and water, required for intimacy to survive and thrive on a day-to-day basis. Withdrawal basically shuts off the food supply, leaving intimacy to die of starvation. Withdrawal blocks the sun and all life in the relationship withers and dies. Relationship research has shown that withdrawal from expressions of vulnerability is even more strongly predictive of marital deterioration than open conflict.

Withdrawal, however, is an understandable reaction to being hurt, and perhaps in small doses it may even be a necessary reaction that allows us to brush ourselves off, take a deep breath, and gather our wits before approaching our partner to reestablish connection. However, chronic, repetitive, and consistent withdrawal not only suffocates the relationship, but it deadens us as well. One cannot simply withdraw some parts of oneself and not others. In other words, when we choose to withdraw, we withdraw completely and lose just that much more contact with the world as a whole. We make ourselves numb through withdrawal, like a mild general anesthesia, gradually draining the world of color and vibrancy. By withdrawing, we not only seem to lessen our exposure to hurt, but we also lessen our exposure to joy and happiness and as a result vastly increase our susceptibility to unhappiness in our relationships and despair in our lives.

If withdrawal becomes about avoiding your partner and avoiding coming to terms with the friction points in your relationship, then it becomes corrosive. If withdrawal is simply to center yourself and clear your head, before resuming full contact and openness, then it serves a healthier function.

COMMUNICATE HURT KINDLY

We are all susceptible to *reacting* to intimate hurt by either retaliating or withdrawing. The key to a successful, healthy, loving long-term marriage may be how we learn to *respond* to intimate hurt instead. One key is to clearly and openly communicate our hurt (or frustration, worry, concern) from a place of openness and mutual compassion. Rather than only reacting to hurt with anger and retaliation, we can also (perhaps sometime later) clearly communicate, in a non-blaming way, our actual experience in a vulnerable and generous way. For example, a common occasion for hurt in intimate relationships involves feeling unappreciated for the work we do and the compromises we make, especially when our partner expresses frustration with us for something that we haven't done or haven't compromised on. Often in this sort of situation we respond to feeling unappreciated by either striking back ("well, you're not perfect either") or by angrily withdrawing ("if you want it done so badly, do it yourself"). If, instead, we neither retaliated nor withdrew, but simply put words on our actual experience, then intimacy may not only be saved from damage, but may actually be strengthened. For example, we might say, "Sometimes when you complain about what I haven't done, I feel unappreciated for the things that I work hard to do." This involves noticing that we're feeling hurt and responding to that hurt by saying something about it, rather than simply reacting to it.

When we react to feeling hurt, we *are* usually trying to communicate our hurt to our partner, but in a way that is self-protective, indirect, and often extremely ineffective. The simplest, most direct, and most intimacy promoting way to let your partner know that you have been hurt is to simply *say it*, as directly and compassionately as possible. Saying, "I'm feeling hurt," "I'm feeling angry," "I'm feeling picked on," "I'm feeling unappreciated," "I'm feeling ignored," "I'm feeling insulted," "I'm feeling lonely," or "I'm feeling worried" is a much more skillful way of responding to the day-to-day hurts that result from true intimacy than reacting either offensively or defensively. It feels risky and vulnerable-making to admit these things out loud, but again that is the first essential step to establishing and nurturing real intimacy and the only way to insure the ultimate payoff of feeling safe and secure being your true self with your partner, and of establishing that solid intimate base from which to draw strength and comfort.

LISTEN GENEROUSLY

Similarly, all of us will hurt our partners at times and will find ourselves listening to our partners' telling us that we have hurt them. This can be a difficult thing to hear and our response is almost always to become defensive. In my own research I have studied couples talking about hurt and it is becoming increasingly clear to me that even in the healthiest of couples our first response to being told that we have done something that has hurt our partner is to become defensive and to deny that we did it, deny that we meant it to be hurtful, or accuse our partner of being too sensitive or of taking us the wrong way. What seems to distinguish the healthiest couples, however, is that after the initial shock of being told that they have done something hurtful, the most responsive partners begin to really hear and acknowledge their partner's hurt and to apologize for that hurt whether they meant to be hurtful or not. For example, this apology and acknowledgement often sounds something like, "Ok, I understand what you're saying. I'm sorry I hurt your feelings. I'll try to be more careful." Notice that this type of statement (a) acknowledges that the other person's hurt is real, (b) apologizes for causing that hurt whether it was purposeful or not, and (c) expresses respect for the person's feelings. This is yet another price to be paid for admission into a healthy intimate relationship, we must be ready, willing, and able to listen deeply and respond compassionately to the hurts that we will inevitably cause our partners. This does not mean that we will not disagree about things, some of which we may never agree upon, but it does mean that we take seriously our responsibility for the loving care of our intimate partners.

RECOMMENDATIONS FOR STRENGTHENING INTIMACY

If we recognize that our relationships, like our physical body, can be fit, trim, strong, and resilient or out of shape, weak, and susceptible to illness and injury, then we are in a better position to engage in everyday practices that can strengthen us and make us healthier. In terms of building strong and healthy intimacy, there are several recommendations that I can make based both on what we know from the research done by relationship scientists and by the work of practitioners deeply involved in working to strengthen couples on a day-to-day basis.

STAY CURIOUS

Constructing an Imaginary Partner

When we first fall in love with our partners, they are mysterious to us and we are drawn to that mystery. On the one hand that mystery makes us curious and pulls us into that wonderful process of getting to know each other. On the other hand, that we don't really know our new partners in all their moods, in all their strengths and weaknesses, in all their perfections and imperfections, allows us to project onto them all of our idealized fantasies, all of our hopes and dreams of perfect love, all of our yearning for unconditional acceptance and our dreams of a partner who is unconditionally acceptable. We often begin to encase the real human being inside an artificial cover constructed from our own imagination. For brief moments, we may catch quick glimpses of the real person, that real human being that exists independent of our imaginations, but often as we grow comfortable that we know our partner inside and out, we lose sight of the real person. Instead we insert between ourselves and our partners a cold, two-dimensional cut-out constructed from what we *think* we know about our partners, from what we have come to assume about who he or she is, from the stories, mostly imagined, that we have come to tell ourselves about this other person. In the process, we lose sight of our actual partner in the here-and-now and form a relationship with an imaginary partner of our own construction. We, in a sense, develop a relationship with ourselves and believe that we are in a relationship with another human being. It is no wonder then that we often find we feel so lonely.

There is a well-researched and natural human tendency to create shorthand, general assumptions about ourselves, the world, and other people. Some scientists argue that we need to use these shorthand assumptions so that we can move around efficiently in the world without being constantly distracted by the complexities within which we are constantly immersed. Although this point is currently being debated (e.g., there is recent evidence that mindful awareness actually makes us more effective than mindlessly assuming), this tendency to quickly form assumptions and then to *form relationships* with those assumptions is particularly pernicious in intimate relationships because it steals our real partners from us in exchange for simplistic, artificial, wholly assumed partners.

This had become the case with Bill and Susan. They each clung desperately to the person the other used to be and feared the implications of the person the other was quickly becoming. As they began to realize how hard they flinched in reaction to each other's growth and how hard they flinched at the other's flinching, they began to be better able to practice staying open and honest with each other.

WE DO NOT KNOW OUR PARTNERS

The key to retaking the richness available in our relationships and continually nurturing intimacy is recognizing a few truisms about intimacy. The first is that no matter how long we have been together, and no matter how much we have learned about each other, we do not *know* our partners. As much as we might think we do know our partners, that "knowing" is just that, a thought, an imagined construction. In truth, what we actually know about our partners is but the smallest thimbleful compared to the ocean of complexity that they really embody. Much more often than not, we have no earthly idea what our partners are thinking. Most of the time we don't even know what we ourselves are thinking, how could we possibly really know what is going on inside our partner's head? Intimacy appears to be best served when we recognize that when we think we know what our partners are thinking, we are in the grip of a strong delusion. When we recognize that we are deluded by our own assumptions, then we wake up to the very real opportunity to connect with this real, flesh-and-blood person standing here with us.

We do not really know our partner's history, not in its full complexity and not as it changes with the new perspectives that our partner constantly brings to it. We do not really know our partner's emotional world. We do not really know our partner's hopes and dreams, aspirations and fears, suffering and joy. We may sometimes make good guesses. We may have had a pretty good idea about some of these things yesterday, and maybe even somewhat today if our intimate relationship is strong and healthy, but we know nothing of who our partner will be tomorrow or even later today. Our partners are constantly changing and have been since the day we first met and they will continue to change every day until the day we will, inevitably, be parted. We do not know in what ways our partners have grown and changed since the day we stopped paying attention. We cannot know in what way our partner will grow and change over the course of today, tomorrow, this week, and this year. And perhaps it is this genuine mystery that actually scares us into the fantasy world in which we live comfortably, if numbly, with the imaginary partner who we have constructed for our own convenience. Maybe we, in part, construct and cling to these fabricated partners to protect ourselves from how scary it seems at first to acknowledge that our partner will forever be a mystery to us and that our future with our partner is utterly unknowable.

It is this un-know-ability that caused Bill and Susan to panic. And it was precisely that anxiety that they slowly learned to better tolerate. For Susan and Bill the oak tree became a powerful metaphor. Like a strong and healthy oak they had to grow to live. Like separate branches, they each grew in unique and independent ways. Although the apparent separateness of that growth could be scary for them, faith in the depth and strength of their shared roots allowed them to better tolerate the somewhat unpredictable quality of continued growth.

OUR PARTNER IS NOT PERMANENT

This leads to the second intimacy promoting truth about our partners. They are not permanent. We will eventually, one way or the other, be separated from each other and we can never know when that evaporation will occur. The healthiest of partnerships are dissolved by disease and death. The less healthy are dissolved by separation and divorce. Regardless, the person you are with today is a temporary and precious gift.

So many of us let our fear, our escape to fantasy, rob us of the astonishing and beautiful gift that is *this* day with this intimate other.

Just these two truisms, that we are constantly and irrevocably changing, and that our time together is short and unpredictable, if truly grasped are enough to allow us to *really* see the riches that are available to us in each moment with our wives and husbands, children and parents, friends and siblings and fellow beings. Truly recognizing these two truths fosters in us the seeds of genuine intimacy: vulnerability, gratitude, affection, courage, compassion, happiness in the joy of others, and curiosity about our partners and ourselves.

Curiosity may be the key to awakening from our tendency to let intimacy go stagnant in our relationship. Curiosity acknowledges that we do not know, but that we want to know our partner, even as she changes. The partner you are curious about today will not be the partner you can be curious about tomorrow. It is by embracing that mystery that we are best able to stand closely with our partners. Truly embracing that not-knowing with curiosity opens up the sacred in the ordinary and can replace despair with wonder. When we embrace that curiosity, we start to pay deliberate attention to our partner again. What does he or she really look like today? What does his or her voice really sound like? How does she move? What makes her happy? What makes him sad? Questions arise that are almost endlessly available to explore. Tell me about your mother? Tell me about your father? What are the values that you hold most dear and how have they changed recently? What has been on your mind lately? There is research evidence to suggest that even simple questions, like "what are you going to do today?" and "Tell me what you did today?" are powerfully intimacy enhancing.

BE A SAFE PLACE

Again, what we are seeking to achieve is a secure sense of being accepted, emotionally close, and safe being vulnerable. Given that, we strive to be generously attentive both to the everyday minutia and to the deeper meanings underlying everyday grumblings. We also strive to be attentive to our responsibility to be kind and warmly accepting of our partner's vulnerabilities.

STRONG VULNERABILITY

One of the best practices for maintaining a strong sense of intimacy in your relationship is to actively strive to make yourself open to being known. Again, this can be as simple as sharing with your partner the little details of your day, from who said what and what you thought about it, to what you had for lunch. One of the leading scholars in the field of relationship science, John Gottman at the University of Washington in Seattle, has found that one notable characteristic of strong relationships is that partners ask about and tell each other about what their day is going to look like, what they'll be doing, what meetings they'll be attending, what projects they'll be working on. Then, at the end of the day, these partners talk again about what actually happened during each other's day. This appears to strengthen intimacy by providing an opportunity to know and be known and by providing a regular opportunity for both partners to be curious about each other and supportive of each other. Sharing and being curious about the mundane details of each others lives may seem too simple, too ordinary to really contribute substantially to a healthy intimate connection, but the truth of the matter appears to be that it is exactly these day-to-day connections around seemingly ordinary things that deeply embeds us in each others lives, that thoroughly interweaves who we are with who our partners are, and that solidifies and strengthens the secure intimate base that we form together. The key here then is to actively and regularly share with your partner the day-to-day goings-on of your life and that the little things matter as much as the big things.

Being open to making ourselves known about the big things is also vitally important and is another exercise for strengthening intimacy that can be of inestimable value to you and your partner. This involves openly and actively sharing with your partner your deepest thoughts, wishes, and beliefs. It involves talking about the things that are most deeply personal and most deeply meaningful. About the things you struggle with and the things you treasure. Topics for these types of conversations can be wide ranging. What life values do you most want to pass on to your children? What is your relationship to the sacred? How do you personally make sense of your place in the world? What do you want your life to stand for? What do you want others to think of you when you're gone? What are the values that you hold most dear? What are the things in life that you fear most? What are your most profound dreams and aspirations? What are the personal weaknesses that you struggle with the most? Sometimes these big questions can be the most revealing about who we are and the direction of our lives. Many times we have no idea how to even answer these questions, but wondering about them out loud with our intimate partners and being openly curious about ourselves with the support of our partner can profoundly strengthen our connection to each other. Sometimes these big questions can seem completely beside the point and that is also completely fine. At the same time, exploring the deeper meanings of our lives with our partners can greatly strengthen our intimate connection.

STRIVE TO FIRST DO NO HARM

Partners often find that of all the people in their lives, they are harshest with each other. We often find that we are most irritable, least polite, most openly cranky or hostile, and least careful with each other. There is something about the process of intimacy that often convinces us that we can "take the gloves off" with our partner, both with regard to ordinary everyday life, and perhaps especially when it comes to actual conflict. Arguments between intimate partners can often be akin to the fights that break out at a hockey game, the gloves fly off and each partner starts swinging wildly. Even during our day-to-day lives, we are often much more likely to be snappish, rude, or dismissive of our intimate partner than we would ever dream of being with anybody else. In fact, oftentimes we are much more polite and forgiving of acquaintances and strangers than we are of our own partners. The same intimacy producing process that can lead us to feel safest and most completely ourselves around our partner also leads us to believe that we do not have to be as careful with our partner as we have to be with other people. Of course, nothing could be further from the truth. Because intimacy makes us most vulnerable to our intimate partners and makes them most vulnerable to us, the truth of the matter is actually that we need to be more careful with our intimate partners than with anybody else. A snappish comment that might be easily brushed off by a mere acquaintance is much more likely to be deeply hurtful to someone who has made themselves intimately vulnerable to us. We are ultimately profoundly responsible for the emotional well-being of those people who we have invited into intimate relationship with us and those intimate relationships are best served when we take that responsibility very seriously.

The recommendation therefore is not to take off the gloves, but to put on even cushier gloves, to be even more gentle and respectful and polite, tender and careful with our intimate partner than with anybody else, because we know that of all the people in the world, this one, my intimate partner, is most vulnerable to being hurt by me. I suspect that if we can keep that responsibility and that attitude of caring for the most vulnerable clearly in mind, then we will all naturally find ourselves interacting more effectively and more gracefully with our partners, and that our interactions are much more likely to build and strengthen intimacy than to harm intimacy. If the central principle is to first do no harm, then when we are cranky, stressed, or angry, our first response will be to take care of ourselves and to be mindful of how we most want to communicate that crankiness, stress, and anger so that we are both gentle and open to being known. In much the same way that we wisely manage our emotions when we are caring for very small children, we want to wisely manage our emotions when we are interacting with our intimate partners. Again, in these cases, it is most conducive to the health of our intimate relationships to respond to our strong emotions by talking about them, rather than by only acting them out. It is better to say; I'm feeling cranky, stressed, or angry, than to just act cranky, stressed, or angry. In this way we take seriously our responsibility to care for our intimate partner, as well as our responsibility to care for ourselves and our intimate relationship.

This principle of first do no harm can be applied even in those instances when we are in genuine conflict with our partners. For example, if my partner has been habitually coming home later and later from work and I am beginning to feel lonely and taken advantage of, if I keep in mind how easy it is for me to even inadvertently hurt my partner, then I might be more likely to say something like "I know your work is very important to you and it is important to me too, but I'm starting to feel upset by the amount of time your spending there, and I wish you could find a way to come home a bit earlier more often." Although perhaps less than perfect, this sort of complaint is likely to be much more effective and nurturing to our relationship than saying, "You're a workaholic and care more about your job than you do about me and the kids." If you don't believe me, try it both ways yourself and see which one works better.

In sum, the essence of this point is to always approach your partner keeping in mind how profoundly vulnerable to you he or she is, especially when you are angry, irritable, or hurt.

RECONNECT, REPAIR, AND HEAL

Given that being emotionally close to someone else guarantees that we will hurt each other occasionally, perhaps the best advice for strengthening and maintaining intimacy is to actively and consciously seek to mend and nurture your intimate connection with your partner following times that you have been hurt or have been hurtful, even when that hurtfulness has been accidental, but especially if it has been purposeful. Relationship scientists find that one thing that differentiates happy from unhappy couples is their willingness to approach each other following conflict to seek and give each other reassurance and soothing. In fact, even during conflict, these couples are much more likely to reach across to each other, to touch each other, to smile or joke reassuringly, than are couples who have shredded their intimate connection. Oftentimes, however, because we are hurt, prideful, full of righteous indignation, or feeling punitive we willfully fail to seek a reconnection with our intimate partner following a hurtful incident. These wounds, even small wounds, do not heal properly by themselves. If we do not actively attend to mending the loving connection between ourselves and our partners, those wounds grow infected and fester, sickening our emotional connection and corroding the foundation of our relationship.

The key to this intimacy strengthening practice then is to conscientiously seek repair every time something hurtful happens between you and your intimate partner. Seek to be nurtured and to be warmly nurturing. Seek to forgive and to be forgiven. In fact, these reconciliations often work best when we seek first to nurture and forgive, rather than when we seek first to be nurtured and forgiven. We will discuss forgiveness in more detail in a later chapter.

This ultimately is what saved Susan and Bill from the chasm in their marriage. Bill was able to acknowledge that he had learned to keep his feelings to himself in his family of origin and that he rarely shared himself openly with Susan, even when talking about his spiritual growth. As he became more willing to risk being vulnerable, trusting Susan's ability to stay open herself, and trusting his own ability to tolerate and forgive the occasional disappointment caused by their shared panic, the sense of intimate connection between them began to grow at a healthy and powerfully satisfying pace. Susan also became determined to stay open and engaged with Bill even when she was scared of the unknown, or hurt and disappointed by their sometimes fumbling attempts to connect. Embracing their vulnerability, falling down in their efforts to stay open and then getting right back up again, and acknowledging their faith in the deep roots of their marriage, connected Susan and Bill in the most human and heartfelt of ways. They smiled more. They laughed more easily. Their work with me was done.

HOW CAN I TELL WHEN IT MIGHT BE TIME TO HIRE A THERAPIST OR RELATIONSHIP COACH?

Intimacy can be thought of as the canary in the coal mine of strong marriages. If you find yourself consistently feeling more emotionally unsafe than safe with your partner for more than six months, and your active efforts to be loving, open, careful, forgiving, and reassuring have not shifted the momentum of the relationship toward greater intimacy, then that is a very good sign that you might need to hire a good couple therapist. We will discuss in much more detail the ins and outs of hiring a good couple therapist or coach in a later chapter.

2

EMOTION SKILLS IN MARRIAGE: PRACTICING EMOTIONAL GRACE

Marriage and intimacy are emotionally complex and that emotional complexity is always present. At any given moment both you and your partner are experiencing some kind of emotion; about each other, about life, or about nothing in particular. Emotion researchers tell us that we are always experiencing emotion at some level. The emotion may be strong enough to grab your attention or it might be so subtle that you hardly notice it. Similarly, that emotion might be positive and welcome or negative and unwelcome.

Many emotion researchers say our constantly fluctuating emotional experience can be thought of as occurring along two dimensions. One dimension goes from positive to negative and the other goes from high intensity to low intensity. High intensity negative emotions would include rage and grief. High intensity positive emotions would include joy and ecstasy. Low intensity negative emotions would include mild disappointment and sadness. Low intensity positive emotions would include feelings of contentment and peacefulness. The main point being that, whether we are aware of it or not, we are always emotionally engaged in our lives.

Given that, our intimate relationships are probably the principal arena within which we live out our emotional lives. Intimate relationships are inherently emotionally complex and we all grapple with the emotional ups and downs of being in complicated adult relationships. We experience our entire emotional palette within our intimate relationships. Even those emotional experiences that are not specifically about our relationships are lived out in relation to our intimate partner. At times, our relationships make us feel happy, content, joyous, and loving. At other times, our relationships make us feel sad, angry, embarrassed, anxious, and lonely. Over the course of our lives we will also experience grief, worry, anger, joy, and pride about things completely outside our relationship, like our jobs, extended families, and friendships, and we will experience and express those emotions within our relationships. When someone close to you dies, you express your grief within your relationship and your partner grieves with you. When your boss treats you unfairly, you are still angry when you get home and your partner experiences your anger with you, whether you know it or not. Because of the nature of intimacy and closeness, it is within our marriages that we experience the largest part of our emotional lives, and of all the domains of life, marriage and family are often the most consistently emotionally challenging.

Because intimacy is an inherently emotional process and because we are always living our emotional lives out loud (even when we are hiding or denying those emotions), how we live our emotions plays a powerful role in how strong and healthy our marriages are. In this chapter, we'll refer to how we live out our emotions as our "emotion skills." Our emotion skills consist of the variety of ways that we have learned how to understand and express our constantly varying emotional experiences. Consider for example the fact that we all experience emotional hurt from time to time during our lives. No one gets to be in a deeply loving relationship without getting his or her feelings hurt on occasion. It is part of the price of admission to true intimacy. However, not everyone enacts their experience of hurt in the exactly the same way. Some people act out their hurt by withdrawing into themselves, getting quiet and maybe showing some subtle signs of sadness. Others act out their hurt by hiding it and putting on their best "no problem" or "whatever" face. Other people act out their hurt by becoming angry and confrontational or angry and withdrawn. Still others act out their hurt by crying or by talking about their hurt feelings with their partner or friends. The point is that the same emotion can be acted out in many different ways and the ways that we have learned to act out our feelings are learned over the course of our entire lives.

An important implication of this is that how a person acts out an emotion may or may not tell us about their underlying emotional experience. Sometimes hurt is acted out as anger. Sometimes anger is acted out as sadness. Sometimes loneliness is acted out as dismissiveness. We are all responding to each other with the same basic set of emotions, but we all act out those emotions in our own unique ways, learned over our own unique lives.

What matters most to the health of our marriages is that some emotional expressions are better for our long-term marital health than others. For example, acting out hurt as vindictive anger or icy withdrawal has been shown to be toxic to marital health. On the other hand, acting out hurt through genuine self-disclosure or clear, assertive communication has been shown to improve intimacy and a sense of emotional connection. Again, the basic emotional experience is the same, but the way that emotional experience is acted out has a significant effect on our marital health.

So, in this chapter, when I use the term emotion skills, I am talking simultaneously about two things. First, I am referring to the fact that in addition to having an emotional experience (like hurt), we also *act out* that emotional experience (for example, by pretending that we aren't hurt). Second, I am referring to the fact that some ways of enacting an emotion are healthy for your marriage (e.g., clearly identifying and communicating that emotion) and other ways of enacting an emotion are destructive to your marital health (e.g., withdrawal and avoidance).

LEARNING EMOTION SKILLS

We learn our emotion skills over the course of our entire lives. Most likely, the largest part of what we learn about how to experience and express our emotions is learned from our family while we are growing up. For example, some families are generally more stoic and emotionally inexpressive compared to other families who are more emotionally expressive and demonstrative. We also learn a great deal about what is appropriate and inappropriate in terms of emotional expression from our culture and community. Some of us learn a way of doing anger that is open and brief. Others learn a way of doing anger that is hidden and slow burning. In many respects, we learn how to do our emotions by watching the people around us and learning to do what they do. For example, it is likely that you enact sadness in a way that is very similar to at least one of your parents.

In other ways we learn how to do our emotions based on what we were punished or rewarded for. We might have been punished or mocked for open displays of sadness, but reinforced for aggressive displays of anger. The point is that we have essentially *inherited* our emotion skills and bring that inheritance into our marriages regardless of whether they are healthy or not. Unfortunately, we are usually completely blind to the fact that we are acting out an emotional repertoire that we learned at home (or on the street) and that may or may not be good for our marriage and family.

An example of this involves a couple I saw recently with two very different ways of experiencing and expressing anger. During therapy, it became clear that one of the main things they suffered from was a difference in their anger styles. He expressed anger easily, was quick to show anger and just as quick to let it go and move on. She, on the other hand, rarely showed her own anger and when she did show her anger she experienced it as deeply embarrassing. She felt in the aftermath of their angry arguments a profound sense of shame and humiliation. Consequently, she tried to avoid angry conflict at all costs. When such conflict occurred, she found herself crying and wondering what had gone so terribly wrong in their marriage. He found her response to conflict utterly baffling and tried hard to convince her that things were fine between them and that they had a good and normal marriage. He was particularly distraught because she had begun talking about leaving him and moving back to be closer to her extended family. For him, her desire to leave seemed to come completely out of left field and they presented desperately wanting to figure out how to keep their marriage together.

One of the first important lessons that we learned in our therapy together was just how different their life lessons about anger and conflict had been. He recalled a family life in which conflict was common, open, often loud, and involving few if any long-term negative consequences. For him, overt expressions of anger were normal and completely nonthreatening. He had learned over the course of his life that overt expressions of anger were, for the most part, "no big deal." In his family, they got mad at each other, expressed that anger passionately and then dropped it and moved quickly back into normal day-to-day interactions. Thus, in his marriage, without thinking about it at all, he naturally expected that his way of enacting anger was the way everyone enacted anger, that it was normal and expected, and essentially no big deal. This is why he found himself completely flummoxed by his wife's devastated response to his anger.

In contrast, she recalled a family history that involved virtually no overt displays of anger between her parents. Her memory was that her father would come home at the end of the day, kiss his wife and tell her he loved her, and then they would all sit down to a family dinner characterized by stability and warmth. By way of demonstrating the virtually complete absence of angry expression in her family home, she recalled an incident in which one day her father came home and simply said "Hi" to his wife, but did not kiss her and tell her loved her. That night she remembered that she and her siblings were very worried about their parent's relationship because it was the first time any of them could recall that their father hadn't kissed their mother warmly when he returned from work. She recalled learning that open displays of anger were shameful and uncivilized. Anger, if expressed at all, was to be discussed coolly and rationally. In a well functioning and presentable marriage, partners simply did not ever raise their voice to each other, particularly in front of the children.

In short, although both of these partners experienced anger in the context of their marriage, what each had learned about how to express that anger was very different. As they came to see this difference between them, they found they were better able to experience anger in their relationship in ways that allowed for their basic differences, rather than in ways that created emotional confusion and chronic emotional pain. He was better able to modulate his expression of anger in deference to how unnerving his anger could be to her. She in turn found herself better able to tolerate non-hostile expressions of anger, both her own and his, with less experience of shame and self-loathing. This not only allowed them to get to know each other better, but to become better friends and more intimate partners. Although the basic difference between the two of them did not go away (nor was it ever likely to), they found that a greater understanding of that difference helped them both to cope with this sensitive area of their marriage with more compassion and grace.

The main point of this chapter is to help each of us begin to think about and see our emotional repertoire more clearly and get a sense for whether that repertoire is helpful or hurtful to our marriages. To the degree that we can each see from the other's perspective what we have learned about how to do our emotions, we will each be in a better position to make wise choices about how to express our emotions in maritally healthy ways.

This chapter is also intended to help you assess the quality of your own emotion skills and provide guidelines for practicing greater emotional skillfulness. The take home message is that intimacy is emotionally challenging and is the main arena for partners' emotional experiencing as adults. The full range of emotions can be enacted in ways that are either conducive to relationship health or destructive to relationship health. Your self-assessment will show you which end of the spectrum you tend to fall on and the chapter will provide you with research and theory-based guidelines for practicing relationship healthy emotional expression.

Table 2.1. The Emotion Skills Questionnaire

Definitely Something We Need to Improve 1	*Could Use Some Improvement* 2	*Neither a Strength nor Area for Improvement* 3	*Something of a Strength* 4	*Definitely a Strength* 5

_____ 1. We understand our different emotion styles (e.g., how we do anger differently).
_____ 2. I have a good sense of how I have learned how to act out my basic emotions like hurt, anger, sadness, affection, and love.
_____ 3. I have a good sense of how my partner has learned how to act out his or her basic emotions like hurt, anger, sadness, affection, and love.
_____ 4. I express my emotions in maritally healthy ways.
_____ 5. My partner expresses his or her emotions maritally healthy ways.
_____ 6. I let my partner know when she or he has hurt my feelings in a gentle and assertive manner.
_____ 7. I communicate my anger with my partner in an open, respectful, and assertive manner.
_____ 8. I do not express my anger in a hostile or disrespectful way with my partner.
_____ 9. I know a lot about what makes my partner happy.
_____ 10. I regularly do things that make my partner feel loved.
_____ 11. I make sure my partner feels loved every day.
_____ 12. I pay attention to the things that my partner cares about.

LEARNING HOW TO "DO" EMOTIONS

In the beginning, we are born into an unknown stew of emotions that can be overwhelming. At this stage, babies may be closest to the truth about basic emotional experiencing because they experience only that they are broadly happy or content or that they are broadly unhappy or distressed. Parents often spend a lot of time trying to figure out exactly what their baby is feeling. We can tell when a baby is clearly upset, but it isn't always exactly obvious whether he or she is hungry, tired, scared, lonely, uncomfortable, itchy, sick, or angry. And the truth of the matter is, the baby doesn't know either. All she knows is that she doesn't feel right and she counts on her parents to figure out how to make it better.

This is where we all start, a purely undifferentiated mass of emotional experience spanning the range from pleasant to unpleasant and from low intensity to high intensity. It is at this point that the people around us begin to teach us, through their own words and actions, how to stand in relation to our emotions. Our family and community teach us which emotional experiences to pay attention to and which ones to ignore. They teach us which ones they consider important and which ones they consider trivial. They teach us which of our experiences to even label as "emotion" and what words to use to describe those experiences. Do we call that emotion we experience when our brother takes our teddy bear "anger," "frustration," "irritation," "sadness," or "hurt"?

Our family also teaches us which emotions we should consider "good" and which ones we should consider bad or even shameful. And these lessons vary from family to family. For example, in some families feeling proud is regarded as a "good" feeling and something that you should work to earn. In other families, expressing pride is considered "bad" and something you should work to avoid in favor of a "better" emotion like humility.

This process of learning about emotions from our families is talked about in the research literature (for example by Professor John Gottman of the University of Washington) as "emotion coaching" and the results are talked about by other researchers (such as Dr. Carolyn Saarni of Sonoma State University) in terms of "emotional competence." Emotion coaching refers to what your family taught you about emotions. And keep in mind that they might not have taught those lessons on purpose, with plans and goals and a well thought out and coherent philosophy about emotions. In fact, more often than not, parents simply pass on some version of the lessons that they themselves learned about their own emotions.

Emotional competence, like emotion skills, refers to whether what you learned about emotions served you well in your life as a child. Did those lessons help you cope with strong emotions in mentally, physically, and relationally healthy ways? Or, did those lessons make it more difficult to cope with strong emotions in healthy ways? For example, when other children teased you, how did you learn to deal with your emotional reaction? Did your response have positive or negative consequences for your relationships with your classmates?

What I most want you take away from this section is the idea that emotions are, in and of themselves, neither good nor bad. What we have learned about emotions we can regard as tools from which we can consciously pick in the service of living a healthy and meaningful life. The point is not to "blame your parents" or necessarily to give your parents credit. It is to see your inherited understanding of emotion from a perspective that will give you greater freedom to relate to your emotional experience with wisdom and compassion.

EMOTIONALLY SKILLFUL HURT

So, we are always experiencing some flavor of emotions, we always act out some learned repertoire about how to experience, regard, and enact that emotional experience, and some of what we have learned is good for our health and some isn't. Now we can begin to carefully examine the lessons we've learned to see where we might want to practice healthier habits.

Let's begin by considering more closely the emotion of hurt. Because of the connection between intimacy and vulnerability, hurt may be among the most common negative emotions experienced in intimate relationships. Consider what you have learned about hurt (for example, is it normal or a sign or weakness) and what you have learned about how to act when you are feeling hurt. Some of us learn that it is okay and normal to occasionally have hurt feelings, so we grow up feeling no particular inner conflict about feeling hurt. Others of us learn that feeling hurt is for babies or weaklings, that feeling hurt is shameful, that strong people don't feel hurt, that a thick skin and letting things "roll off our back" is good, and that "letting" things hurt us or "letting" people "get to" us is pathetic. If we have learned that feeling hurt is shameful and weak, then we grow up having learned to deny an unavoidable feeling, hiding hurt from ourselves and others, and condemning ourselves and others for ever feeling hurt.

In our research laboratory, we often ask partners to think of something their partner does that hurts their feelings. We ask this sort of question to better understand the role of emotion skills in marriage. During this task, I have been repeatedly surprised by how many people, most frequently men, deny any experience of hurt ever caused by their partners. One partner I remember particularly well said, "I just don't let her get to me in that way." What was particularly striking about that statement is that it was made by someone who was newly engaged to be married for the first time, so it wasn't the product of a long history of emotional conflict between them in which he had begun to shut himself off emotionally. This was a product of what he had learned about the normal experience of hurt over the course of his entire life prior to becoming engaged. Being hurt meant you had let someone "get to you" and letting someone get to you was clearly contemptible. The implication, from the perspective of marital health, is that not letting someone "get to you" also means not letting someone get close to you, essentially stunting the growth of intimacy and weakening the foundation of the relationship.

So, on this continuum, what have you learned about how okay it is to feel hurt? Are you closer to the person who has learned that hurt feelings are normal and legitimate or are you closer to the person who has learned that hurt feelings are abnormal, shameful, illegitimate, and weak? Knowing where you fall on this continuum is important because our data suggest that more open and genuine expressions of hurt are better for long-term relationship health than hurt that is either covered up or denied, or hurt that is converted into hostility.

How have you learned to act out your hurt feelings with your partner (and with your children)? Some of us learn to turn hurt directly into anger and then we act out our anger repertoire instead. Others of us learn to hide our hurt completely. We learn to pretend that we haven't been hurt and to push those feelings down, hiding them from both ourselves and our partner. Some of us learn to withdraw when we are hurt, pulling away either physically or emotionally. Maybe we learned to go off by ourselves when we are hurt. Some people learn to withdraw as a way of getting their partner to come after them to try to make them feel better. Others learn to withdraw as a way of hiding a shameful emotion and they stay withdrawn until the feeling goes away. Some of us learn to express hurt feelings as a means of pressing our own advantage or manipulating others into giving us our way. In the best of all possible worlds, however, we learn to openly express feelings of hurt as a way of seeking understanding and repair, as a way of maintaining love and intimacy in a relationship.

Think deeply about how you usually react when your feelings have been hurt. Do you approach? Do you withdraw? Do you hide? Do you get angry? Do you seek revenge? Do you communicate? Do you shut up and shut down? Perhaps you respond with a combination of these things. Again, to the degree that you can begin to see clearly how you usually act out your feelings of hurt, you can begin to make an accurate assessment of how that response affects your long-term physical, mental, and relational health. The evidence from the research is fairly clear that emotional withdrawal and angry retaliation are damaging to our marital health both in the short and long run. On the other hand, open and assertive communication of hurt feelings from a perspective of mutual compassion appears to facilitate and maintain intimacy and relationship health.

MUTUAL COMPASSION

The key to relationally healthy emotional expression is mutual compassion. Mutual compassion means simultaneously respecting your feelings *and* your partner's feelings. It means first noticing your own hurt feelings with a sense of compassion, as if saying something like, "My feelings are hurt and that's okay. It doesn't mean anything bad about me or about my partner. It just means that my feelings are hurt and I need to act with kindness toward myself." This first emotionally skillful step is just about identifying the feeling accurately and beginning to move in a direction of kindness.

The next step is to find a way to communicate your experience of hurt to your partner in a way that takes your partner's feelings and perspective into account. Your partner has done something that has hurt your feelings (maybe unintentionally). If you keep it to yourself, your relationship will suffer. If you take your hurt feelings out on your partner, your relationship will suffer. The alternative is simply to let your partner know that your feelings are hurt. The closer you can come to saying something like, "It hurt my feelings when you did *x*," the better. For example, "It hurt my feelings when you snapped at me." Simple, direct, assertive, non-blaming descriptions of how you are feeling communicate clearly what is true for you and minimize the buildup and escalation of small things.

You won't necessarily tell your partner about every little thing that he or she does that irritates or bothers you. Most of the little things will simply go unnoticed anyway because when things are going well in a relationship we tend to wear rose-colored glasses about our partners. We are simply less easily hurt when things are going well between us. At the same time, if something hurtful happens, then more times than not, it is best to be authentic with your partner about that. That doesn't mean that you have to "teach your partner a lesson" and force an apology. It does mean that you have to stay transparent and present so that your partner can learn what hurts your feelings and how to move more gracefully with you. It also means staying fully human and not lying to yourself or to your partner about who you really are and how you really feel. It is just this sort of openness about how you and your partner affect each other that creates and maintains intimacy and a deep, shared knowledge of each other. It allows you both to be fully human with each other in a warm, complicated, and engaging intimate relationship.

EMOTIONALLY SKILLFUL ANGER

Everyone experiences anger at their intimate partner from time to time, however, some ways of being angry with your partner are more likely to lead to greater satisfaction in the long run and some ways of being angry with your partner are more likely to erode relationship health. Anger that is communicated respectfully and managed effectively has been shown to increase marital satisfaction in the long run, whereas anger that is communicated in hostile and disrespectful ways has been shown to rapidly corrode the foundations of a healthy marriage.

There is evidence in the relationship science research literature that suggests that legitimate and respectful expressions of anger are unpleasant in the short run and healthy for the relationship in the long run. The explanation seems to be that while hostile expressions of anger corrode the foundations of a healthy relationship, respectful and compassionate expressions of anger are essential to clear and open communication. In a close and intimate relationship, we will on occasion make each other angry. Stuffing that anger or withdrawing appears to be the most damaging thing we can do to our long-term marital health. Similarly, acting out our anger in ways that are intentionally hurtful and disrespectful is like trying to grow a healthy garden by stomping on it.

Let us think for a moment about how we have learned to act when we are feeling angry. Probably the first place to look is to how your parents acted out their anger. One of the most common ways that we learn is through modeling others, so it should not be a surprise to find that we learn a great deal about how to "do" anger from how we saw our parents "doing" anger. And they in turn likely learned their anger repertoires from their own parents.

In general we can think about three broad categories of "ways to be angry." The first involves withdrawal. There is the sort of "hot" withdrawal that involves storming out, stomping, and slamming doors as you go. This way of acting out our anger definitely communicate to others that we are angry, but in an indirect way that is hard to stay close to. We know that withdrawal is bad for a relationship in the long run, especially if it becomes chronic and partners don't come together again to openly address their issues.

That being said, taking time to cool down when you are particularly angry is a very good thing because even the best of us tend to be a little emotionally destructive when we are furious. We'll talk about that in a bit more detail later.

The other flavor of withdrawal is "icy" withdrawal. This is the storied "cold shoulder" and may in some ways be even worse for a relationship in the long run than "hot" withdrawal because in addition to communicating anger, it also communicates a sense of disdain and emotional rejection. Icy withdrawal also tends to be more chronic, which is extremely corrosive to a marriage. Both of these types of angry withdrawal sever lines of communication and hinder our ability to learn how to move more gracefully in relation to each other.

Rather than withdrawing, many of us learn to act out our anger in an aggressive and often scary way. We learn from our lives that this way of acting out our anger has a powerful effect on the people around us, sometimes even working in our favor in the short run. For example, you might force an apology out of your spouse with an angry display or you might force your spouse to do what you want by really dragging them through your anger.

We tend to try to communicate all kinds of different things through approaching our partners with hurtful forms of anger. We communicate that we have been hurt, disappointed, scared, or ashamed. More often than not there is a very important and necessary message behind aggressive displays of anger. Unfortunately, those important messages are virtually guaranteed not to be heard when they are packaged in aggressive and emotionally painful forms of anger.

Aggressive and emotionally painful ways of acting out our anger, or what we will call "dirty" anger, have several qualities that tear at the fabric of our relationships. Dirty anger often involves name-calling or attacks against the other person's character. For example, if we are angry with our partner for not doing the dishes, we might call him a slob (name calling) or say something like, "You've always been inconsiderate and lazy" (attacking his character). You might also bring up several examples of other times that he has shown how lazy he is, all the while letting him know what a disaster you think he is as a person.

Sometimes, in the very worst of cases, dirty anger involves physical violence or touching the other person in an angry way. These acts can include throwing things at your partner, hitting your partner with hand, fist, or foot, grabbing your partner in an angry way, choking your partner, blocking your partner from leaving, raising your hand in a threatening way, getting in your partner's space in an intimidating way, or even beating your partner up. These forms of physical violence are weapons of mass destruction in a marriage and are cause for serious and immediate concern and efforts to seek safety.

There are two broad negative effects of dirty anger. First, dirty anger completely pollutes whatever message you might have been trying to get across. It is virtually impossible to accurately hear a partner who is screaming at you and calling you names. You might be trying to communicate that your life feels better and more peaceful when you are both working together to keep your home clean and orderly. Your partner however will not hear about the sense of calm satisfaction that you get from pitching in together and so won't be motivated to join with you as an ally, friend, and partner. What your partner will hear instead is that you don't like him, that he is only worthy of your love and respect when he or she diligently toes the line, and that she or he is not safe with you. He might find himself working hard at household chores, but it will be out of a sense of fear, resentment, anger, and bitterness. He will be further removed from you emotionally and you will understand each other less and less well.

This leads to the second negative effect of dirty anger. Like a strong acid, it actively corrodes and permanently damages the very foundation of your marriage and family. Things said can never be unsaid. That remains true even if you "really didn't mean it." Names called always remain names called. The injuries of open emotional attacks never return to normal. Displays of dirty anger are essentially like trying to build a beautiful and solid house with a chainsaw, flamethrower, and wrecking ball.

THE SOFTER SIDE OF ANGER

Neil Jacobson and Andrew Christensen, two leaders in the field of couples research and therapy and the codevelopers of a very powerful approach to couples therapy called Integrative Couples Therapy, have made the case that anger is almost always accompanied by other emotions. In almost every case, our experience of anger is rooted in some other, more vulnerable emotion. For example, as we mentioned before, anger is often the way that we learn to cover up feelings of hurt. It can also be how we react to feeling lonely, embarrassed, worried, tense, confused, frustrated, or overwhelmed. Identifying and communicating those hidden emotional experiences maintains an honest understanding between you and your partner, ultimately benefiting your relationship health.

Rather than emphasize a formula to follow when you are feeling angry, I want to emphasize where to stand emotionally in relation to your loved ones so that what you say or do is both true and healthy. There *are* formulas that can be followed that involve taking appropriate amounts of cool-down time, focusing on I-messages, avoiding blame, focusing comments on behavior rather than character, and being reassuring and respectful, but at this point we will focus on a more general way of understanding anger in intimacy.

Again, there is good data in the research literature to suggest that clean and clear communication of anger, while unpleasant in the short run, is healthy for a marriage in the long run. When we were discussing intimacy, I noted that we all have personal and interpersonal boundaries that we must respect in order for a healthy marriage to flourish. As in the example of the couple with different anger styles, you might have a boundary around "yelling" in your relationship. You might find yelling not just unpleasant, but entirely unacceptable to you. If your partner yells, you consider that completely stepping over the line. If you were to simply allow your partner to step over that line without comment, then ultimately you would both end up unhappy and resentful. If you were to retaliate against your partner for crossing that line, you would also end up unhappy and resentful. However, if you were to notice your anger about crossing the "yelling" line and that your anger comes mixed with feelings of fear and a sense of being overwhelmed, then you might be able to communicate your anger in a relationship healthy way.

COMPASSIONATE ANGER

How do we communicate our anger in relationship healthy ways? One ingredient again is mutual compassion. That means behaving with compassion toward yourself, behaving with compassion toward your partner, and behaving with compassion toward your children, all simultaneously. Compassion toward yourself will lead you to want to take loving care of yourself by clearly communicating your upset to your partner. Compassion toward your partner means that you take loving care of him or her while you are expressing your anger such that you speak to your partner with kindness, respect, and empathy. Finally, compassion toward your children means that you remain aware of their feelings while you are communicating your anger and that you take care to be reassuring and respectful toward them as well. With this attitude of mutual compassion, you will be in a much better position to trust what comes out of your mouth.

Although anger may be inevitable in an intimate relationship, it need not be relationship corrosive. If you clearly recognize when you are feeling angry and what softer emotions you might be hiding behind your anger, you are in a better position to communicate that anger in a healthy way. You must also be committed to your partner's emotional well-being. If I need to let you know that I am angry and, I also need to be gentle with the gift of your love and trust, then I am much more likely to communicate my anger in ways that are both clear *and* gentle. There is a whole world of difference between telling my partner that I am mad at her for not following through on a promise that she made to me ("Honey, you said that you would take care of it and you didn't and I'm kind of pissed off and worried about it.") and angrily attacking her ("I don't know what made me think I could trust you with this.") or angrily withdrawing from her ("I can't even look at you right now."). The first, although not entirely pleasant to hear, is at least genuine, respectful, and clear about the underlying issue. The other two are completely unclear about the underlying issue and are irresponsibly careless. A "clean" expression of anger is likely to lead to a useful discussion, greater understanding between you, and a continuing sense of being "in it together." The other two, less emotionally skillful ways of expressing anger are likely to lead to greater misunderstanding, escalate into even more emotionally upsetting arguments, result in no useful outcomes, and perpetuate a sense of greater isolation between you.

RESPONSIBLE ANGER

The second ingredient of healthy anger is accepting responsibility. What I mean by accepting responsibility is that you are conscientious about your responsibilities when you are angry. You are responsible for yourself, you are responsible for the gift of your partner's vulnerability, and you are responsible for the impressionability of your children. Again, accepting your responsibility for the well-being of all the members of your family can help shape the expression of anger toward greater health, warmth, and gentle assertiveness.

In the example above in which your partner has crossed the "yelling" line, you might recognize that you are angry *and* that mutual compassion and accepting responsibility necessitates that you communicate that anger to your partner. You might also recognize that while being assertive, you must be gentle and empathic toward your partner. Finally, you might recognize that your children will learn a life-long lesson from you about how to behave when they themselves are angry and that the lesson you model will likely be passed down to your grandchildren. From that perspective, you might find yourself saying something like, "I know you're pissed and I want to know what's going on, but you don't get to yell at me. It pisses me off and it's scary and confusing. If you can tell me what's wrong without yelling, then I want to keep talking. If not, I think we need to take a break and try talking about this later."

Notice here that there is strength in vulnerability. In this example, you are able to lead with your vulnerable feelings (fear and confusion) while assertively taking care of yourself. You are being responsible to yourself by saying what you need to say, you are being responsible to your partner by being respectful and loving, and you are being responsible to your children by showing them that adults can be angry with each other in a safe and non-threatening way.

GOOD ANGER SKILLS

The final ingredient is having good anger skills at your disposal. The first, and perhaps most underrated tool is the appropriately timed cool-down period. John Gottman in his research into the physiology of marital distress has found that when partners become angry at each other, their heart rates can sometimes increase dramatically. Sometimes couples sitting down and arguing can have heart rates as high as when they are physically exercising. Dr. Gottman's research has found that when we are over-stimulated by how upset we are (for example, a heart rate around 120 beats per minute) it becomes infinitely harder to communicate clearly and effectively. Dr. Gottman calls this moment of physiological over-arousal "flooding." He cautions that once partners have become emotionally flooded, it is virtually impossible for them to have anything positive or healthy come out of continuing the struggle without first taking sufficient time to cool down.

He has also found that it takes an average of thirty to forty minutes for a person's heart rate and blood pressure to return to normal. The implication is that it is important to notice when you or your partner might be flooding, ("Honey, I think we're overheating the system here") so that you can take a health promoting time-out ("Let's take a break and come back to this in thirty minutes or so"). It is hard to over-emphasize the importance of a good time-out. Although it may feel artificial and forced, well-timed time-outs can prevent unnecessary and avoidable damage to your marital health. We are all simply less effective and more reactive when we are flooded. At the same time, we retain our responsibility to manage our anger well and to take cool down time when necessary. In fact, there is decent evidence that simply taking a time-out, without any further intervention, can be sufficient to dramatically improve the quality of conversation afterwards.

An additional anger tool involves focusing on what we used to call "I" messages. Using "I" messages simply means talking about yourself and not talking about your partner. Talk about your feelings, your motives, and your thoughts. Do not assume anything about your partner's feelings, thoughts, or motives. You say things like, "I'm feeling ignored," rather than "You're ignoring me." Or, "I was scared" rather than "You're inconsiderate." It is much easier to hear someone talking about their own thoughts and feelings than it is to hear someone talking about our thoughts and feelings. Even when they are right, we tend to resent it. I go over this in much more detail in the communication chapter.

Another anger tool is mindful breathing, which we'll go over in more detail in another chapter. In short, however, it is helpful to have some strategies for calming our anger before communicating it and one very helpful strategy is focusing on the breath for ten or fifteen minutes. To do this, you can sit, stand, or walk while paying deliberate attention to each consecutive in breath and out breath. The idea is to lightly lift your attention off of your angry thoughts and feelings (though you will still be able to feel them) and place your attention on the physical sensations of breathing in and out. You can focus on wherever in your body you feel your breath moving whether that is your nostrils, your throat, or your belly. You can say to yourself while you are breathing in, "breathing in, I am right here right now." On the out breath you can say to yourself, "breathing out I am calming my anger." After ten or fifteen minutes you will find yourself in a much better place emotionally from which to communicate your anger gently to your partner.

Finally, if you must complain about your partner, complain about his or her *behavior* rather than about who he or she is as a person. If he hasn't been picking up his dishes and it is making you mad, tell him "you haven't been picking up your dishes and it's making me mad" not, "Can you please stop being such a pig." If she is being carelessly snappy with you and it is making you mad, tell her "you've been short with me all morning and it is making me mad," rather than, "you're a jerk." If you focus on *behavior* you allow that your partner is still a lovable and complicated human being who sometimes does things that get under your skin. If you focus on your partner's character, you imply that there is something about who he or she is as a person that is fundamentally unlovable. No one responds well to that kind of message.

In summary, there is certainly such a thing as emotionally skillful anger and it is to the enormous benefit of you and your family that you find ways to learn and practice this kind of emotion skill. Without these skills you risk the health of your marriage and you risk passing poor skills on to your children.

EMOTIONALLY SKILLFUL LOVE

What does it mean to love someone skillfully? Perhaps first and foremost it means recognizing that love is a verb. Love is something that we do; it exists only in the acts we engage in. Love means behaving in a loving manner. To love someone fully means to act lovingly toward him or her in both big and small ways, consistently and without pause. If love only describes a feeling and is not a way of behaving toward others, then it is dead. No one thrives on dead love.

When we choose to love someone, we are not necessarily guaranteeing that we will feel warm, fuzzy, loving feelings toward that person day in and day out, at every moment for the rest of our lives. Intimacy is much too complicated for something so small. When we choose to love someone, we commit to loving that person in what we do and what we say, in how we stand next to him or her; in how we live our lives, and in how we spend our time. That means that sometimes you will behave in loving ways toward your partner when you are feeling warm and positive feelings and sometimes you will behave in loving ways toward your partner when you are feeling angry, disappointed, or confused. The commitment to love actively is far too important to entrust to the ups-and-downs of day-to-day positive and negative feelings. Emotionally skillful love means allowing for the ups and downs of human intimacy while committing to the steady and generous offering of loving behavior.

HOW DO *YOU* "DO" LOVE?

Emotionally skillful love means saying it out loud. It means being affectionate. It means providing steady support. It means fostering joy. It means doing what you can to ease your partner's burden. It means moving with grace and gratitude. It means seeing your partner with fresh eyes, every day, and not letting your view of your partner become obscured or jaded by old assumptions. Love means remaining curious about your partner, respecting his or her independence while honoring your interconnectedness. Love is generosity. It is generosity with your time, with your attention, with your affection, with your voice, with your whole being. Love means showing up with every fiber of your being, completely undefended, and with a generous attitude.

The genuine practice of love is selfless. It is not to be confused with feeling positively about our partners (though that feeling is a common side effect). Positive feelings might result from loving behavior, but they are not love in action unless they translate into loving behavior.

Unhealthy and unskillful love is motivated by greed. Rather than being unselfish and focused on the well-being of the other, unhealthy love is selfish and focused on our own benefit. If when I think of love, I think only of how loved *I* feel or how warm my feelings are for my partner, then it is easy to get lost. If my actions toward my partner are only motivated by how loved or loving I feel, then my relationship will be fragile and unhealthy. If, on the other hand, my actions are motivated by my *partner's* experience of joy and happiness (his or her experience of feeling loved), then I am practicing emotionally skillful love. Granted, feelings of love are complicated and can be confusing. Granted, as well, however, that loving *behavior* is not so complicated and is often quite obvious and clarifying.

The emotionally skillful part of love involves both the intention to behave lovingly toward our partner *and* the necessary knowledge and skill required to bring real joy, happiness, contentment, security, support, and vibrancy into our partner's life. In this case, intention, while important, is not sufficient. Emotionally skillful love is a real skill and one requiring ongoing attention, curiosity, and practice. The odds are quite good that none of us are as emotionally skillful in this area as we could be. Like any skill, this one requires regular practice.

Ask yourself, what do I know about what makes my partner happy? Do I know how to be comforting to her? Do I know how to bring him moments of joy? How much do I know about how best to love her? If you cannot easily list a variety of loving gestures that you *know* add brightness to your partner's life, then (1) you are not alone, and (2) your next loving act is to open your eyes and get actively curious. Open your eyes and ears and try to see your partner anew. Keep asking yourself about what makes your partner happy for the next few days while really paying attention. Use your curiosity and your empathy and do your level best to solve the mystery. Once you have several guesses to work with, start trying them and allow for the process of trial and error to teach you how to skillfully love your partner. After you have been practicing for a while, you might also *ask* your partner to tell you about some of the things that make him or her happy. You might find that your partner knows some things, but not others and the two of you might discover new things together that neither of you would have found on your own. Recognize that this is lifelong learning because your partner will continue to grow and change for the rest of your lives together.

Be patient with yourself and allow that not many of us know as much as we should about how to be skillfully loving. Start from wherever you are and simply begin to learn and practice. Do what you can every day and you will find that with time and patience and persistence, you are becoming a more skillfully loving person.

In some respects this may seem like a simple point, but it is all too common to meet people in both my research and practice that have forgotten, fallen asleep, or become neglectful of the practice of loving. It is also surprising how powerful simply picking up the practice again can be. I would like to encourage you, from wherever you are, to pick it up and start practicing, with your partner, with your children, and with yourself. Try to practice love in action every day and the benefits will become obvious.

CONCLUSION

There are several things to keep in mind when considering your own emotion skills. First, I believe that it is important to keep in mind that we are always under the influence of some degree of emotional experiencing. Emotional experiencing is simply part of the fabric of all of our lives. Next, it is important to recognize that you have learned how to behave in the context of your emotions over the course of your entire life. You have learned how to behave when you are hurt or sad. You have learned how to behave when you are angry or disappointed. You have learned how to think about and act out feelings of love, compassion, and joy. In other words, there is a distinction to be made between *feeling* angry and how each of us has learned to *act* when we are angry. Third, it is important to recognize that how we act out our emotions can have either a positive long-term effect on our marriage and family or a negative long-term effect on our marriage and family. More emotionally skillful ways of loving, of being hurt, of being angry or sad, foster strong and healthy relationships that flourish in the good times and are resilient in the bad times. Less emotionally skillful ways of loving, being hurt, angry, or sad weaken our relationships making them vulnerable to permanent damage during the bad times and incapable of positive growth during the good times. Fourth, when we are open-eyed and honest with ourselves about our own emotion skills, then we are in the best position possible to begin consciously practicing more skillfully. Finally, the key to identifying healthy emotion skills is a perspective of mutual compassion. When what you most want in the moment of interaction between you and your loved one is motivated by empathic concern for everyone involved, then you can trust yourself to begin moving in emotionally skillful ways. As long as you stay open to the effects of your actions on others, your own ongoing experience of trial and error will lead you to grow in ever more skillful ways.

3

COMMUNICATION: HEALTHY MISCOMMUNICATION

Unhealthy communication between couples has been shown by research to predict marital distress, divorce, domestic violence and physical ill-health. It has also been associated with behavioral and emotional problems in children. Our biggest misconception about communication is that we think we're any good at it. We tend to assume we communicate well and understand clearly. We think we say exactly what we mean and we think we hear exactly what was meant. The truth of the matter is that even in the best of relationships with the best of communicators, we miscommunicate more than we communicate. We misunderstand more than we understand. Misunderstanding is the natural state of the world and of intimate relationships like marriage. Miscommunication is easily the most common form of communication. We are mostly deaf and mostly blind when it comes to understanding each other. It requires patient, deliberate, and loving work to hear each other clearly and understand each other well.

The main point of this chapter is this. It is a monumental challenge to understand ourselves and an even greater challenge to understand each other. We must learn to embrace how much we don't know about ourselves and our partners. We must practice the art of patient and curious listening to allow us to get to know each other better, even as we continue to misunderstand, change, and grow. The goal of this chapter is to present some of the tried and true methods studied by relationship researchers that have been designed to help us practice the art of healthy miscommunication.

HOW WELL DO WE COMMUNICATE? A BRIEF MEASURE

Look over your strengths and areas for improvement. First, as always, appreciate your strengths. Your strengths are the stable foundation of your marriage and it is important to your overall health to acknowledge them. I recommend spending a moment thinking about how you can capitalize on your strengths to further the health of your marriage. You might want to write some of these ideas down and even share your positive assessment with your partner.

You'll notice that this questionnaire focuses almost exclusively on you as an individual rather than on either your partner or your relationship as a whole (except for the first couple of questions). The reason for this is that it is vitally important for us to take full and personal responsibility for how we communicate in our own marriage. It is also astonishingly easy to find ourselves blaming our partners for any communication issues we might be having. As personally satisfying, and maybe even true, that kind of blame may be, it is completely worthless to us. Believe me, if blaming our partners were an effective solution to communication issues, I would be all for it. It's easy and it comes so naturally. Oddly enough, it so often feels like something of a relief to blame our partners. If only it were so easy. As with all such things, the only real answers lie in the direction of courageously accepting our own responsibility, our own "ability to respond," by attending more conscientiously to our own attitudes and behavior.

Now, take a look at those items that you rated as needing improvement. Without judging yourself and regarding yourself with an attitude of kindness, recognize that we all have areas we need to improve and these are often lifelong projects. With that in mind, let's press on.

Table 3.1. The Marital Communication Checkup

Definitely Something We Need to Improve 1	*Could Use Some Improvement* 2	*Neither a Strength nor Area for Improvement* 3	*Somewhat of a Strength* 4	*Definitely a Strength* 5

_____ 1. My partner and I make time to communicate with each other on a regular basis.
_____ 2. My partner and I communicate well with each other.
_____ 3. When I talk to my partner I focus on sharing my thoughts and feelings rather than on pointing out my partner's shortcomings.
_____ 4. When my partner is trying to talk to me about something I tend to give him/her the benefit of the doubt.
_____ 5. I am careful not to jump to conclusions about what my partner is saying.
_____ 6. I am careful not to assume I know what my partner is talking about.
_____ 7. I try to be aware of how easy it is to miscommunicate and misunderstand.
_____ 8. I try to say what I mean directly, openly, and assertively.
_____ 9. I strive to always speak to my partner with kindness and respect.
_____ 10. I try to listen closely and with empathy to what my partner says.
_____ 11. I listen to understand my partner, not to judge or argue or to defend myself.
_____ 12. I try to double-check that I've understood my partner correctly.
_____ 13. I clearly and effectively communicate my wants and needs.
_____ 14. We chit chat regularly with each other.
_____ 15. We talk about the things that matter most deeply to us.
_____ 16. I try hard to empathically understand my partner when we are talking.
_____ 17. I openly communicate my positive feelings to my partner.
_____ 18. I kindly and directly communicate my negative feelings to my partner.
_____ 19. I don't carry around negative thoughts and feelings without sharing them.
_____ 20. I don't withdraw from difficult conversations.
_____ 21. When we're having a difficult conversation, I know when we need a break.
_____ 22. I'm willing to work hard to communicate clearly.

CHAPTER 3

MISCOMMUNICATION IS NORMAL

As I have noted, we miscommunicate more commonly than we communicate accurately. Some level of miscommunication is a normal part of any conversation. If you think about it for only a moment, this state of affairs begins to make sense. When we have something that we want to communicate to our partner, we are first faced with the task of trying to figure out exactly what it is that we want to say and, as we all know, that task is not always easy. The task becomes even more difficult when what we have to say is very important to us or in some way emotionally complicated. Somehow we have to put words on our experience and much more often than not, the words we have are at least somewhat inadequate to the task. If our partners could just crawl inside us and directly know what we mean, then we could be truly understood. Unfortunately, we are stuck with this very clumsy means of trying to package and carry our meaning across to our partners through language and words. Much gets lost in the translation.

The first words out of our mouths are often poor reflections of what we really mean to say. We might at times even want to take our words back and try again. But once those words have left our mouths, our partners are already responding to whatever clumsy jumble we coughed up and we get caught up and lost in whatever that cycle of misunderstanding and confusion is that we fall into again and again. We are rarely given the chance to try to figure out the distance between what our words meant to us and what they meant to our partners. In fact, more often than not, we don't know ourselves what we are *really* trying to say, and we have to hear ourselves say *something* before we can even begin to figure it out. Most conversations simply unfold too fast to allow us to clarify, even for ourselves, what we really mean to say. The bottom line is that starting a conversation, especially an important one, is a tricky business.

Now, add to the dilemma how complicated it is to clearly *hear* what our partner is saying and *translate* their unique way of saying things into our unique way of hearing things with any degree of accuracy. What I mean is that even though we and our partners might technically speak the same language, all of our words mean something slightly different to each of us than to anybody else. We learn the meaning of words, both their broad meanings and subtle nuances, from our accumulated experience with them over the entire course of our lives. Simple words like "angry" can have strikingly different associations for some people than for others. One partner might have grown up in a household where the word "angry" was used to refer to passionate, open, but relatively civil interactions about frustrations and disappointments that were emotionally skillful, generally respectful and always safe. Another partner might have grown up in a household where the word "angry" was used to refer to devastatingly frightening parental tantrums that were emotionally chaotic, hateful, and traumatizing. Now, as simple a statement as, "I'm angry with you" is going to mean *very* different things to these two partners, *regardless* of what it might mean to the person who said it. And people rarely clarify by saying, "Now what I mean by 'angry' is 'let's sit down and talk respectfully about how frustrated and hurt I am by your behavior,' and not 'I am about to completely lose control and say hateful and humiliating things to you.'" We are left instead having to infer meaning from our own unique experience.

In less exaggerated forms, this same process of accumulating different understandings of the same words happens for all of us for all words, so even though we often understand each other well enough to get by, there is a great deal of misunderstanding built directly into the system. So, despite the fact that Bob and Gina are both speaking English, Bob is really speaking "Bob-English" and Gina is translating into "Gina-English" and the translation is never perfect. Now keep in mind that Bob himself is not entirely certain what he is trying to say or what he really means and it becomes surprising that we ever understand each other at all. If you further add to that mix any emotional upset or any competitive drive to "win" an argument rather than understand a partner, and it is no wonder that miscommunication and misunderstanding are the norm and not the exception.

A PARTICULARLY DESTRUCTIVE COMMUNICATION PATTERN

Rick approached Karen wanting to talk about "the big picture." He wanted to talk about the future, kids, what they both want to do with their lives, and really just play with all the possibilities ahead of them. Rick loved having these types of conversations and considers them playful and fun. Karen heard him say, "So, let's talk about where we want to be in five years," and panicked. She found these conversations unsettling and felt like they were really about all the ways in which Rick wanted her to change, to be more cheerful, more optimistic, more relaxed, and, well, more playful. So she told him she was tired and didn't feel like talking about anything big. Rick felt pushed away and shut down and started pushing to get the conversation going, "Come on. It'll be fun. Why do you always have to run away like that?" Karen responded, "I don't *always* anything. I just don't want to talk right now. Give it a rest." That's when the argument really got going.

Professor Andrew Christensen of UCLA and his colleagues have spent many years studying a particularly pernicious form of miscommunication they call "demand-withdraw." A demand-withdraw pattern involves one partner "demanding" change while the other partner withdraws from the conversation physically, emotionally, or psychologically. In other words, while one partner approaches the other seeking some kind of change, the other partner does everything he or she can to withdraw from the conversation and avoid the requested change. I suspect all couples fall into this pattern from time to time, but the more common it is in your relationship, the more likely that your marriage is suffering some ill-health.

Research has repeatedly shown that the demand-withdraw pattern of communication is associated with worsening relationship distress. This pattern has also shown a very interesting gender difference. In most of the research into the effects of this pattern, results have shown that wives are most often in the "demand" position and husbands are most often in the "withdraw" position. Originally, researchers guessed that the effect might have something to do with typical "maleness" and "femaleness," however, further research revealed that the pattern has more to do with who is asking for change than with gender per se. Professor Christensen and his colleagues found that if you asked partners to simply pick the most significant issue in their relationship to talk about, the chosen topic was almost always one in which the wife was heavily invested in seeking change. If, however, the researcher specifically asked the husbands to talk about an issue in which they were heavily invested in seeking change, then the demand-withdraw pattern reversed in almost all cases. In other words, the more demanding partner appears to be the partner most invested in seeking change, regardless of whether that partner was the wife or the husband.

More recent research conducted by Dr. Kathleen Eldridge at Pepperdine University and Dr. Christensen at UCLA and their colleagues found that the extent of this reversal in the demand-withdraw pattern was affected by how severely distressed the couple was when they entered the study. Christensen originally found that most, but not all couples reversed the pattern when the husband was the partner seeking change. Dr. Eldridge's research has found that the most severely distressed couples appear to be locked into a wife-demand and husband-withdraw pattern. Interestingly, these researchers found that even if these very distressed couples were talking about a change that the husband wanted to make in himself, as opposed to a change that the wife was seeking from him (e.g., he wanted to exercise more or lose weight), they were still just as prone to the wife-demand and husband-withdraw pattern.

MIND READING IS A MISTAKE

Karen thought, "Damn, here we go again. Now we're going to fight about all the ways I'm constantly disappointing him." Rick, however, was thinking, "Things have been going great between us. I bet this would be a great time for us to daydream about our future together." Unfortunately, both partners assumed something about the other that turned out not to be true.

Because effective communication is so complicated, we find ourselves relying too often on mindreading. Most conversations unfold at such a breakneck speed that there is no time to try to clarify what we or our partners really mean to say and instead we are left with our clumsy guesses. We end up responding to our guesses instead of to our partners. In other words, we settle for poor mindreading over accurate understanding. That is why when you really listen deeply to two people having a conversation, it often sounds like they are having two completely separate conversations and just happen to be facing each other.

We settle for mind reading because we simply don't know any better alternative. The task of accurate communication is so challenging that mind reading somehow just seems easier and more efficient. That it usually leads us completely astray rarely enters our minds. In fact, it very rarely occurs to us that what we think our partner means and what our partner actually means might be two very different things. We simply assume that our interpretation is 100 percent accurate and go from there. Unfortunately, that interpretation is often wrong and simply going from there can do more harm than good.

THE IMPORTANCE OF COMMUNICATING DIRECTLY, OPENLY, AND ASSERTIVELY

Step Up and Say It

Although communication is a tricky business, it is also the lifeblood of any healthy relationship. These are simply deep waters that you must dive into over and over again, until you are comfortable with their challenges and able to be playful in their depths. So, you must step up and say something, and you must do it over and over again. Allow that the first words out of your mouth will be imperfect. Starting a conversation is always a rough draft, merely the beginning of something that you and your partner will shape together. You might think of beginning a conversation as coming together with your partner around an unformed block of clay and then beginning to work together to shape a clear and shared understanding between you.

A healthy marriage simply requires that we maintain an ongoing conversation with our partners. Some of that talk is the regular chitchat of everyday life and some of that talk is about the most important things that need to be said and understood. We have to say something even though what we say might not be perfect.

Unfortunately when couples begin having real trouble in their marriage they often stop talking completely. As the health of their marriage begins to deteriorate, they find that the difficulty they have communicating with each other makes the whole process feel like more trouble than it's worth. Each time an effort to communicate becomes hopelessly stuck in a pattern of miscommunication, the partners become more reluctant to try again. However, given that healthy marriages require healthy communication, unhealthy marriages are in even greater need of patient and deliberate talk. Ultimately we can't stop talking to each other just because the process is difficult. We have to step up and say something.

As we come to accept the fact that communication is a tricky business, we are likely to be more forgiving of the awkward process of stumbling around trying to figure out what we mean and how to say it. When we accept that the first words out of our partners' mouths are only poor approximations of what they ultimately mean to say, then we are more likely to give them the space that they need to figure out what they mean and how to say it. We're also less likely to react to our first misinterpretation as if it were 100 percent accurate. The bottom line is that it is infinitely better to start an imperfect conversation, knowing that it is imperfect, than to either avoid talking to each other at all or to assume that miscommunication is rare.

Keeping It Short

Clear or muddled you must say something. Once you start talking, and with your partner's help, you'll have the opportunity to begin to discover what you mean to say through the process of saying it, saying it again a little differently, and saying it yet again a little differently. Eventually, with patience and understanding, you and your partner will begin to understand each other better. Perhaps the most important point here is recognizing again that the first words out of our mouths will be imperfect and off-target, even to us, and that we will need several tries before we stumble on the meaning we are after.

One important step in communicating openly, directly, and assertively is to keep what we say relatively short. Listening well is difficult enough as it is without having to listen for a long time to many different things. Granted we may be trying to figure out what we really mean to communicate while we are talking, but we also have to grant our partner time to take it in and digest it. We want to make sure that what we have to say to our partner is in small enough chunks to be heard well. Otherwise, even if our partner is trying hard, she is likely to only hear the first thing we said, maybe the last thing we said, and a lot of "blah, blah, blah" in between.

We often hold onto the floor and go on for too long because we're concerned that we won't get the floor back from our partner once we stop or because we know we're being misunderstood and continue

piece. In this way, conversation is more like a game of king of the hill than it is like an actual conversation.

We are so practiced at constructing our rebuttal in the space that we should be listening, that at first this can be a very challenging practice. That being said, we must try, and a metaphor that we often use in therapy can be helpful.

Holding the Basket

The analogy that we use in therapy for listening without constructing our rebuttal is called, "holding the basket." When our partner is talking, we listen as if we were holding a basket and collecting everything our partner is saying into that basket to show to him later. When he is done talking, we look closely in the basket to see what's in there, and then we pull it out and show it to him and ask him if that is what he *meant* to put in there. The basket analogy can help us to remember that our job is to gather, sift, and understand. It can also help us to hold what our partner is saying gently and lightly, rather than taking it immediately to heart and taking it personally before we've made sure we heard it correctly.

Listening and Having Emotions at the Same Time

Good listening is, of course, easier when we are not flooded with emotions. If we are concentrated, calm, able to focus and non-defensive, then listening well requires less effort. Unfortunately, our emotional state can make both speaking and listening significantly more challenging. It is simply more difficult to listen well when we are having strong emotions at the same time and, very often, strong emotions are involved when we are talking to our partner about something important. The point of noting this isn't so much to change it as to help us cope with it more gracefully. If we know that we are having a harder time listening well when we are having strong emotions, then we are more likely to give ourselves and our partners the benefit of the doubt and to take what we think we are hearing with a grain of salt until we do enough empathic listening to be sure we're understanding each other well. In other words, if you know you are having a hard time listening well to your partner because you are emotionally flooded, then you can make wiser decisions about how to proceed. For example, you might actively use some of the listening techniques described later in the chapter to help you both slow down and work harder to understand each other clearly. You might also choose to call a time-out and take some time to recover yourself before attempting the conversation again. Many times after returning from a calming time out, the conversation will go noticeably more smoothly.

EMPATHY AND MUTUAL COMPASSION

What is empathic listening? Empathic listening involves, as noted earlier, listening with your whole body, both heart and head. You want to listen with the question in mind, "what would make me say what she is saying in the way that she is saying it?" "What is it like to experience the world from his perspective?" The effort is to feel your way into your partner's perspective. If we try to understand from inside our partner's shoes, we will discover that we hear our partners much more thoroughly than we would otherwise. We start to understand not just the literal meaning of the words we are hearing, but the emotional and subtle meanings underlying them.

We all want to be listened to in this way. We all long to be heard not just for the words that we say, but for the meanings behind those words. Especially in intimate relationships, we want to know that our partner is listening with an open heart.

For example, our partner might say to us, "You're home late." On the surface, this is just a statement of fact. Underneath the surface however, if we listen from an empathic perspective, we might hear both the irritation that we are late *and* the real worry about our well-being. If we just hear the statement of fact, the interaction isn't likely to be satisfying to either of us. Similarly if we just hear the irritation, we are likely to become defensive and unhelpful. But if we hear the worry and respond to our partner at that level, then he or she is much more likely to feel understood and our whole interaction will go more smoothly and in a much healthier direction.

LISTENING FOR COMPASSIONATE UNDERSTANDING

It is unavoidably true that much of what our partner says to us when he or she is upset, irritated, or angry is difficult to cuddle up to. Given that, part of active listening involves striving to listen through the interference and to understand our partner from a perspective that elicits our compassion and understanding. This usually involves listening with just that intention and starting with the assumption that there *is* a way to understand what our partner is saying that we can empathize with. Listening for compassionate understanding means listening for the meaning *behind* what our partner is saying; listening with that part of ourselves that knows our partner's background, that knows our partner's history, that knows how he or she was raised, that knows what she's afraid of, what she worries about, what she cares for, what matters most deeply to her, and trying to take all of those things into consideration in trying to understand what has brought her to us in this way, what has made her say *these* things. It can take some doing to listen in this way. When we have achieved what we are after however, the experience that we have will be like a lightbulb going off. We'll have that kind of "Aha" experience in which we say, "Oh, now I get it!" The moment we begin to resonate with what our partner is saying, we will know it as though we were saying it ourselves. Thus the goal of listening is not just to hear, but to experience empathy and compassionate understanding.

One of the keys to active listening is to use our own emotions and our own experience to try to see the world as our partner sees it. The way that we experience emotions and the way that our partner experiences emotions are not all that different. If you use your own emotions and experience to understand what your partner is saying, then you are really listening with your whole body. You're much more likely to hear accurately from this empathic perspective than from any other. You can then check your empathic understanding through paraphrasing.

PARAPHRASING

What is the most important thing to know about paraphrasing? The most important thing to know is that paraphrasing can be easy. Good paraphrasing is more about the attitude that we bring to it than it is about any particular skill we do or don't have. What is the right attitude? Essentially, the right attitude is the humility to accept that we don't know what our partner is trying to say to us, that what we think our partner means and what he or she really means are not the same thing.

With that attitude you will find that your most natural instinct is to ask your partner to help you understand. "Okay, honey, it sounds to me like you are saying that I don't help out enough around the house and that you think I'm lazy. Is that right?" This will give your partner the chance to clarify what she means. She might say, "No, it's not that I think you are lazy. I know you work hard. It's just that I feel overwhelmed by the housework and wish it felt more like we were doing it together rather than completely separately."

Once we have done our best to hear what our partner is saying, the next step is to double-check what we think we heard. Since, it is more likely than not that our first hearing has been imperfect, we want to share that first hearing with our partner and make sure that he has had a chance to hear himself from our perspective. In couples therapy, this often takes the form of saying something like, "Okay, what I think I heard you say is that you're angry that I've been coming home late without calling and that you get worried when I do that. Is that right?" This example is a little formal and it is possible to do this much more informally, but the basic practice remains the same. And that practice is to recognize that our first hearing could be wrong and that because of that we want to get our partner's help making sure that he said what he intended to say and that we heard it the way he intended for us to hear it. When in doubt, double-check and since you should always be in doubt, you should always be double-checking.

VALIDATING

Another function of paraphrasing is to validate what your partner has said to you. Validation can go a long way toward meeting the ultimate goal of communication, which is to understand and to feel understood. Although we often think that the goal of communication is to identify problems and then to work toward solutions to those problems (if there *are* any solutions), more often than not the goal is not problem solving, but understanding and connection. Validating what your partner is saying simply involves communicating what you have understood from an empathic perspective. Of course, this means more than simply saying,

"I understand." It means showing your partner that you understand empathically by sharing that understanding with her and asking her if you're on the right track. Essentially, that is what a paraphrase is. It is showing someone that you understand by putting your compassionate understanding in your own words.

Validation does not mean agreement. You can validate what your partner is saying without necessarily agreeing with it. Oftentimes people fail to show their partner that they understand because they believe that if they do then that means that they agree with their partner, even when they don't. For example, your partner may be complaining that you haven't been doing enough around the house lately and you disagree because you know you have been working hard. It is still possible to validate your partner's feelings by saying, "I know you're upset because you feel I haven't been carrying my share of the load lately. I completely understand where you're coming from. I think I would feel the same way in your shoes. At the same time, from my own perspective, I feel strongly that I have been working hard around the house. We should probably talk about where we're seeing things differently."

The bottom line is that we don't have to dismiss our partner's perspective just because we disagree with it. One of us might be wrong or we might simply have two different views. Accurately understanding and validating where your partner is coming from should actually make it easier to clear up misunderstanding or to recognize simple differences of opinion.

Professor Keith Sanford at Baylor University has found that whether we expect to be understood by our partner or not has a significant effect on how well we tend to communicate. His research has shown that if we expect that our partner is going to listen well and try hard to understand us, we are much more likely to speak in healthy and constructive ways. On the other hand, if we expect that our partner is not trying to understand us then we are much more likely to speak in ways that are defensive, self-protective, and attacking. There is also evidence to suggest a self-fulfilling prophecy is involved such that expecting your partner to listen well increases the odds that he or she will listen well. However, expecting your partner to listen poorly appears to increase the odds that he or she will do just that. The implication appears to be that we can benefit ourselves and our relationship by carefully examining our assumptions about how engaged our partner is in listening to us.

PARROTING

What is parroting? Parroting is what you do when you simply try to follow the rule that you "should" paraphrase, rather than simply listening empathically. If you simplistically follow the paraphrasing rule, then when your partner says, "All you ever do is hide down in the basement with your music and I just can't stand it anymore," your paraphrase will be, "So, it sounds like you're saying that all I ever do is hide down in the basement with my music and you just can't stand it anymore." Technically, you *are* checking to see if you heard your partner correctly, but this kind of word-for-word repeating of what your partner said is parroting, and is, unfortunately, not as useful as a genuine empathic paraphrase. It is less useful because it can be done without any attempt to experience empathy. The effort that it takes to genuinely reflect your understanding of what your partner has said is an empathic effort. It requires you to try to see and feel the world from your partner's perspective and then put your own words on your empathic experience. It is this empathic experience that is at the heart of building genuine understanding between you and your partner.

FEEDBACK ABOUT THE PARAPHRASE

When you are trying to communicate something to your partner and he or she has made a valiant attempt at empathic listening and paraphrasing, then it can be helpful to let your partner know if he or she has understood you well. If your partner asks if he has understood you correctly, it will come relatively naturally to say, "Yes, exactly, that's what I mean," or to say "no, I guess what I really mean to say is. . . ." It is this process of checking and clarifying that builds genuine understanding. You say something imperfectly, your partner feeds back to you his imperfect understanding of your imperfect statement, and then you begin the process of clarifying, back-and-forth, until you both together come closer to a shared understanding.

It is important to keep in mind that this kind of conversation requires patience. Our usual way of talking to each other unfolds quickly and feels like real forward movement, even though it can often be a lot of smoke and noise creating more confusion than clarity.

Good communication that builds real understanding is necessarily slow. In fact, communication strategies are deliberately designed to slow the process down so that you aren't proceeding from one misunderstanding to the next, but are instead slowly and conscientiously building solid understanding.

Good communication is a process of trial and error. We start out hoping to understand each other and through a process of trial and error, we inch our way toward clarity. The point of this chapter is to help you understand that most conversations start with misunderstanding and build greater misunderstanding from there. Like a game of telephone in a circle of children, one mishearing gives rise to an even more ridiculous mishearing, ultimately turning "Mary had a little lamb," into "Larry likes to eat green jam." Really getting to know your partner requires building a foundation of accurate, well-constructed understanding and that requires a deliberate process of speaking openly, listening empathically, checking for misunderstanding, clarifying misunderstanding, and speaking openly again.

Once you feel that your partner has understood what you have been trying to say, then you can switch roles from the one who is seeking to be understood to the one who is seeking to understand. We talk about this as a floor switch, from you having the floor to your partner having the floor. We can also think of it as seeking understanding. Seeking understanding is something that you both do together. You both work together to understand where you are coming from, then you both work together to understand where your partner is coming from. This is the practice of mutual compassion. This process of trying and trying again, stepping out on a limb and speaking from the heart, listening openly and empathically, humbly checking and clarifying our understanding, ultimately results in our getting to know each other and ourselves in a way that few other processes can ever hope to achieve.

COMMUNICATING NEGATIVE FEELINGS

Communication is essential. And, of course, communication is not just about the positive things that feel good in a relationship (although that kind of communication is also indispensable). It is also about the things that don't feel good in a relationship, about the things that bother us and make us feel crummy. Communicating negative feelings is one of the more difficult things for couples to do and yet it remains one of the most important. Part of the normal experience of intimacy is the discovery of friction points between us and our partners, the discovery of little things that annoy us as well as big things that make us wobble. Some of those points of irritation are minor and short-lived and some of those things are more challenging and chronic. It is essential to the long-term health of our marriages for us to communicate openly and frequently about these things. While it is true that we don't want to be constantly harping about the things that irritate us, it is equally true that if we don't say anything the relationship will become unbalanced and unhealthy.

Because communicating about negative feelings is particularly tricky business, many couples find that they avoid saying anything about negative feelings, which leads them to avoid saying much at all, which in turn leads them to start to avoid each other altogether. For some couples this cycle culminates in a huge fight during which everything that has gone unsaid over the course of the last six months all comes out in one huge tidal wave of sound and fury. Sometimes these fights serve as a type of course correction for the relationship and things might even get better again between the partners for some time or at least until what has been left unsaid builds up again to the point where it sets off another huge fight. Unfortunately, these major and only periodic expressions of negative feelings are emotionally draining and sometimes damaging, and often makes us even more reluctant to bring up negative feelings in the future for fear of setting off another big fight.

Frequent small course corrections are infinitely better than infrequent, emotionally turbulent, course corrections. Many couples avoid saying the little things like, "could you please not move my things. It drives me crazy trying to find them," because they are afraid that saying anything like this will set off one of their huge semi-annual blowouts. However, if partners are making these minor course corrections with each other more often, then they simply won't have to make major course corrections later. If you deal with things as they come up rather than letting them accumulate, you will actually find yourself feeling closer and more connected to your partner. It is in many ways a lot like dancing together. If you aren't constantly giving each other feedback about how you're moving through space, then you are going to step on each other's toes a lot more often. That can really start to hurt after awhile.

A crucial part of maintaining a healthy intimate relationship involves being open and honest enough to say, "I don't like that" and being open and generous enough to say, "Okay, I'll try." You simply *have* to be able to say "that hurt my feelings, that ticked me off, I'm feeling lonely, please don't do that, could you please try to remember to . . . , I'd prefer it if you didn't . . . , it scares me when you . . . , I wish you wouldn't . . . , and I wish you would. . . ." These are all part of negotiating living in close physical and emotional proximity to another whole and complicated adult. The more open you are in giving and receiving these minor complaints and course corrections, the better your marital health will be in the long run. When you take care of the little things right away, then they don't pile up into huge messes that require emotionally taxing and relationship damaging blowouts to clear up.

If your partner does something that bugs you, say "that's bugging me." If you're starting to feel lonely, say "I'm starting to feel lonely." If your partner is stepping on your toes, say "Honey, you're stepping on my toes." Again, this is part of the openness that builds and maintains intimacy.

On the other side of the equation, when your partner says, "that's bugging me," listen to him, acknowledge your own tendency to get defensive and accept that that is normal, then validate your partner's feelings and do what you can to adapt. The reason I like to talk about this process in terms of course corrections is because in any healthy relationship we are constantly and actively navigating around the tricky parts of being close to another human being. We will regularly drift off course and that is very normal. Maintaining a healthy and happy relationship means catching that drift early and often and making the little frequent corrections that keep you on course. It is essentially like steering a car down a winding road. You have to keep your hands on the steering wheel and be constantly adjusting to stay between the lines. If you only put your hands on the wheel when you have drifted onto the shoulder, then getting back on track is going to be a more dramatic and scarier maneuver.

COMMUNICATING POSITIVE FEELINGS

As important as it is to communicate when your toes are being stepped on, it is equally important to communicate when the dance is going well and you are having a wonderful time. Many of us easily take the good things for granted and so stop saying anything about them or maybe even stop noticing them altogether. Some people believe that if you love your partner then you shouldn't have to say it out loud. Maybe writing it in an anniversary card once a year should be enough. A healthy marriage, however, requires regular care and part of regular care involves regularly communicating positive feelings. Everybody wants to hear good things about themselves and we most want to hear those things from the people we love most dearly.

Communicating positive feelings usually only requires that we amplify what we are already feeling by simply saying it out loud. When you are feeling loving toward your partner, say "I love you." When you are proud of her, say "I'm proud of you." When you think he has done a good job on something, say "I think it looks great."

This doesn't mean paying compliments just for the sake of paying compliments. In other words, it doesn't mean to mindlessly follow a rule about compliments. Unfortunately this advice is often given as "compliment your partner every day." When we try to follow that rule strictly, our compliments can often seem forced and hollow. I am not asking you to go out of your way to find something nice to say about your partner. I'm asking you to tune into and notice your own feelings. Notice those feelings of love, closeness, comfort, fun, joy, ease, happiness, attraction, pride, gladness, thankfulness, excitement, surprise, and contentment as they come up. When you notice those feelings, say something. Just open your mouth and let something spill out. "I love you, I like you, this is fun, you look great, I like spending time with you, you make me happy, and you're sure cute." Turning the volume up on these feelings as they pass by feeds your relationship in ways that nothing else can.

COMMUNICATING POSITIVE AND NEGATIVE FEELINGS

Researchers at the University of North Carolina at Chapel Hill, including Drs. Elizabeth Schilling and Donald Baucom, have found that marital education can help couples learn how to deliberately increase their positive communication and decrease their negative communication. Their research also seems to indicate that relationships benefit most when men learn these skills. Interestingly, they found that increases in wives' positive communication has been associated with decreases in marital satisfaction. Marital researchers have repeatedly found that wives' positive communication is related to self-reports of marital happiness in the short run, but indicators of marital ill-health in the long run. As unexpected as these results were initially, recent evidence suggests that the underlying issue may have more to do with how engaged partners are in communicating with each other about both positive and negative things, rather than with whether the topic of conversation is positive or negative per se. Evidence has begun to suggest that when wives decrease their negative communication in relation to their positive communication it may indicate an increase in conflict avoidance. Refusing to talk about the negative things appears to be bad for your relationship health in the long run.

What I'm talking about here is not destructive negative communication, but instead simple assertive communication about real relationship issues. The bottom line is that whatever leads to more and better communication is better for your marital health. Anything that contributes to stifled or poor communication causes real marital health problems. In husbands, increases in positive communication appears to signal increased engagement in communication in general, whereas increases in positive communication by wives appears to signal decreased engagement in communication in general. In sum, communication about positive and negative things are both vitally important to your marital health and it appears that we shouldn't neglect giving voice to either one (with the caution of course that destructive ways of communicating are never healthy).

CHIT CHAT

Usually when people think about communication in marriage, they are thinking about communicating about the big and important things. Communication about the little things, however, is just as important. In fact, it is difficult to keep a relationship healthy if you aren't regularly shooting the breeze with your partner. This type of regular daily conversation about not much in particular is an important part of the glue that keeps us together. If you think about it, it makes sense. It is out of these little daily conversations that we really weave our lives together.

Research by Dr. John Gottman of the University of Washington has shown that couples who regularly spend a little time talking to each other about their day are healthier than those couples who don't. This research further shows that these conversations don't have to take a lot of time. A few minutes at the end of the day catching up on each other's lives helps you to stay connected and helps you to keep your partner in your thoughts. We like to feel like our partner knows what is going on in our lives and cares enough to keep up with the plot as it unfolds.

Couples today are extremely busy. It can be easy to lose track of the details of each other's lives and to end up feeling disconnected and alone. We want to feel like we have a partner and an ally even in the mundane details of our daily lives, because, let's face it, much of our lives is built out of the little details and if we can't connect around those then there isn't much left to connect around. Dr. Gottman recommends spending five minutes in the morning sharing your plans for the day and then five minutes in the evening talking about how the day actually went. Although it can seem like these little conversations about nothing in particular or about the little daily details of our lives couldn't possibly make that much of difference to our overall marital health, research suggests otherwise. These little talks are the ties that bind. Big talks may set the course and communication about negative feelings helps to keep us on course, but little talks, our daily chit chat keeps the whole thing going.

CLEARLY AND EFFECTIVELY COMMUNICATING OUR WANTS AND NEEDS

I have met many partners who think their spouse should "just know" their wants and needs without being told. In fact, they often say that having to tell their partner their wants and needs sort of spoils it. I think this is understandable. We all want to be known so thoroughly by the people who love us that we don't have to struggle to communicate our wants and needs. Unfortunately, if we're really honest with ourselves, we're just too complicated and constantly changing for anyone to be able to always know what we want and need. And since there is no such thing as mind reading and communication is difficult enough even when it's done out loud, we are simply stuck with having to *say* what we want out loud, on purpose, and as clearly as humanly possible.

TALKING ABOUT THE BIG STUFF

The last type of communication that we'll mention here is communication about the big things in life. This type of communication involves talking about those things that we find most meaningful. These might be talks about deeply held beliefs, philosophies of life, questions about meaning, fears about death. What are the things that inspire you? What are the things that scare you? What are your hopes for the future; for yourself, for your partner, for your children, for your country, for your world? What gives your life meaning? What are the things you're most thankful for? What are your beliefs about God? What do you want your life to stand for? What life lessons would you pass on to your children?

Talking about the big things is another way to get to know your partner and for your partner to get to know you. Fortunately, the answers to these questions are always changing, so there is always something to talk about and discover about yourself and your partner. Talking about the big things helps you to understand why your partner does what he does, why she likes what she likes, why he dislikes what he dislikes. Maybe it helps you to understand why you tend to clash about certain things or why you tend to see eye-to-eye about certain other things. These conversations about the big things don't have to be that frequent, but they should be frequent enough to keep up with the changes your partner experiences and to keep you both connected on this deeper level.

Communication is all about understanding and being understood. It is the tool we use to break through the two-dimensional life-sized cutout that we construct out of our assumptions about our partners. Communication is the tool we use to continue learning about this ever-changing person we have married. Through communication we get to know one another, we identify and solve our problems, we build love and intimacy, we develop compassion and understanding, and finally we create meaning and purpose together. The bottom line is that communication is how we connect and stay connected. Without it we will inevitably drift apart and the relationship will get sick and die. With it, our relationship will grow strong and deep; more beautiful, more vibrant, more able to withstand the ups and downs of life, and finally more nurturing for ourselves and our children.

KAREN AND RICK COMMUNICATE

Here is the conversation that Rick and Karen eventually had, following many of the guidelines presented in this chapter.

Rick: "Apart from that last fight we had, it feels like we've been getting along really great lately. I think it's fun to daydream about the future with you."

Karen: "It sounds like thinking about the future is your way of sort of playing and dreaming."

Rick: "Right. Exactly."

Karen: "It's just that these conversations bring up all my insecurities about our relationship and make me think that you really just want me to be a different kind of person."

Rick: "It sounds like thinking about the future actually makes you worry about us."

Karen: "Yeah, I guess it does."

Rick: "I guess I think we're going to be fine, Karen. In fact, more than fine. I love you and I want us to build a future together. I know I do things that drive you crazy and you do things that drive me crazy. I don't care about that. I want us to live life and grow old together."

Karen: "Me too. I guess I just worry sometimes."

Rick: "I know. It's okay. We're okay."

PUTTING IT ALL TOGETHER: A COMMUNICATION EXERCISE

The following exercise will help you and your partner to communicate effectively about even the trickiest of issues. The structure provided here summarizes what I have presented in this chapter. It helps to focus the conversation on clarification and creating mutual understanding. I recommend that you practice using this structure several times and use it deliberately whenever you find yourselves struggling to get through a particularly sticky issue. These steps are a version of the speaker-listener technique described by Drs. Howard Markman, Scott Stanley, and Susan Blumberg in their excellent book, "Fighting for Your Marriage."

1. Find a comfortable place where the two of you can sit facing each other without being interrupted.
2. Decide who will begin in the role of speaker and who will begin in the role of listener. It is vitally important that these two roles be kept strictly separated.
3. Pick an object like a coffee mug or magazine that you can use to indicate who the speaker is. We call this object "the floor" so that we literally see who is "holding the floor." We find that a visual reminder is often necessary to prevent partners from switching roles accidentally.
4. Whoever is holding the floor begins the conversation by trying to communicate what is most true for him or her about the issue being discussed. We often call this a focus on "I" messages versus "you" messages. If you are the speaker, the key is to focus on talking about your own thoughts, feelings, and experiences. It is important to avoid talking about your partner's rather than your own experience (i.e., "You think this, you feel that, you do or did this"). Focusing on the other person doesn't help him or her to understand you any better and only makes that person defensive. Thus rather than saying, "You are never happy. You should focus on what's good about our relationship." You might say instead, "When I think that you're unhappy, I worry and wish that I or you or somebody could do something to make you feel better about us."
5. The speaker should be careful to keep the message short. This is not the place for long soliloquies. Listening is hard enough work without having to keep track of a lot of material. Take it easy on your partner and insure that you'll be understood better by keeping your message as short as possible.
6. The person in the listener role should "hold the basket." Listen carefully with your whole body and from an empathic perspective. Remember that your job will be to reflect your empathic understanding of what your partner has said, so pay careful at-

tention. If your partner is giving you too much material you can gently hold up your hand and ask for an opportunity to paraphrase first before he or she continues.

7. Now the listener should paraphrase. Remember that the goal is to reflect your empathic understanding so that both you and your partner can begin to clarify your shared understanding.
8. As the speaker, when you have heard your partner's paraphrase, you get to notice where it sounded like what you most wanted to communicate and perhaps where it seemed to miss the mark a bit. If your partner's paraphrase has made you feel like he or she understood what you were trying to say, then you can say something like, "Yes, that sounds right," and pass the floor to your partner so you can switch roles. When you switch roles, return to Step #4 and work your way through again with the new speaker.
9. If, however, you as the speaker feel that the paraphrase missed the mark in an important way, you should keep the floor and try again to get your meaning across in as succinct a way as possible. You and your partner should repeat this cycle of until you both feel that your meaning has been understood. Please remember that this should only be a small bite and not the whole meal. You want to make sure that you both get plenty of turns as speaker and listener. Floor switches should ideally be happening frequently so that you are having a conversation with each other and not simply talking at each other. If you make frequent floor switches, you will both feel thoroughly heard. If, however, you hog the floor, you'll both end up feeling frustrated.
10. Once you have each had a handful of turns as speaker, stop, give each other a hug and take a break. This can be exhausting work and it is important not to walk away from this exercise feeling like you have been put through the wringer. Make sure to keep the whole conversation short enough so that you don't begin to feel that every time you sit down to do this you're going to leave exhausted.
11. Ideally, here is what a cycle between you and I should look like.
    a. You speak and I listen.
    b. I paraphrase and you clarify.

c. I paraphrase again and you agree that I have understood.
d. I speak and you listen.
e. You paraphrase and I clarify.
f. You paraphrase again and I agree that you have understood.
g. Repeat.

4

MINDFULNESS: LEARNING TO LOVE IN THE MOMENT

The main point of this chapter will be to help you assess the quality of your "marital mindfulness" or your ability to attend to and appreciate your relationship with your partner in this moment. Research has begun to show that partners who are better able to attend mindfully to the here-and-now enjoy a higher quality marital relationship. Drawing on psychology's growing interest in mindfulness, this chapter will describe what we mean by mindfulness and will provide you with exercises to practice mindfulness as a couple and strengthen your capacity for mutual loving-kindness.

UNDILUTED PRESENCE

Mindfulness is the quality of being fully present in the here and now. In the simplest terms, mindfulness involves closely attending to your experience right here and now. It is a particular type of attention. Mindfulness is specifically moment-to-moment *nonjudgmental* awareness of your life as it is happening right now.

Normally we spend our lives perpetually distracted by thoughts and feelings about the past or the future. Although we can really only live here and now, we pay almost no attention to our present experience and let our lives pass by without notice. We are, more often than not, simply on "autopilot." We go through the motions of our lives with our partners with little thought or attention. The time we share together is often on automatic pilot. The conflicts we have with each other have a life of their own, often proceeding from start to finish with little sense that we have any control over their direction or intensity. Even the supposedly positive times we spend together are often so habitual and automatic that they feel dull and bland. The time that we do spend together, what little of it there may be, is often spent distracted by thoughts about the past or worries about the future. Mindfulness brings you home: home to your life, home to your marriage, and home to the love that is available to you right here and right now.

When is the last time you really *looked* at your partner with "fresh" eyes? I'm sure you glance at your partner all the time, but how often do you look deeply, past your expectations and habitual ways of seeing your partner? We all fall into habitual ways of looking at our partners, expecting them to think and act in predictable and unsurprising ways. So much so that we start to simply look past them, at home with our preconceptions rather than at home with our actual partners. Can you see past who you have come to *think* your partner is, to really *see* your partner for who he or she is today?

When is the last time you really *listened* to your partner? Again, I'm sure you hear your partner talking (or not talking) all the time, but how often do you really *listen* with all your attention and all your empathy to what your partner is saying *this time* both in words and actions. More often than not, we listen to our partners with only half an ear. We listen while thinking about other things, distracted by thoughts and feelings of the past and future, or formulating our response before our partner has even finished talking. How often do you give your partner your full attention when he or she is talking to you?

Perhaps the most important gift that you can give to your partner and to your marriage is the gift of your undiluted presence. Being truly present and attentive may be the most effective thing you can do for your marital health. We will spend some time together in other chapters considering how important healthy communication is to the long-term health of your marriage. In this chapter we will consider how important it is to show up *all the way* when we are with our partners, rather than showing up half distracted by the rattle and hum of our busy lives and the thoughts and feelings in our heads. Looking and *seeing* our partner for who he or

Table 4.1. The Mindful Relating Questionnaire

Definitely Something We Need to Improve 1	*Could Use Some Improvement* 2	*Neither a Strength nor Area for Improvement* 3	*Somewhat of a Strength* 4	*Definitely a Strength* 5

_____ 1. I am often pleasantly surprised by seeing my partner "in a new light."
_____ 2. I am aware of how my partner is changing and growing every day.
_____ 3. I don't make too many assumptions about what my partner thinks and feels.
_____ 4. I don't take my partner for granted.
_____ 5. When I am spending time with my partner, I don't get lost in thoughts about the past or future.
_____ 6. I can see past my assumptions about my partner to who he or she really is today.
_____ 7. I am careful with my partner when I'm angry.
_____ 8. I communicate how I am feeling to my partner.
_____ 9. I do not ruminate on my negative feelings for my partner.
_____ 10. I remind myself of my loving feelings for my partner.
_____ 11. I listen closely to my partner and give him or her my full attention.
_____ 12. I am fully present when making love with my partner.
_____ 13. I am able to be sad with my partner when he or she is sad.
_____ 14. I am able to be happy with my partner when he or she is happy.
_____ 15. I am able to give my partner all of my attention even when he or she is experiencing unpleasant feelings.
_____ 16. I almost always give my partner the benefit of the doubt.
_____ 17. I do not carry grudges toward my partner. I am able to let go of past injuries.
_____ 18. I am curious about and interested in my partner.
_____ 19. Often, when I look at my partner, it's like I'm seeing her or him for the first time.
_____ 20. I'm emotionally tuned in to my partner. I feel in myself his or her sadness, happiness, anger, and joy.
_____ 21. When we make love, I am not distracted by other thoughts and feelings. I feel completely present.
_____ 22. When we are disagreeing, I am aware of and careful with my partner's feelings.
_____ 23. I appreciate the time I spend with my partner.
_____ 24. I try to remain aware of my partner's likes and dislikes.
_____ 25. I deliberately do things on a daily basis that bring my partner joy and ease his or her burdens.
_____ 26. I feel like I'm always learning who my partner is.

she really is today and not just who we *think* he is or who we *wish* she'd be requires that we practice mindfulness. Showing up in a way that fosters genuine intimacy requires present-centered attention. All of the ingredients of a strong and healthy marriage benefit from our bringing to them greater mindfulness and fuller presence.

MINDFUL RELATING

I want to show you what mindfulness is and how it can benefit your marriage and family. First it is important to keep in mind that mindfulness is more a skill than a concept, so it is better to think of mindfulness as similar to playing a sport or a musical instrument. Rather than something you simply know how to do, it is something that you practice and the more you practice, the better you get. In order to illustrate the practice of mindfulness, consider the following simple example.

Consider the difference between absentmindedly eating an apple while you are busy doing something else like watching TV versus deliberately paying close attention to all the sensations of eating an apple undistracted by anything else. In the first case, it is easy for us to eat an apple all the way down to the core without tasting a single bite or enjoying a single moment of it. In the second case, we experience the apple as the small miracle that it actually is. Try it now, with an apple or with whatever else happens to be handy.

- First, look closely and really examine the apple before biting into it. Notice the variety of colors in the skin and the way the light bounces off of it as you turn it in your hand.
- Next, notice how it smells and how it feels in your hand. Pay attention to the texture and the weight.
- Now, bite into it and notice the "pop" of your teeth breaking the skin, the flavor of the juice and flesh, the texture and smell as you chew.
- Chew slowly and deliberately, really experiencing the flavor and texture thoroughly before swallowing.
- Feel it travel the whole way down your throat and into your belly.

Now, compare the two experiences. What is it like to eat an apple mindfully versus absentmindedly? You probably noticed that eating mindfully is a much richer and more enjoyable experience. You may have even discovered something you hadn't noticed before about apples and the eating of them. Now consider that if the experience of eating an apple mindfully versus absentmindedly is so dramatic, what might the difference be between relating mindfully versus relating absentmindedly?

Think about the normal experience of being with your partner when you are distracted by thoughts about something else. Maybe you are thinking about something that you have to accomplish tomorrow, or maybe you are thinking about something that happened earlier today that upset you, or maybe you are just thinking about what you are going to say next and aren't really listening to what your partner is saying now. When you are distracted from what is happening right in front of your face or from what is happening in your life right now, that is absentmindedness. When, instead, you are paying full attention, when you are listening actively to your partner and hearing clearly what he or she is saying, when you are seeing clearly what is right in front of your face, and you are clearly aware of what is happening right now, then that is mindfulness.

Mindfulness refers to our ability to direct our attention toward our ongoing present experience with an attitude of curiosity, openness, and acceptance. Mindfulness is our innate capacity to simply experience what is true right now without first judging it as good or bad. It is our natural capacity to be fully present with our immediate experience even as that experience continues to change. Notice that what I am describing as mindfulness is in somewhat direct contrast to our most common way of being in the world, which tends to be characterized by various degrees of distraction by thoughts and feelings about almost any other moment *except* this one. We think about the future, we think about the past, we worry, we ruminate, we plan, we regret, we are constantly time traveling in our head away from ourselves, away from our partners and children, and away from our lives. This is so much the norm for all of us that we completely fail to notice that we are even doing it. At the same time, we are also capable of various degrees of being fully present, and we all have had many experiences of being fully present throughout the day. Those experiences are usually brief, but a capacity for mindfulness is something that we all have and use to some degree.

A SIMPLE MINDFULNESS EXERCISE

Since mindfulness is a type of skill, it is something that we can get better at with practice. Practicing and getting better at mindfulness requires that we find something that is always with us here in the present moment and deliberately focusing our attention on it. Maybe the simplest practice is to pay close and deliberate attention to the physical experience of breathing in and out. What is nice about choosing the breath as the object of mindful focus is that it's always with us, it's always in motion, it's always in the present moment, and we can feel it with our whole body. We can use our breathing as our anchor in the present moment and by deliberately shifting our attention to the sensations of our breathing we immediately become more mindful of the moment.

Here is a simple and time-tested mindfulness exercise you can do right now.

- Adjust yourself so that you are sitting comfortably with good posture, feet flat on the floor, lower back slightly away from the back of the chair, head up and chin in.
- Lower or close your eyes so you are looking at nothing in particular.
- Shift your attention to the physical sensation of your breath entering and exiting your nostrils.
- Notice the coolness inside your nose as you breath in and the sensation of your belly rising.
- Notice the warmth of your breath as you exhale and the sensation of your belly falling.
- Notice that if you allow your body to take a deep breath and release it slowly all the way, that you can feel your whole body relaxing.
- Simply follow your breath without forcing it. Some breaths will be deep and long and some will be short and shallow. Follow each with equal attention.
- Move your attention to the sensation of breathing with your whole body. Feel your whole body breathing in and your whole body breathing out.
- Breathe in and out through the parts of your body that feel relaxed.
- Breathe in and out through the parts of your body that feel tension.

- Count your in breath as "One."
- Count your out breath as "Two."
- Continue counting breaths until you reach ten. If your mind wanders, gently guide it back to breathing and counting.
- If you have the time, continue this breathing exercise for 15 minutes. If you don't have the time right now, schedule some time later today to sit down and practice mindful breathing for 15 minutes.
- If you pay close and deliberate attention to your breathing for 15 minutes, you are likely to find that your thoughts and emotions are less scattered. As a result you are better able to attend to what is truly right in front of you, and perhaps more importantly, *who* is truly right in front of you.

You will notice initially that maintaining your attention on your breathing is quite challenging and that your mind has a strong tendency to wander rather aimlessly. You will also notice that with practice maintaining your attention on your breath becomes easier. As with any skill, the more you practice, the more skillful you will become. At first it may be quite a challenge and you will have to repeatedly remind yourself to bring your attention back to the sensations of your breath. It is unavoidable that you will frequently be distracted by other thoughts and sensations. This will be your lived experience of discovering your own God-given talent for mindfulness and the positive effect that practice can have on improving this natural skill. The key is to practice regularly, just like practicing a musical instrument or a sport, and to be gentle with yourself as you wander back and forth between being distracted and being mindful. Each instance of this wandering back and forth is one more bit of good old-fashioned practice. Try it one more time now for a few ten-breaths and then when you're ready; move on to the next section.

WHAT IS MINDFUL RELATING?

Mindful relating is simply the application of our capacity for mindfulness to our most important relationships. An emerging area of research has begun to show a clear relationship between mindfulness and marital health. Within my own lab we have been studying the possibility that a more open and receptive attention to the present moment promotes a more accepting and less avoidant orientation to the emotionally challenging nature of intimate relationships, such that we become more capable of responding to ourselves and our partners in ways that promote and maintain our marital health and genuine intimacy.

More mindful partners literally see each other more clearly, regard each other more non-judgmentally, behave more responsively toward each other, and navigate the emotionally challenging waters of intimacy more gracefully. Our own findings suggest that greater mindfulness is associated with greater relationship satisfaction, more warmly affectionate interactions, and greater inter-partner harmony across a range of marital domains.

The practice of mindful relating is itself a skill that improves with practice. For example, mindful listening is the practice of listening to your partner with your full attention. As in the breathing exercise, when you find your attention drifting away from listening to your partner, gently guide your attention back to what he or she is saying and to the emotional meaning behind it. In fact, an excellent way of practicing mindful relating is to use the speaker-listener technique described in the communication chapter while deliberately focusing on listening mindfully.

All of the ways in which you interact with your partner can be done mindfully. In addition to listening mindfully, we can also speak mindfully, attending closely to what we are saying and the likely impact of what we are saying on our partner. We can also look at our partners mindfully. Rather than simply glancing cursorily, try looking deliberately and with your full attention into your partner's eyes. Really look him or her in the eyes. Notice the color and shades, the forms and patterns, and the emotion communicated by them. Eyes are really quite lovely and vivid when seen mindfully. We can also touch our partners mindfully. Whether that touch is a brief hug and kiss before parting for the day, holding hands while walking together, or making love, we can pour our full attention into the experience of contact between us. The following is a simple exercise in mindful relating.

A SIMPLE EXERCISE IN MINDFUL RELATING

Talking is good. Not talking is also good. This is an exercise in mindful hugging. You and your partner should both read through this exercise before practicing it and you should both commit freely and fully to practicing it together.

- Begin by simply entering into a hug in whatever fashion is most natural to you both.
- Position your body so that it is in a natural and comfortable position and you are not straining in any way. As the exercise progresses, feel free to shift around within the hug to maintain your body in a comfortable position.
- First, close your eyes and breathe deeply into the hug. Let your body relax into the contact between you. Attend fully to the warmth and softness, the pressure of contact between your two bodies.
- Breathe your partner in. Allow yourself to become aware of scents and the experience of breathing in and out with your partner.
- Breathe into your whole body, both places of tension and comfort.
- Continue to breathe into the experience of holding and being held for at least 5 minutes. Stay present to all the experiences of your five senses. As your attention drifts away, gently guide it back into the present moment and the lived experience of hugging your partner.

You might also want to practice with longer periods of time, perhaps up to 15 minutes or more because this type of practice is fundamental to mindful relating. For some, this type of practice will come fairly easily, although sustaining mindfulness is a challenging practice for everyone. For others, this type of practice will be surprisingly challenging. Make note of the challenges that emerge and simply allow them to move in and out with the breath, without judging them, grappling with them, or pushing them away. With time, those challenges will get bored and wander away, leaving you and your partner alone with each other.

WHAT DO WE KNOW ABOUT THE BASIC BENEFITS OF MINDFULNESS?

Many scientists have begun to study the effects of mindfulness on a range of psychological and physical phenomenon. For example, researchers have consistently reported that people who are practicing mindfulness experience improvements in their mood. Studies have also shown similar improvements in the symptoms of depression and anxiety. For example, a 1998 study by Professor Shauna Shapiro of Santa Clara University showed that medical students engaging in the same sort of mindful breathing exercises presented above reported fewer depressive symptoms and fewer anxiety symptoms than medical students who were not engaging in any kind of mindfulness practice. A similar study conducted in 2003 by Dr. Steven Rosenzweig and colleagues at Thomas Jefferson University found improvements in medical students' experience of tension, anxiety, fatigue, and mental confusion for those who had been practicing mindfulness versus those who had not. Besides pointing out that medical students experience a lot of stress, anxiety, and fatigue, these and other similar studies show us that even under the most stressful of conditions, our own efforts to stay grounded in the experience of the present moment allow us to function more effectively and more happily both emotionally and cognitively.

In other words, we are all prone to making stressful circumstances even more stressful by losing sight of what is right in front of us because we are over-focused on worries about the future or ruminations about the past. This is as true in our intimate relationships as it is at work. Genuine intimacy and a healthy marriage can be emotionally demanding and cognitively complicated. The rich rewards of a truly healthy intimate relationship are most available to those who practice staying grounded in the here and now. Those rewards are most difficult to achieve for those who are most lost in their worries about the future or distracted by their memories of the past.

Scientists have found similar beneficial results of increased mindfulness even for those individuals struggling with more serious challenges. For example, Drs. Miller, Fletcher, and Kabat-Zinn of the University of Massachusetts in a 1995 study found that anxiety and depression amongst individuals meeting criteria for generalized anxiety and panic disorders were significantly reduced following a period of training in mindfulness-based stress reduction.

One of the current challenges being addressed by clinical scientists is the relatively high rates of relapse experienced by people who have suffered an episode of major depression in their lives. Research by Dr. John Teasdale and colleagues in 2000 found that individuals who were taught how to practice mindfulness in their daily lives were less likely to experience a relapse of their depressive symptoms over the long run. These individuals appeared to become better able to experience challenging emotions and thoughts without becoming distracted by those thoughts and feelings. They seemed to be better able to stay richly engaged in the world both when their thoughts and feelings were pleasant and when their thoughts and feelings were more unpleasant. The presence or absence of pleasant or unpleasant thoughts and feelings were less able to distract them from living their lives in vivid and personally meaningful ways.

Even challenging or psychologically painful internal states can be observed to dissipate when one chooses not to elaborate on the thoughts or feelings, but to simply notice them. With greater mindfulness it is possible to develop an understanding that negative feelings can be tolerated and even accepted, allowing us to be less reactive and more wisely responsive to emotionally challenging situations. In other words, we appear to be better at coping well with even the most challenging conditions when we are regularly reminding ourselves that everything that is most alive and most available for loving and effective action is right here in the present moment. We cannot return to the past for even an instant, just as we cannot leap forward into the future. We literally can only be alive right now. And it is from this place that we are most lovingly effective in our lives and relationships, no matter how challenging or simple right now may be.

More recent studies of naturally occurring mindfulness (how mindful we usually are without any real practice), have found that people who are naturally more mindful in their daily lives are also healthier across of number of psychological domains. For example, people who are more naturally mindful experience less anger in their lives. They are also more optimistic and less pessimistic, more likely to see the glass as half full than half empty. More naturally mindful people are also less painfully self-conscious and less unwisely impulsive. They report experiencing greater well-being, experiencing more positive emotions, being generally more satisfied with their lives, having higher self-esteem, as well as generally feeling more free, more competent, and experiencing greater intimacy.

Although a greater ability to engage our lives mindfully can be cultivated through specific mindfulness practices like the breathing practice described earlier, the ability to attend clearly to the present moment is a type of activity that humans engage in naturally to varying degrees. Those who tend to reside naturally in a more mindful state of awareness are more likely to behave skillfully with their emotions due to the level and quality of attention that they are directing to their internal and external environment. Because of this greater capacity to be clearly aware of what really matters both in ourselves and in our partners, we become better able to know what we are feeling, to empathize with what our partner is feeling, and to communicate in an empathic and effective way. The quality of our marital health cannot help but benefit from this type of loving attention.

A SIMPLE EXERCISE IN MINDFUL LOVING

A loving attitude toward our partners is also something that we can practice mindfully. The following is a simple exercise in mindful loving.

- Begin by sitting and breathing mindfully for a few 10-breaths.
- Now, visualize your partner looking happy, content, and loving.
- Think of all the kindnesses he or she has done for you over the years, all the ways in which he or she has ever moved lovingly in relation to you. Bring to mind all of the things that you love most about this person.
- Feel your love and respect for this person and shift your attention to the bare quality of this feeling.
- Let this feeling of love for your partner become the focus of your mindful attention. As your attention wanders away, gently guide it back to this feeling of love and respect for your partner.
- Let the feeling fill your whole body. Let these loving feelings fill your partner's whole body.
- Breathe into these feelings of love for your partner for several minutes.

EMOTIONAL CLARITY

Knowing what we are feeling when we are feeling it is of great benefit to our marital health. Studies have shown that those who are better able to identify their emotions while they are having them, rather than denying that there is any emotional content to their lives or being confused about what that emotional content is, experience greater love and happiness in their marriages. A greater ability to stay mindfully engaged with our own emotional experience in any given moment vastly improves our ability to know what we are feeling when we are feeling it and thus to behave wisely toward ourselves, our partners, and our children. The more mindfully present we are, the better able we should be to access the full range of our emotional experience.

Paying close attention may be particularly difficult during emotionally or psychologically stressful times. For example, when you are having a conflict with your partner, the less mindful you are the more likely you are to misread the emotional complexities of the moment and thus the more likely it is that you will do or say something unwise and destructive. On the other hand, the more mindful you are in that moment of conflict, the more likely you will be to recognize all the different emotions you are experiencing, *and* all the different emotions your partner is experiencing (clear-sighted empathy relies on present centered attention). Misunderstanding becomes less likely and mutually compassionate action emerges more naturally.

This can be as true in our interactions with our children as it is in our interactions with our spouses. For example, recently during my four-year-old son's nighttime routine, he became very upset just at the point where we usually brush his teeth. He was tired, I was tired, and he just really didn't want to brush his teeth. He became angry with me for trying to talk him into brushing his teeth and I became angry with him for getting so resistant in a spot that usually goes very smoothly. As I became angry I could feel all of these strong impulses beginning to emerge around forcing him to get back on my agenda. I could feel myself wanting to yell at him, give him a time out, and win this test of wills between us. At the very same time I could see that he was legitimately upset in a way that wasn't "just" angry and I wanted to help him feel better. So I stood there for a moment, noticing all of these strong and unpleasant feelings and thoughts coursing through me and rather than battle myself or battle him I found a little more room to make choices. I chose to look closely and find out more about what was upsetting him. I still had angry thoughts and feelings on board and I certainly didn't like the way that felt, but with a little bit of mindfulness I was a little better able to choose a wiser course of action than that suggested to me by my angry feelings. As it turned out, my son had skipped his usual bedtime snack and knew he wouldn't get to have it after he brushed his teeth. I gave him some time to himself to calm down, and then we went downstairs for his snack, brushed his teeth, and got him in bed on time and content. I'm quite sure that if I had reacted as angrily as my whole body was prepared to at that moment, the rest of the evening would have gone much less smoothly. I would have become more upset, he would have become more upset, and the whole emotional tone of the household would have suffered. We would likely have missed the bedtime goal and the only lesson my son would have learned would have been about coercion and disrespect. Instead he had an opportunity to learn about mutual respect, cooperation, and emotion skills while still maintaining the boundaries of a well-structured family environment. In this example, mindfulness was the key to engaging my challenging emotions more wisely. Again, we can apply the same type of mindfulness to conflict with our partners, increasing our chances of turning conflict into mutually respectful compromise rather than embittering coercion or stalemate.

UNDERSTANDING COMPLICATED FEELINGS

Greater mindfulness in the moment can also help us to recognize when we are experiencing more than one emotion at the same time. We call these "blended" emotions and more often than not our most common conflicts tend to be a product of blended emotions that we are not openly acknowledging and communicating. Probably the most common example of the type of emotion blend that causes us trouble in our relationships is the blend of anger and hurt. As described in the chapter on emotion skills, we often mask hurt with anger because anger makes us feel less vulnerable. At the same time, acting out our anger in hostile or withdrawing ways also makes it less likely that conflicts will be resolved well. Greater mindfulness can help us to acknowledge and tolerate the hurt underlying our anger such that we are in a better position to communicate that hurt effectively. If we are only aware of our anger and the messages that anger is giving us about "injustice," revenge, and coercion, then we are much less likely to reach for the loving response we need in that moment. One of the principle benefits of any kind of mindfulness practice appears to be an increased tolerance for our own unpleasant feelings. This is particularly beneficial because we will all continue to have unpleasant emotional experiences throughout our lives. If we are intolerant of our unpleasant thoughts and feelings then we tend to react to those moments of our lives much less skillfully, to the detriment of ourselves and everyone around us.

KNOWING WHAT YOU'RE FEELING AND HOW TO TALK ABOUT IT

Studies in my own research lab have found that more mindful partners are indeed better at identifying their own emotions, as well as being better at communicating their emotions to others. Our capacity to know what we are feeling as we are feeling it requires a certain level of mindful attention to our moment-to-moment experience *and* a willingness to tolerate those feelings. Our feelings tend to change from moment to moment both in terms of their content (worry to anger to guilt, etc.) and in terms of their intensity (from barely noticeable to completely overwhelming). To the degree that we are distracted from our present experience, our ability to identify our own emotions is compromised, which in turn compromises our ability to engage fully in the emotional processes of intimacy.

Being fully present means, in part, openness, curiosity, and acceptance of our emotional experience as well as of the emotional experience of our partner. Fear is usually what keeps us from being fully present. We are often at some level afraid to have the feelings we are having; afraid of what they mean, afraid they will run out of control, afraid they will overwhelm us, afraid they are shameful, afraid we will be judged harshly for having them, so we run away from them and in the process run away from our own lives. Greater mindfulness allows a place to stand where we can be courageous in our acceptance of whatever our experience is right now and equally courageous in accepting whatever our partner's experience is right now. We can approach our own lives with our partners with great curiosity rather than fear.

CHAPTER 4

EMPATHY, COMPASSION, AND LOVING-KINDNESS

Some of the most recent research exploring the relationship between mindfulness and empathy shows that our ability to be in tune with our partners and our availability to experience concern for another's feelings are a product of our attention to the present moment. Empathy refers to our ability to be sensitive to another person's emotional state and to be able to show that person that we genuinely understand and *feel* how she or he is feeling. In other words, empathy is an emotional experience as much if not more than a cognitive experience. There can be a world of difference between knowing our partner feels sad and *feeling* their sadness. Real empathy requires genuine presence.

Relationship scientist Mark Davis at Eckerd College has described empathy as having three parts. The first part is "perspective taking" or being able to stand in your partner's shoes and see things from his or her perspective. The second part is "empathic concern" or the ability to express caring about our partner's welfare and compassion toward his or her experience. The third part is "personal distress," or the degree to which we tend to become overwhelmed by the suffering of others. To the degree that we find other people's pain personally intolerable, we are less available to experience and act on feelings of empathy.

The results of studies in my own lab with my graduate student Karen Wachs has shown that greater mindfulness is associated with a greater capacity for empathy. We think this may be because a greater ability to stay grounded in the present emerges with a greater capacity to accept those thoughts and feelings that we experience through empathy for others. Feeling your partner's pain is actually personally painful. If I can't tolerate my own pain, it will be difficult for me to empathize with the pain of others. Compassionate acceptance of our own unpleasant feelings allows us to maintain empathic contact with the suffering of others.

Empathy emerges as a natural outgrowth of our greater openness to the experience of others. Being less distracted by thoughts and feelings about the past and future means more of our attention is available for taking our partner's perspective. We are born capable of great empathy and as long as we are not distracted, as long as we are not avoiding or running away, as long as we are able to just stand quietly next to our partners, empathy will flow as naturally as breathing.

LOVING YOUR PARTNER AS PERFECTLY IMPERFECT

Another interesting thing that seems to result from more regularly paying attention to the totality of our present experience is a greater ability to love our partner "warts and all." We talk about this as loving your partner as perfectly imperfect. It seems like we all know that "nobody's perfect" but that we often fail to deeply understand that our partner's imperfections will always be part of what makes him or her absolutely perfect. You are exactly who and what you are right now, "warts and all," and there is something about that that is, quite simply, perfect. Similarly, your partner is exactly who he or she is right now, "warts and all," and there is also something about that that is just right and without flaw. The same could be said for your relationship as a whole. All relationships emerge with "natural flaws in the fabric" and when we can settle down into our lives, fully embracing those flaws in a spirit of loving cooperation, then we nurture and protect the health of all those we love.

It is also likely that as we practice being mindful in our marriage and with our children that we find ourselves more naturally chalking up our partner's and children's "less than pleasant" behavior to something having more to do with passing circumstances than with something fundamentally "wrong" with who they are as people. Relationship science research tells us that more distressed couples tend to attribute their partners' unpleasant behavior to something about them that is internal, stable, and global. That means that they see the cause of their partners' unpleasant behavior as something about who they are as a person rather than something having to do with passing circumstances. For example, if your partner leaves a mess in the kitchen, a more distressed attribution would be "he left a mess because he's a pig." A more positive attribution would be "he left a mess because he was distracted by something else." Notice the first "because" leads us to see our partner in a particularly negative light and probably to confront him with his character deficit in an effort to get him to see the error of his ways. The second "because," leads us to see our partner in a more neutral or even compassionate light and more likely to simply remind him that he left a mess or even to help straighten it up ourselves.

There is something about being more fully present in the moment that predisposes us toward more positive attributions for our partner's behavior and this is likely the result of greater empathy. Scientists who have studied attributions have discovered that we are much more likely to attribute our own negative behavior to external, temporary, and specific circumstances and more likely to attribute the behavior of others to internal, stable, and global character flaws. Increased empathy makes it much more likely that we will treat our partners just as gently as we tend to treat ourselves.

GENTLE ANGER

Finally, when we are more mindful we also tend to be more inclined toward thoughtful, considered responses to our partner even when we are feeling negative emotions, like anger. When we commit ourselves to practicing more mindful relating, we experience an increased tolerance for both our own and our partner's negative emotions and as a result we find ourselves less impulsively reactive to points of friction between us. When we are better able to notice and tolerate the discomfort of feelings like disappointment, frustration, and shame, then we allow ourselves an opportunity to actively adapt and cope through perspective taking and compassion, rather than simply through reactive displays of anger.

It may be that a more present-centered orientation to our lives ultimately diminishes the intensity of our negative emotions by rendering them less aversive. In other words, we tend not to make our negative emotions even more negative by struggling to deny or get rid of them or by trying to force those around us to deny or get rid of them for us. When we can relate to our unpleasant emotional experiences as simply something else that happens to be true right now, then somehow they don't seem to be quite as unsettling. When our own emotions are less unsettling to us then we are much more available to be gentle with both ourselves and our partners and much less likely to cause damage in a panicky tantrum against what amounts to emotional "spilled milk."

Secondly, some ability to keep the "noise" of our own minds down to a dull roar should allow us to take better care of those relationships which we value most deeply, even when we are stressed and upset. For many of us, when we become upset we find ourselves thinking about, and virtually reliving all the slights, minor and major, that our partners have perpetrated against us since the beginning of time and to project those slights forward into our future together as far as the mind can see. Relationship researchers refer to this phenomenon as "kitchen-sinking" because in such moments we tend to throw everything and the kitchen sink into the argument. Greater attention to the details of the moment and the resulting greater ability to "let go" of resentments about the past and fears about the future means we can take better care of what is true right now.

Thirdly, the more we can practice bringing our full attention back to right now, the more likely we will be able to avoid engaging in all those tired and destructive patterns of interaction that are eating away at the foundation of our marital and family relationships. We almost all come to our adult relationships with patterns of behavior acquired in our past. Maybe our father was a screamer when he was angry. Maybe our mother withdrew into icy silence when she was upset with us. And yet as much as we know from our own experience how painful and destructive those reactions were to us, in our own moments of mindlessness we find ourselves behaving in exactly the same ways and perpetuating exactly the same injuries.

As we practice being more consciously attentive to what is true right now, we become better able to stay out of these habitual responses and better able to choose wiser and healthier responses. We become better able to notice our habitual impulses without actually playing them out. We might for example feel like yelling but noticing that feeling from a perspective of nonjudgmental acceptance, choose to respond with empathy and compassionate assertiveness. The more mindful we can be, the more likely it is that we will wake up to our habitual patterns and explore healthier alternatives. We will find ourselves more aware of what is unique to each situation as it arises without reacting as though it is the same fight, with the same fighters and the same moves from hundreds of past bouts.

What patterns do you notice in your own marriage? Where do you find yourself reacting with the same blame, the same judgment, the same angry flinch or lash? What happens if you take a deep breath and remind yourself to look deeply and with respectful curiosity at what is happening both inside and outside? Do you see options emerge from the fog of anger that maybe you hadn't seen quite so clearly before? Do you find yourself at least a little more aware of how fragile this moment is and how you might choose to take good care of yourself, your partner, and your children in *this* moment?

SEEING YOUR REAL PARTNER

I noted earlier that perhaps the greatest gift that you can give to your partner is your undiluted presence. A facet of that undiluted presence is really seeing your partner for who he or she is today and not for who you think she is or wish he was or thought he used to be. It is a very common psychological phenomenon for us to put the people around us into artificially constructed boxes that let us move around them without having to pay too close attention to them. The clear downside to this natural tendency, however, is that it leads us to dramatically oversimplify the people we love. We become incurious about them and bored with them and convince ourselves that we know everything there is to know about them. We treat our partners as though they haven't changed one iota in the last ten years and completely blind ourselves to the fact that they are not even the same people they were yesterday. We tend to construct two-dimensional representations of our real partners and insert those life-sized cutouts between us and them. Then the relationship we have is with the two-dimensional cutout and not with our real, changing, complicated partner.

Greater mindfulness reminds us to remain curious about our partners on a day-to-day basis. The more present-centered we are, the better able we are to see that our partner today is not exactly the same person we were married to yesterday, and we get to be curious about who this new person is today. The bottom line being that with greater mindfulness comes greater capacity to be curious about the people we love and see them with fresh eyes and listen to them with renewed interest.

In a sense, if you are bored, you're just not paying attention. Worry about the future and resentment of the past obscure our capacity to revel in the loving partnership that is right here before our eyes. If we can follow our breath into the present moment, then we can wake up to what treasures we already have. Gandhi said, "If you don't see God in the next person you meet, you need look no further." Allow yourself to see God or the sacred in your partner, in your relationship, in the quality of your actions toward your spouse and children. If you can genuinely and palpably experience that sacred presence, then you are truly home.

5

ACCEPTANCE: GOD GRANT ME THE SERENITY

PRAYING FOR SERENITY

Many people are familiar with a prayer about coping with the many challenges of life called the Serenity Prayer. The words of this prayer perfectly capture the attitude of acceptance that we are exploring in this chapter.

"God grant me the serenity to accept the things I cannot change, the courage to change the things that must be changed and the wisdom to know the difference."

The main point of this chapter is to convey to you, the reader, the essential nature of acceptance and how fundamentally important acceptance is to the overall health and quality of your marriage and your life. In a later chapter we will explore in more detail the courage to actively seek change.

What is acceptance? The Serenity Prayer itself does not actually define acceptance, and yet somehow we seem to have an intuitive sense of what it means to accept the things we cannot change. In this short prayer, acceptance is placed in contrast with the courage to change the things that must be changed. By this contrast we get a sense for what acceptance is not. It is not the struggle to try to change what is simply so or to make the world as it is conform to our wishes for how it should be. Yet knowing what to try to change and what to practice accepting does not necessarily come easily to us, and so we ask for the wisdom to know the difference. When that wisdom is granted, and we begin to clearly recognize that some aspects of our lives, of our marriage, of our partner are unlikely to change in the manner we most wish, then what opens up for us is the practice of acceptance. And yet, what exactly is this alternative? What is acceptance?

Based on recent theoretical and empirical advances, this chapter will help readers to get a sense for the necessary role in a healthy marriage of mutual acceptance. How accepting are you of your partner's shortcomings, foibles, and mistakes? How accepting is your partner of you, just for who you are, "warts and all?" This chapter will present a research-based discussion of the positive power of acceptance on marital health and happiness and will provide exercises for nurturing greater degrees of acceptance both for yourself and for your partner.

Table 5.1. The Acceptance Questionnaire

Definitely Something We Need to Improve 1	*Could Use Some Improvement* 2	*Neither a Strength nor Area for Improvement* 3	*Somewhat of a Strength* 4	*Definitely a Strength* 5

_____ 1. I feel like my partner accepts me as a person, "warts and all."
_____ 2. I accept who my partner is as a person "warts and all."
_____ 3. My partner is accepting of who I am, faults and mistakes included.
_____ 4. I am accepting of who my partner is, faults and mistakes included.
_____ 5. My partner accepts my faults and weaknesses.
_____ 6. I accept my partner's faults and weaknesses.
_____ 7. My partner doesn't call my attention to my weaknesses.
_____ 8. My partner appreciates the "real me."
_____ 9. I am comfortable just being myself around my partner.
_____ 10. My partner is comfortable just being himself or herself around me.
_____ 11. I have come to terms with things that once bothered or upset me in our relationship.
_____ 12. When my partner disappoints me, I am able to let it go.
_____ 13. My partner likes me for me.
_____ 14. I don't dwell on my partner's weaknesses.
_____ 15. I'm happy with my partner the way he/she is.
_____ 16. I am able to take the bad with the good in my relationship.

WHAT IS ACCEPTANCE?

The Target: The Things We Wish Were Different

Acceptance begins with something that we wish were different and that we pour too much life and suffering into trying to change. We do not generally find ourselves thinking about change and acceptance when it comes to the things that we like. We seldom recite the Serenity Prayer when confronted yet again with our partner's good habits and loving, attentive behavior. Instead, the main targets of an accepting attitude are those things about our partner and our marriage (and ourselves) that we find distasteful, the things we don't like, and wish were different. If you spend a couple of minutes thinking about it, I bet you can come up with several things about your partner that you regularly find yourself wishing were different. Keep one or two of those things in mind as you read through the rest of this chapter and explore what it might be like to take a step or two in the direction of greater acceptance.

The Response: Run Away, Attack, or Avoid

When confronted by something that we find aversive, our first instinct is to try to escape from it or change it. We identify it as a problem and immediately set off to solve it. We are all natural born problem solvers and for the most part our good problem-solving skills work very well for us on a day-to-day basis. If we have an itch, we scratch it. If we need money, we work. If we're lonely, we find people to hang around with. If our car breaks down, we get it fixed. If we are lost we ask for directions. If we are stuck, we ask for help. Almost all the problems that confront us on a day-to-day basis lend themselves relatively well to our natural problem-solving inclinations.

For example, consider a couple in which Dick and Jane have different tolerances for clutter versus tidiness around the house and Dick is upset by the many messes that Jane leaves around the house. Dick's first response is likely to be simple problem solving. To solve the "clutter problem" he either cleans up himself or maybe asks Jane if she could try being neater. So, we have a situation that Dick finds unpleasant and wishes were different. We also have a change driven problem-solving response that Dick hopes will make the problem go away.

The fact of the matter is, however, not everything can be changed. And some things are less amenable to change than others. For example, our partner's basic personality is very unlikely to change, no matter how sophisticated our problem-solving attempts or unassailable the force of our arguments. The same can be said for many of the ways that our partners are just plain different than us, like different tolerances for clutter, different emotional reactions to money issues, or different needs for closeness or sex. Unfortunately, the harder we try to change something that won't change, the more it feels like we are beating our head against the wall, the more likely we are to start using more coercive and maritally destructive strategies.

If like Dick, our attempts to change our partner fail repeatedly, then we are likely to shift our problem-solving strategy to more openly angry and aggressive ways of trying to force change. For example, Dick might start to complain bitterly about Jane's messes and criticize her repeatedly for not picking up after herself. He might become angrier and angrier and more and more pushy in his attempts to force Jane to change, perhaps hoping that if he is just forceful enough she will capitulate and become a tidier person. Unfortunately, this strategy is likely to work in the short run, with angry outbursts being followed by short periods of time in which Jane tries to be tidier, even if just to avoid the drama. However, Jane is likely to resent feeling pushed to meet Dick's expectations and if the issue is essentially about a fundamental difference in their personalities, then any changes brought on by arguments are unlikely to last for long. Jane will eventually drift back to being who she is, her naturally more cluttered self. Regrettably, the price the marriage pays for these short periods of compliance is likely to be very high.

Another way that partners sometimes react to those things about each other that they find aversive is by withdrawal or avoidance. For example, Dick might react to Jane's greater comfort with messiness by withdrawing into his own space or by trying to stay away from the house as much as possible. In other words, he solves the problem by trying to avoid it as much as he can. Of course, the main problem with this type of solution is that by withdrawing from and avoiding the problem, he simultaneously withdraws from and avoids Jane. And, as I've noted before, there is good research evidence to suggest that withdrawal and avoidance are even more corrosive to the basic health of marriage than repeated unsuccessful change attempts and active criticism (as bad as those things are). In fact, withdrawal is often the last stage in an accumulation of hopelessness that results from our desperate struggle to change something that refuses to bend to our will.

The Consequent: Doing More Harm Than Good

If fruitless attempts to change the unchangeable about ourselves, our partners, our marriages, and our lives were harmless, then we would have little to worry about. However, much more often than not, it is these very change attempts, and even more the bitter sense of dissatisfaction that underlie them, that corrode our capacity for health and happiness. In other words, despite what we find ourselves convinced of, it is not those things that we dislike that make us suffer, it is the fact that we dislike them. This is particularly true when it comes to those things that will not change. By trying to change these things about our partner, we both explicitly and implicitly communicate a rejection of something about them that is simply true and goes all the way down to the core of who they are. It is a rejection of them; a rejection of the people who counts on us above all not to reject them. Even if our partner goes along with our criticism, taking deeply to heart our desire that he or she be different, something inside him or her shrivels and withdraws; pulling away from us and the life we share together. A distance opens up between us and in that space, rot sets in.

This shriveling and pulling away is even more likely in those cases where our aversion is acted out in the form of personal criticism, a generally judgmental attitude, or other forms of pushing angrily for change. Not only does the gap open up, but defensiveness, counter-criticism, returned anger, and bitter resentment grow up beside it. Partners find themselves moving into opposite corners and begin to see themselves as adversaries rather than allies. No one ever responds to an angry attack against their character with a sudden flash of insight and a deep sense of gratitude. Instead, the most natural reaction to being pushed is to push back, to become unassailably defensive, or to withdraw in hurt and anger. None of this is conducive to change or long-term marital health.

In the final analysis, attempts to change the unchangeable always do more harm than good. When we struggle to change things about ourselves that are not available for change, we tie ourselves into knots of self-loathing that pollute everything we touch. When we struggle to change the unchangeable about those we love, like bulls trustingly allowed into a shop of priceless China, we recklessly crush the irreplaceable, leaving dust and pain where once was the promise of genuine intimacy.

WHAT IS ACCEPTANCE? PART II: LETTING GO AND EMBRACING

The Moment of Recognizing That Change Is Not the Answer

There are many things that simply do not lend themselves well to a change agenda and in particular there are many things about living intimately with another human being that do not lend themselves easily to change. Acceptance, or developing an accepting attitude, involves "coming to terms with" those unpleasant things that you cannot change. It means letting go of our efforts to change those things and letting them be as they are, unmolested by us. Acceptance in one respect means letting go of our efforts to change those things about our partner that we wish were different.

If we are extremely lucky, there will come a time, perhaps this very moment, when it will dawn on us that the struggle to change is not the answer, that maybe there is another way that flows more gracefully within the currents of our own lives. It is at this moment that the possibility of acceptance arrives to save us from ourselves.

THE ACCEPTANCE CONTINUUM

Bitter Rejection

Acceptance exists on a continuum from bitter rejection to what Professor Marsha Linehan of the University of Washington has called radical acceptance. On the extreme negative end of the spectrum is bitter rejection. This is the attitude that says "My partner's irritable mood is totally unacceptable and he had better snap out of it if he wants any positive regard from me at all." In other words, bitter rejection involves rejection not just of your partner's unpleasant behavior, but of your partner himself. When we adopt a bitterly rejecting attitude we take back our love and esteem for our partner until he or she "earns" it by behaving only in a fashion to our liking. Bitter rejection means our love is conditional. We only provide it when our partner jumps through all our hoops and not when she disappoints us, bugs us, or does things that get under our skin.

Tolerance

Moving up the continuum from bitter rejection we pass through a middle point we call tolerance. This is where rejection and acceptance come together in equal parts. Although we continue to thoroughly dislike that thing our partner does that gets under our skin, we put up with it, if somewhat grudgingly. For example, in one couple I worked with, the wife enjoyed going out with her friends at least once or twice a week and the husband couldn't stand it. They argued frequently about it and were on the verge of divorce when they came to see me. She was simply unwilling to give up her freedom and had come to feel that if she couldn't enjoy the company of her friends without having to fight with her partner about it, then maybe divorce was the best option. He, on the other hand, simply couldn't see why going out with her friends was so important to her and given that it made him feel so left out and jealous, he couldn't understand why she wouldn't just stop and stay home with him instead. As we worked on developing a greater degree of mutual acceptance between them, there came a point in therapy where he had begun to develop some greater degree of tolerance for her freedom, although he clearly continued to fall short of a more thoroughgoing acceptance. He would report that she had gone out with her friends and that although he felt upset by it, he "bit his tongue" and didn't criticize her for it. He began to see that his greater tolerance improved the overall quality of their lives together and she clearly appreciated his efforts to accept her individuality. Both, however, were clearly aware that tolerance, while a step in the right direction, was not the goal they were ultimately after. In other words, tolerance was clearly better than bitter rejection, but it still didn't feel entirely right, it still felt like a compromise, if perhaps a necessary one, for both of them.

Radical Acceptance

While it is the case that tolerance is sometimes the best that can be hoped for, the ultimate goal of acceptance is something much closer to what we'll call generously embracing or radical acceptance. It is that point on the continuum where the aversive properties of the situation are outweighed by compassionate understanding, an appreciation of the differences and complexities that are essential to a real, human, intimate relationship. Genuine acceptance comes from beginning to see those facets of a previously aversive situation that might actually be embraced. It involves discovering aspects of the issue, angles of compassionate understanding, that shift how we see and experience what we previously only wanted to change.

Sometimes this shift involves discovering genuinely embraceable aspects of what had been previously seen as wholly aversive. For example, you might find that you actually appreciate the financial stability that results from your partner's frugality, despite the fact that you could initially only see that behavior as "cheap" and "penny-pinching." When seen as cheap and penny-pinching, we can't help but want to change it. When seen as frugal and responsible, it becomes instead something we genuinely value.

Other times, genuine acceptance results from a clearer recognition that what you had previously complained bitterly about is so much an inextricable part of the warp and weft of your partner that it becomes loveable as an endearing flaw in a loveable whole. Maybe your partner is a worrywart and initially you struggled to get him to stop being so anxious and to "just let it go." Over time, however, with the advent of a more accepting attitude, you may find that your partner's worrywart qualities are an endearing, if perhaps at times frustrating, part of who he is as a whole and if you were to get rid of that part of him, he simply would no longer be the same person you love and married.

In general, each step up the acceptance continuum, from bitter rejection to radical acceptance, is a step in the direction of greater marital health. Learning to pick your battles and to simply let go of unwinnable struggles to change your partner will add immeasurably to your store of marital happiness and peace of mind. At the same time, do not necessarily expect saint-like levels of acceptance from yourself. Sometimes part of moving in the direction of greater acceptance is coming to terms with the fact that there are some things about your partner that are always going to rub you the wrong way and that being bugged on occasion is a small price to pay in the grand scheme of things. In fact, this may be the ultimate form of radical acceptance, allowing ourselves to fully experience our partners without rejecting or holding off even those parts that can get under our skin.

WHAT WE CAN LEARN FROM COUPLES IN THERAPY

Acceptance is a kind of change. It is a change in you. Rather than struggling to change something that cannot be changed, acceptance means changing the way we relate to those things that we wish were different. It is an internal change in how we perceive or understand the source of our current frustration. Acceptance is complicated, however, because accomplishing acceptance involves both making conscious decisions and developing a more compassionate understanding of that which we seek to accept. In other words, some aspects of achieving acceptance involve things that we can "do on purpose" and some aspects involve more of the type of "aha" experience that comes from seeing something in a new light. For example, coming to terms with the difficulty a partner might have expressing affection involves both a willingness to try moving in the direction of greater acceptance and a willingness to pursue a deeper understanding of the issue. It also involves developing that deeper understanding in a way that allows you to experience the issue from a more compassionate perspective.

One couple I saw struggled with this issue explicitly. Much of the difficulty in their marriage stemmed from a pattern in which he craved and pursued affection and she could at times find affection cloying and beside the point. Because of this fundamental difference between them, they were stuck in a pursue-withdraw pattern in which the more he pursued affection, the more she withdrew from it and the more she withdrew from it, the more he pursued it. Although in many respects this was treated as a pattern that emerged *between them* based on their individual differences, treatment also involved coming to understand the roots of her discomfort with affectionate expression. Over the course of therapy it became clear that her difficulty expressing affection had deep roots in her childhood attachment experiences. She recalled growing up in a household in which she really had no one to turn to with her more difficult emotions, so instead she learned to keep them to herself. She also talked about how chaotic and turbulent the relationship between her parents was from her earliest memories until she was in her preteens when they finally divorced. After her father left the household, she remembered continuing to have a very turbulent relationship with her mother until she moved out several years later and moved in with her father, who she reported forming a good relationship with. It became clear that growing up in this environment taught her that expressions of affection were rare beasts indeed and that her own needs for affection were simply disappointing to have and, again, beside the point.

In her adult relationship with her husband, she described very much wanting to have an affectionate relationship with him and at the same time finding the whole "affection thing" often annoying. It is interesting to notice here that her basic underlying need for affection was still there, despite a history that provided very little room for it. So, as an adult, her experience of affection, both needing it and receiving it, was complicated. On the one hand, her basic human nature craved it and reveled in it, on the other hand, affection felt so much like all the disappointment that she felt as a kid that she withdrew from it and retreated into the other aspects of her life.

As both partners gained this more thorough understanding of why she had the difficulty she did with expressions of affection, they both found themselves becoming more tolerant of this issue in their lives and more compassionate toward her struggled-with ambivalence about affection. He became more accepting of the difficulty she had expressing and accepting affection as he came to realize that the issue wasn't so much about him as it was about her attachment history before she ever met him. He also found himself more accepting because he was able to see more clearly that this was something that she was struggling with herself and that she did, at a fundamental level, want to have an affectionate relationship with him. Seeing her struggle more clearly helped him to appreciate the issue from a more compassionate perspective and put him in a better position to tolerate her ambivalence about affection without becoming irritated and defensive. He also became better able to tolerate his own experience of sometimes wanting affection when she wasn't really available to give it. At the same time, she herself gained a more compassionate understanding of her own experience and was better able to forgive herself for carrying this particular struggle in her life. I think it's important to note that acceptance, when we genuinely nurture it, is much more often than not a two way street in which we simultaneously experience greater compassionate acceptance for ourselves and our own challenging experience as well as for our partner and his or her difficult struggles.

Both partners came to better understand the roots of this particular issue in their marriage. They began to come to terms with the likelihood that she would continue to struggle with issues of affection for many years to come, if not for the rest of their marriage. Similarly, he in turn would continue to occasionally want more affection than might be legitimately available from her and his owning that want without becoming demanding played its equal part in their overall experience of greater acceptance. By developing this more accepting stance, they were better able to come together as partners in relation to issues of affection in their relationship. They were better able to work on the issue as partners, together and on the same page, rather than as they had been doing before, as opponents in the affection wars.

Although this example comes out of therapy, it is possible for you to foster an atmosphere of greater mutual acceptance on your own (although a few sessions of therapy can help if you're feeling stuck). Again, all of us want to feel accepted by our partners and not just for those things about us that are easy to love, but also for things about us that we know are our flaws and weaknesses. We are all so much better off when we feel we have an ally in our struggles with our own defects than when we feel that we have yet another vicious critic.

HOW TO TELL THE DIFFERENCE BETWEEN SOMETHING THAT MUST BE CHANGED AND SOMETHING THAT MUST BE ACCEPTED

Acceptance is not about accepting things like psychological and physical abuse or the sorts of things that diminish us or others. Acceptance is not hopeless resignation in the face of things that can and must be changed for the mutual benefit of the whole family. Although the distinction between change and acceptance is not hard and fast, there are general rules of thumb that one can apply to get a rough idea about the difference between what must be changed and what must be accepted. The most basic rule of thumb is the "more harm than good" rule. If the absence of change ultimately results in more harm than good, then change, if possible, is the only wise answer. The best example involves issues of physical violence. The occurrence of physical violence in an intimate relationship is the most toxic and dangerous of events. Accepting violence as part of a relationship does more harm than good and is a legitimate target for change. Victims of violence must seek out and get the help that they need to escape from violence and the threat of violence.

This includes, by the way, psychological violence. Words and actions that fall short of hitting, but that nevertheless function to instill a climate of fear, control, and domination are the equivalent of physical violence in terms of their detrimental effect on the relationship. In fact, there is good evidence in the scientific literature that psychological violence is as bad, if not worse than, physical violence. Accepting psychological violence does more harm because everyone involved is diminished and miserable.

Apart from the issue of domestic violence, applying the "more harm than good" rule is something that you have to do for yourself. Ultimately, you have to make up your own mind about the limits of tolerance and acceptance in your relationship. Making these decisions is guided by your own deeply held values, including the values you hold most deeply about family and marriage. People do differ in terms of what they are willing to accept for the sake of their values, relationship, and family. For example, for some couples the occurrence of an affair by one of the partners is completely intolerable and the survival of the relationship is beside the point in relation to the intolerability of living in it after having been betrayed. For these people, their values hold that fidelity and trust are the cornerstones of marriage and that once violated, forgiveness is simply out of the question.

Other couples survive infidelity, not so much by accepting the infidelity itself, but by accepting the partner's mistake and accepting the partner's genuine remorse and recommitment to the marriage. This process is never easy and I don't mean to make it sound like recovery from infidelity is quick and painless if only one is willing to forgive and forget. I give the example of infidelity as the most dramatic example of an event that for some ultimately leads to forgiveness and acceptance and for others ultimately leads to dissolution of the marriage.

In general, however, those things that lend themselves most easily to change are those day-to-day things that involve behavior that a person has complete conscious control over. For example, a division of labor in the household that feels unfair is fully available for change because it involves things that you and your partner *do* rather than who you and your partner *are*. By contrast, in almost all couples, one partner is going to be by nature more orderly and organized and the other partner is going to be, by comparison, more chaotic and disorganized. This type of difference has to do with how each partner is made, what their individual personalities are, and their deeply ingrained ways of being in the world. Such things simply are not available for easy and lasting change. Furthermore, to attempt to change each other when it comes to something about who we *are* is not only foolhardy and doomed to fail, but is dangerously corrosive to the foundation of the marriage.

In a nutshell, those things that are available for change tend to be those things that we *do* versus those things that we simply *are*. It may be too simple to say that you can only change what you can change, but fundamentally that is what it boils down to. The challenge is figuring out what is actually changeable and what is worth the price you will pay to try to change it. You have to choose your battles wisely and they should be few and far between. Our fundamental need to feel accepted by the people we love is so deeply ingrained that acceptance of our partner "warts and all" should be given top priority and efforts to change him or her should be limited, gentle, and ultimately in the service of greater health for our partner, for our marriage, for our family, and for ourselves.

HOW TO BECOME MORE ACCEPTING

As I noted earlier, acceptance is the kind of change that we make in ourselves and so it is important to think about how we might come to cultivate a more accepting attitude toward our partner, our marriage, and ourselves. The key here has something to do with "letting go"; letting go of our struggle to change the unchangeable. Letting go starts with beginning to notice that we are hanging on. When we begin to notice that we are twisted up in the wishing that things were different than they are, then in that moment of noticing we are granted the opportunity to begin to let go, to begin to untie that knot of wanting. Beginning with noticing that we are caught in a struggle to change allows us to examine whether letting go might not be the healthier alternative. We can ask ourselves, "What does it feel like to just let this go and accept that this is just part of the wonderfully complicated person who is my partner." In the asking of this question we give ourselves the opportunity to see what acceptance might feel like and although it will be short of the thoroughgoing acceptance that might ultimately have to be cultivated, it can provide us with the taste that whets our appetite for more.

"Trying on" acceptance opens our eyes to the range of alternatives we have for how we live our lives in relation to our partner. Once we begin to see that maybe we can learn to come to terms gracefully with something that we had previously been struggling to change, then we begin to see our partner in a new light and to experience what it is like to love them without the burden of judgment and rejection. For example, what would it be like to "try on" accepting that our partner is more prone to clutter (or neatness) than we are? How does the possibility of acceptance feel compared to the usual stance of rejection?

As we explore the possibility of acceptance, we also grant ourselves the opportunity to discover our capacity for grace and tolerance. We get to explore our capacity to be unconditionally loving. Sometimes what drives our frantic scramble for change is the belief that we cannot handle, we cannot possibly tolerate how we feel when confronted with those aspects of our partner that we find challenging. We believe that we cannot live gracefully with feelings of disappointment, irritation, frustration, and the like. We make *our* feelings our partner's problem and end up blaming him or her because *we* feel something that we would rather not feel. When we begin to explore the possibility of cultivating greater acceptance, we also give ourselves the opportunity to learn our real capacity to live gracefully within a world that is imperfect. We get to test our own strength of character, our own depth of being, and our own capacity to love wholeheartedly. Much more often than not, we discover that we are stronger, more solidly rooted, and more graceful than we originally gave ourselves credit for.

As we explore the possibility of acceptance, we also get the chance to see how our accepting attitude affects our partner and changes the dynamic of the interaction between us. People open up and flourish in an atmosphere of greater acceptance. In turn, relationships strengthen and brighten. Directly making contact with and seeing the beneficial effects of our own more accepting attitude feeds back on itself in a way that strengthens our capacity for even greater acceptance. We notice that we feel healthier and stronger, our partner feels healthier and stronger, our marriage feels healthier and stronger, and our children, somehow, feel healthier and stronger. All of this flowing from a little stretching in the direction of acceptance, a willingness to explore the possibility of acceptance that does not absolutely require us to change ourselves overnight from human to saint. Nurturing a greater capacity for acceptance requires only that we be willing to wonder what it might be like to let go and accept rather than clamp down and reject.

HOW DO I GET MY PARTNER TO BE MORE ACCEPTING OF ME?

Acceptance breeds acceptance. The more accepting you become of your partner, the more accepting your partner will become of you. As is the case with most positive attitudes, acceptance is contagious.

Acceptance talk helps to spread the word. If you talk about acceptance and how important it is and how determined you are to practice acceptance, then your partner will be affected by what you have to say. Even if initially your partner feels challenged by the idea of acceptance and argues against it, in the long run the possibility of acceptance will begin to seep into the relationship and into your partner's attitude.

Acknowledging those things about yourself that your partner tries to change or wants to change or wishes were different and applying your own attitude of acceptance can also help to foster acceptance in your partner. For example, if your partner wishes you would be more cheerful in the morning when you wake up, you can acknowledge that you understand that she wishes you were different in that way and practice accepting that she wishes you were different. This also involves accepting that you are unlikely to *be* different and gently communicating that truth to your partner. For example, "Honey, I know you wish I were a more cheerful person in the morning when I first wake up and I understand that and respect it. I also know I've been like this my whole life and even if I wanted to, I doubt it's something I could change. I do appreciate your willingness to cope with something I know isn't your favorite part of me and I'll do what I can to keep it in check."

SUMMARY: THE WISDOM TO KNOW THE DIFFERENCE

The Serenity Prayer once more in an alternate version by Reinhold Niebuhr

> God, give us Grace to accept with serenity the things that cannot be changed, Courage to change the things which should be changed, and the Wisdom to distinguish the one from the other.

The power of acceptance cannot be underestimated. We all long to be accepted by those we love, as we are, simple, human, and flawed. We also find that we are often caught in the trap of struggling to change the unchangeable and suffering from a world that will not conform to our wishes. As we wake up to the potential acceptance has to improve our lives and our marriages, we step onto a path toward greater marital health. Contemporary researchers have added a substantial emphasis on acceptance to current versions of many therapies, including both individual and marital therapies. The research findings to date support our confidence in the power of acceptance to promote health. As noted earlier, the path toward greater acceptance begins with simply acknowledging that acceptance might be an option and testing out what it might be like to move in the direction of greater acceptance. Our experience of acceptance can be thought of as existing on a continuum from bitter rejection, through tolerance, to radical acceptance and any move up that continuum is likely to result in noticeable benefits to you and your family

If you find yourself beating your head against the same wall over and over again in your marriage, all to no avail, then cultivating acceptance may be a path worth exploring for you. If, however, you find yourself stuck and having difficulty making progress toward a greater feeling of acceptance toward your partner and toward yourself, then working with a professional that understands the process and goals of acceptance work can be a very effective tool in your marital toolbox. Couples therapy is in many respects about helping you to become a better person yourself, someone more available for relationship, someone more comfortable with him or herself, more generous, more compassionate, more centered, less driven by fear and loathing. Couples therapy can be a context of liberation from suffering.

6

FORGIVENESS AND REPAIR: GRACE, GENEROSITY, AND COMPASSION

A good deal of recent research has begun to explore the role played by forgiveness and repair in sustaining marital health. The goal of this chapter will be to help you better understand the nature of forgiveness and its opposite "unforgiveness" in marriage, to share with you what relationship scientists know about the relationship between forgiveness and marital health, and to help you learn how to take advantage of the power of forgiveness to keep your marriage healthy and strong. This chapter will help to strengthen your ability to seek and grant forgiveness and to effectively repair your relationship following hurtful incidents.

FORGIVENESS: THE MARITAL IMMUNE SYSTEM

Forgiveness is essential to all healthy relationships. You simply cannot sustain and continue to nurture a strong and healthy marriage and family without regularly practicing the subtle art of forgiveness. The bonds of emotional intimacy involve moving around in close physical and emotional contact with another complex, unknowable, often irrational human being. Every move you make affects the other person in some way, decisions reverberate for both of you, moods and emotions and

Table 6.1. MC Forgiveness and Repair Questionnaire

Definitely Something We Need to Improve 1	*Could Use Some Improvement* 2	*Neither a Strength nor Area for Improvement* 3	*Somewhat of a Strength* 4	*Definitely a Strength* 5

_____	1. I don't carry grudges against my partner.
_____	2. My partner doesn't carry grudges against me.
_____	3. We tend to forgive each other easily.
_____	4. After a disagreement, we don't stay angry for long.
_____	5. We're good at making up after a disagreement.
_____	6. When my partner hurts my feelings or makes me mad, I don't try to get back at him/her.
_____	7. When my partner has hurt my feelings or made me mad, I don't start to avoid him/her.
_____	8. When my partner has hurt my feeling or made me mad, I don't give him/her the cold shoulder or stop talking to her/him.
_____	9. I tend not to hold on to hurt or anger in the relationship.
_____	10. I can usually feel empathy for my partner even when I'm feeling angry or hurt.
_____	11. I usually apologize when I've hurt my partner's feelings.
_____	12. There aren't any lingering or unforgiven hurts in our relationship.

intentions are contagious. At times the intricacy of this interweaving is heady and romantic, comforting and soothing, a safe and erotic space of love and intimacy. At other times, you will be out of step with each other, out of harmony, saying and doing things that grate and irritate, hurt and disappoint, frustrate and anger. Toes will be stepped on. Harsh words may be said. Expectations will be failed. Hopes will be stranded. Moments will be missed. Trusts will be violated. You will feel lonely, angry, and jealous, hurt, put upon, embarrassed, ashamed, frustrated, interfered with, confused, and anxious. This is the price of admission, guaranteed, no refunds. And this then is the context of forgiveness. If these experiences of hurt are built into the fabric of marital intimacy, then so too are experiences of forgiveness.

Without a capacity for forgiveness of things both big and small, a relationship is without an immune system; susceptible to every injury becoming potentially fatal. Just as a healthy body cannot survive without a strong immune system, a healthy marriage cannot survive without a strong forgiveness system. Just as a long and healthy life involves many periods of being hurt and ill and many processes of repair and recovery, so too with intimacy and marriage. When the immune system stops working or becomes overwhelmed, repair and recovery fail, and health deteriorates catastrophically. The key to a long and healthy intimate marriage is forgiveness.

WHAT IS FORGIVENESS?

Forgiveness is letting go; specifically, letting go of hurt. It is the kind of hurt that comes with a feeling of having been treated unfairly, dismissively, or with ill regard for your worth and dignity. It is the kind of hurt that you tend to hold on to because your sense of what is just and right has been violated. Letting go of that kind of hurt can be uniquely challenging, especially when the injustice done is grave and damaging. It is that letting go of justified hurt that defines forgiveness in most respects. In other ways, forgiveness also often involves reconciliation and repair. In other words, we oftentimes feel like we have fully forgiven only when our relationship with the person who hurt us has been repaired, dusted off, and rejoined with love, affection, and trust.

Forgiveness can also be understood by understanding its opposite, which in the relationship science literature has come to be called unforgiveness. Unforgiveness is characterized by how we tend to feel and act when we haven't yet forgiven a significant hurt. The two main signs of unforgiveness are retaliation seeking and avoidance. Many times when we feel we have to right a wrong that has been done to us by our partner, we find ourselves wanting to make our partner feel just as badly as we feel, to experience the same pain that we have experienced, to actively punish the transgression against us. This is the desire for retaliation manifest. You can feel it in your body as anger and aggression, a powerful and negative energy fueling a desire to lash out and cause harm. For our purposes then, when we are experiencing a strong sense of wanting to seek revenge or retaliation, we will say we are experiencing the opposite of forgiveness.

The second sign of unforgiveness is avoidance or withdrawal. Again, many times when we have been deeply hurt by our partner our first response is to simply get away from them and stay away from them. Sometimes this is as simple as physically leaving and maintaining real physical distance between our partner and ourselves. In other circumstances it is a subtler kind of emotional withdrawal from our partner in which we stay physically close, but shut ourselves off emotionally in small or large ways. This type of unforgiveness can be more pernicious in that it is undercover unforgiveness; unforgiveness that can be unacknowledged, unseen, and unaddressed and therefore silently corrode the foundation of the relationship without making itself available for repair. Again, for our purposes we will define our desire to withdraw from and avoid our partner, physically or emotionally, as the opposite of forgiveness.

Forgiveness and unforgiveness are not necessarily two ends of the same continuum. It is possible to hold onto feelings of injury and righteous indignation without pursuing avoidance or retaliation. We might call this "embittered resignation." The point being that genuine forgiveness is an emotional process ultimately up to the individual who holds the hurt. You can interact with someone, perhaps even in a caring way, that you have not yet really forgiven in your heart. Without genuine forgiveness, however, even in the face of no discernable unforgiveness, you create a space between you where scar tissue forms, deadening your ability to feel fully connected. We have to distinguish genuine forgiveness from simple lack of unforgiveness because a healthy and vibrant intimate marriage requires the openness and vulnerability of real forgiveness. You must decide to let it go.

From this perspective then, the road to forgiveness involves an empathic desire for our partner's happiness and well-being. Also from this perspective, forgiveness most often involves a desire to repair a close and loving relationship with our partner. More technically, forgiveness researcher Michael McCullough of the University of Miami and his colleagues define forgiveness as "the transformation that occurs when motivations to seek revenge and to maintain estrangement from an offending partner diminish, and motivation to pursue conciliatory courses of action increases" (McCullough, Worthington, and Rachal, 1997, p. 322).

WHAT FORGIVENESS ISN'T

It is important at this point in defining forgiveness to mention what forgiveness isn't. Forgiveness isn't giving in, giving up, or tolerating hurtful behavior. A commitment to forgiveness should never result in exposing yourself to repeated harm. The main caution here is if we find ourselves repeatedly forgiving someone for hurting us in the same way over and over again, then what appears to be forgiveness may actually be part of a destructive cycle in our relationship. At the same time, we want to be cautious that our inability to forgive is not the thing that is keeping us stuck in a miserable situation.

Sometimes forgiveness can be difficult because it feels like if we forgive someone we are excusing his or her hurtful behavior. Seeking forgiveness doesn't mean giving up a commitment to mutual respect, trust, emotional safety, interpersonal justice, or the need to create and defend appropriate boundaries of right and wrong. It does mean seeking to heal and strengthen both yourself and your intimate relationship. At times, however, we sacrifice our own well-being and the well-being of those we love in the service of retaliatory "justice" or we wall off our natural human vulnerabilities and call it "being realistic."

FORGIVENESS AND MARITAL HEALTH

Forgiveness is good for your marital, mental, and physical health. Research in each of these areas has been clear and convincing. Studies have shown that unforgiveness is physically stressful and emotionally painful. Researchers have found that people asked to imagine a hurtful incident that they haven't yet forgiven not only subjectively experience greater feelings of stress, but actually produce greater quantities of the stress hormone cortisol and measurably higher blood pressure. Large amounts of cortisol in the circulatory system has been linked to both poorer immune system functioning and the production of micro-abrasions in the vascular system that increase our risk of developing heart disease. So in a very direct way, unforgiveness makes us sick.

Unforgiveness also just feels awful. It is the sort of awful feeling that follows us throughout the day, distracting us and polluting our experience of even the most positive events. Carrying unforgiveness is like strapping a fifty-pound rock to your back and then trying to get on with your life. Getting on with your life is possible, but everything becomes more burdensome, we tire more easily, we're crankier, and just generally feel worse and more run down. The worst part is that we can forget that we ever picked this thing up and started carrying it. At that point we become helpless to help ourselves. We know we feel crummy and weakened, but we no longer know why. We have forgotten that in some very real way we chose at some point to pick up this burden and attach it to our lives. From this perspective it is no wonder that carrying around unforgiveness has been found to make us both physically and emotionally sickly. Forgiveness, however, like strong medicine, returns us to health and vitality.

In addition to physical and emotional health, research has also found a connection between forgiveness and marital health. Couples themselves report that the ability to seek and grant forgiveness is one of the most important factors contributing to a long and healthy marriage. Relationship scientists have shown that the amount of anger in a relationship diminishes in direct proportion to the experience of forgiveness. In fact, relationship scientists Frank Fincham of Florida State University and Michael MuCullough of the University of Miami have both found evidence linking forgiveness to marital health. These scientists posit that forgiveness short-circuits cycles of ongoing destructive argument within a marriage. Chronic conflict is characterized by a state of unforgiveness and has been repeatedly associated with marital deterioration and divorce. As noted by Professor Fincham and his colleagues (2004, p. 78), "Forgiveness may prove to be an important element of marital transactions precisely because spouses often hurt one another and, in the absence of forgiveness, it may be common for lingering effects to exert their influence on subsequent efforts to resolve marital problems." In other words, it is likely that we tend to carry unforgiveness with us into all the other moments of our marriage such that it undermines our ability to deal well with any other areas of friction in our relationship with our spouse. It is simply harder for us to solve the problems that come up between us today if we are still carrying unforgiveness from yesterday. Further, the more unforgiveness we carry around with us, the more poisoned are all the rest of our day-to-day interactions with our intimate partners.

In short, to continue with our immune system analogy, the work of psychological scientists is quite consistent in supporting the view that a strong forgiveness system keeps us healthier across all the domains of our lives, physical, emotional, and marital.

INTIMACY AND FORGIVENESS

As I have mentioned previously, intimacy grows from those times when we respect and comfort each other's vulnerabilities. The intimacy you experience in your relationship is a direct reflection of what you have learned through hard-won personal experience about how safe you are being vulnerable with your partner. The emotional and physical closeness that characterize an intimate relationship means that we cannot avoid being hurt by each other from time to time. While genuine intimacy is the bedrock of a healthy marriage, emotional exposure is the price of admission. Unforgiveness begins when the hurt resulting from that vulnerability is such that it knocks us back on our heels and makes us begin to question the cost of emotional exposure.

For the most part, little hurts are simply absorbed without notice into the ongoing stream of a well-functioning marriage. There is suggestive evidence in the research literature that partners who feel very positively about their spouses are generally immune to the little day-to-day frictions of marriage. Called "positive sentiment override" in the relationship science literature, partners in healthy marriages literally appear blind to what might objectively be seen as negative behavior from their partners (for example, sarcasm or defensiveness). When asked about their partners' negative behaviors following a standard marital interaction in the lab, partners in healthy marriages report that they didn't even notice negative behavior that was easily seen by the researchers. These little day-to-day negativities that essentially fly under our radar are not the targets of our forgiveness system precisely because they are so completely absorbed within the generally positive atmosphere of the marriage that they do not register as hurtful and therefore do not require any deliberate acts of forgiveness.

EVERYDAY FORGIVENESS

It is therefore the larger hurts or the chronic accumulation of smaller hurts that require more conscious acts of forgiveness. Some hurts go by unnoticed, others merely sting; some completely change our perspective on our partner from safe to unsafe, from comforting to discomforting, from a source of intimate safety to a source of intimate threat.

How hurtful any particular event is, is defined by how much it changes how you see and how you experience your partner. This involves a combination of how intimately healthy the relationship is to begin with (how much trust and intimacy characterize the relationship) and how traumatic or chronic the hurtful events are. This is known as a "diathesis-stress model" in which illness is caused by a combination of how susceptible we are to that illness and how exposed we have been to the immediate causes of that illness. Little hurts in the context of very intimately healthy relationships appear to be absorbed without notice in much the same way that minor cold viruses are shrugged off by a healthy immune system.

Hurts that sting enough to grab our attention require a type of everyday forgiveness that is characteristic of a healthy forgiveness system. Sometimes, maybe most times, that type of everyday forgiveness is preceded by an apology of some sort. However, an attention-grabbing, heartfelt apology is not always required for these little everyday hurt-and-forgive interactions to work well. At the same time, it is just these types of hurts, the ones that actually consciously sting, that can accumulate into a chronic state of unforgiveness.

ACCUMULATING AND TRAUMATIC HURT

Accumulating minor hurts can eventually overwhelm our sense of intimate safety, changing our experience of our partner from safe to unsafe. This can be a slow process of gradual accumulation in the absence of frequent positive interactions. As unforgiven hurts accumulate, the relationship becomes sicklier and more vulnerable to serious injury. If your experience of your partner flips from mostly positive to mostly negative, then a deliberate forgiveness process becomes essential to a healthy recovery.

In addition to accumulated hurts, single traumatic hurts can change even the healthiest marriages into sources of chronic pain. The most obvious example of this type of traumatic hurt is an extramarital affair. I will focus on forgiveness and extramarital affairs in a later section of this chapter. Suffice it to say for now that extramarital affairs are uniquely traumatic to marital health and uniquely challenging to forgive. At the same time, affairs are not the only kind of event that can be classified as a traumatic hurt. Marital therapist and relationship scientist Susan Johnson of the University of Ottawa, has coined the term "attachment injury" to identify a type of event in which one partner feels abandoned by the other at a moment of particularly desperate need.

For example, in one couple, the wife was very anxious about the birth of their first child for several very understandable reasons having to do with her age, her career, her own family history, and other well-earned insecurities. In addition, as a couple they had several preexisting vulnerabilities that had not yet caused them any significant trouble. Overall, although vulnerable, their relationship felt healthy to both of them at this point. Very close to her due date, however, the husband chose to go on a very challenging mountain climb despite his wife's objections to doing something so risky so close to her due date. Unfortunately, during the climb he fell and badly broke his leg in multiple places; an injury that essentially crippled him for several months prior to and after his wife gave birth. He was badly enough injured that he was unable to support her during the birth and was essentially unavailable to her during the difficult transition to motherhood. This incident completely shifted her view of him from stable and reliable to undependable and untrustworthy. Despite herself, she found she was unable to forgive him even years afterwards. When they finally presented for couple therapy, it had been close to five years since the incident, during which their marriage had steadily crumbled under the weight of unforgiveness.

In a nutshell, how much forgiveness is required of any particular injury is a product of how healthy the relationship was to begin with and how powerful was the hurtful event. Accumulating minor hurts can severely erode feelings of safety and trust and punctuating major hurts can dramatically and nauseatingly tear a relationship inside out.

UNIQUE VULNERABILITIES

Forgiveness can be particularly difficult because each of us has acquired our own unique vulnerabilities. The things that I find particularly hurtful might not necessarily be the same things that you find particularly hurtful. Maybe you were teased about your looks a lot in school and now find your feelings are particularly easily hurt by things your partner might say (or might fail to say) about your appearance. In contrast, your partner might have been put down in his family for being "stupid" or maybe for being "a sissy." In your relationship now, you might find that his feelings are particularly easily hurt by anything that sounds even vaguely like a reference to his intelligence or masculinity. We all have these unique personal vulnerabilities that we bring with us into our relationships, places where we are particularly easily hurt, places where even the slightest brushing up against that spot makes us wince, regardless of our partners' intentions. The experience of hurt around these particularly sensitive areas can make it hard to forgive. We want so much to protect those vulnerable places that we can react to hurt in powerful ways, ways that might even seem out of proportion to the injury. We might react by completely shutting our partner out in small or large ways. Or we might react by trying to hurt our partner back. Of course, the research literature is quite consistent in saying that such reactions are toxic to our long-term marital health.

When we are unaware of these uniquely personal vulnerabilities, we might find ourselves reacting in ways that are detrimental to our long-term health. On the other hand, if we are aware of those spots where we are particularly easily hurt, then we are in a better position to be both more careful around those spots and more forgiving of the hurts that emerge there. I think it is also essential to recognize how important it is for that forgiveness to flow both ways, for us to forgive ourselves for our own vulnerabilities as thoroughly as we forgive our partners. The only alternative is to smother intimacy and actively diminish the quality of our own lives. Living with unforgiveness is like living with dull and noxious barriers between us and our lives. Those barriers only seem to be protecting us from hurt, when in reality they are slowly suffocating us.

Another thing to keep in mind is that some of us are simply more vulnerable to hurt than others. People with histories that have taught them that intimacy and trust are emotionally dangerous come to their intimate relationships uniquely vulnerable. For example, for some partners, name-calling is experienced as a normal and unremarkable expression of anger. For others, name-calling is experienced as a serious and painful breach of trust. Those of us with particularly painful or rejecting childhoods come to our marriages raw and tender in ways that other people with more secure and supportive childhoods do not. We might try to deny that fact, but such denials only make it harder for us to create true love and intimacy. If I know that the emotional complexity of marriage is perhaps more challenging to me than most, then maturity and wisdom tell me that I will have to take better care of myself and my marriage than others. Perhaps for some people maintaining marital health is easier than it is for me, but that does not mean that I cannot have just as healthy a marriage as they, I simply have to be more diligent and conscientious about taking good care of myself and my marriage.

It is like having a bad back or a chronic medical condition like asthma. Having a bad back or asthma doesn't mean you can't live your life just as fully as people who don't have these problems, but it does mean that in order to do so you have to work a little harder to take care of yourself and your health. Similarly, if you try to deny that you have a bad back or asthma, then you are much more prone to injury and illness than you would be if you were fully embracing your condition and taking proper care of yourself. It is just the same with your marriage. If you deny your vulnerabilities then you are much more likely to find your marriage becoming sick and injured than if you fully embrace your vulnerabilities and take active and loving care of your marital health. Again, in this way, forgiveness flows both ways. You will be in a better position to forgive yourself and your past for having those vulnerabilities and you will be in a better position to forgive your partner for bumping into those spots from time to time.

Notice that when you are able to forgive your partner for something hurtful, you find yourself naturally acting very differently toward him than you did before that forgiveness. Before forgiveness we can feel completely at the mercy of our desire to withdraw or retaliate. After forgiveness, our feelings shift to wanting to repair and reestablish our basic friendship.

EVERYBODY HURTS DIFFERENTLY

Something else to recognize when considering the expression of forgiveness in marriage; there are many ways to act when we are hurt and different people enact their hurt differently. For example, some people withdraw physically when they are hurt. Others withdraw emotionally while physically staying close. Some of us actively confront in angry or hostile ways when we are hurt. Others of us try to pretend that we aren't hurt, but then seek revenge in subtle or sneaky ways. Any way of doing hurt that involves withdrawal, avoidance, or retaliation is unforgiveness.

Alternatively, some people simply show up and let you know in clear and simple ways that you have hurt them. This simple showing up is often one of the first steps in pursuing forgiveness in that it clearly sets the stage for the other person to respond in a warm and forgivable way. Perhaps the main point here is that we don't have to respond to hurt with unforgiveness. It is possible, and maybe even preferable, to respond to hurt by simply and honestly communicating it. Dealing openly and honestly with each other in this way is strong and healthy and does not make us any more easily hurt or any less safe than unforgiveness. We often suffer under the delusion that unforgiveness makes us safer and forgiveness makes us more vulnerable, when just the opposite is true. Unforgiveness makes us sick and weak and forgiveness makes us strong and healthy.

You cannot simultaneously seek retaliation or withdrawal and seek to experience forgiveness. The experience of forgiveness requires that we actively do something to foster that experience. Waiting around for feelings of unforgiveness to dissipate simply doesn't work.

A CONTINUUM OF FORGIVENESS

Forgiveness exists on a continuum from complete unforgiveness to complete forgiveness, with a great deal of distance between those two ends. In most cases any forgiveness is a powerful move in the direction of health. Even small advances in the direction of forgiveness can help us to heal emotionally and physically. If complete forgiveness seems unachievable at the moment, don't give up on the health and spiritual benefits of even a few steps in the direction of greater forgiveness. A little more letting go of unforgiveness, a deeper breath and shaking off of the shackles of hurt, injury, indignation, resentment, and bitterness can be of enormous benefit to the whole of our lives.

It is also possible to forgive someone without necessarily reconciling with him or her. This is a form of forgiveness somewhere between complete unforgiveness and complete forgiveness. Although I might not actively seek out a close relationship with someone who has hurt me deeply, I can let go of the sharp edge of unforgiveness. I can let go of bitterness, a desire for revenge, active avoidance, recrimination, and victimhood. I can free myself from those shackles and get on with the business of living my life. In the context of marriage this might mean forgiving someone but not staying married to him or her. Again, this is clearly a step in the direction of health and in some cases, such as those involving emotional or physical abuse; this move can be the healthiest option.

It is also possible to completely reconcile and repair a relationship through forgiveness such that it is as strong as or even stronger than it was before the moment of hurt. Depending on the extent of the injury and the degree to which the partner actively seeks forgiveness, this can either be a particularly easy or particularly challenging thing to accomplish. Nevertheless, it is possible to accomplish complete reconciliation with a partner in the wake of a hurtful event.

STAGES OF FORGIVENESS

Beginning to move toward forgiveness often involves stages of change. Stages of change are a series of distinct steps toward change originally coined by psychologists James Prochaska of the University of Rhode Island and Carlo DiClemente of the University of Maryland in Baltimore. Stages of change describes the process that people go through when they make substantial changes in their lives like quitting smoking or starting an exercise program. Although a stages of change model can be applied to almost all of our significant moves toward change, it has something particularly useful to tell us about the pursuit of forgiveness in marriage.

Precontemplation of Forgiveness

The first stage of change is called precontemplation. The precontemplation stage of forgiveness is when we have yet to even begin considering forgiveness as an option. We are deep in the throes of unforgiveness and have not even begun to consider moving in the direction of forgiveness. During the precontemplation stage, unforgiveness can seem like the natural state of the world and like something we neither want to change nor could change even if we wanted to. In this stage, moving in the direction of forgiveness is almost literally unthinkable. We are in a trap that we haven't even begun to consider getting out of.

Contemplating Forgiveness

The second stage is called contemplation. We are in the contemplation stage of forgiveness when we have begun to consider the *possibility* of forgiveness, but we have not yet really decided to forgive. In this stage we are often ambivalent about forgiveness. On the one hand, we might be sick and tired of carrying around the burden of unforgiveness and want to be free of it. On the other hand, we might think that forgiveness is unjustified and maybe even unjustifiable. We might feel that forgiving our partner would be a sign of weakness or that it might be shameful or irritating. We might believe that forgiving our partner lets him off the hook and says that it's okay to hurt us. We don't feel ready to release our partner from the pain of our unforgiveness and therefore we aren't ready to release ourselves. It is possible for us to stay stuck in this ambivalence for long stretches of time, acutely feeling both the pain of unforgiveness (and thus the desire to forgive) and the righteous indignation of the hurt we were caused (and thus the unwillingness to forgive).

Determination to Forgive

The third stage of forgiveness is called determination. In this stage we have resolved our ambivalence and decided that we definitely want to move in the direction of forgiveness. At the same time, we may be completely unsure about exactly how to do that. We know we want to experience forgiveness, but we don't know how to make it happen, we don't know exactly what it means to "let go" and we don't know how to move in the direction of reconciliation. What we do know is that we are done with unforgiveness and are determined to forgive, so we start in earnest to try to figure out the forgiveness puzzle.

It is important to note how critically important a conscious and active decision to forgive is to the process of forgiveness. Forgiveness is rarely something that "just happens." Instead, much more commonly, we have to make a deliberate decision to forgive. The decision to forgive is not itself the experience of forgiveness, but it is often a critical early ingredient. Deciding that you are going to try to forgive begins to create the momentum that eventually leads to actual forgiveness. This also highlights that the decision to forgive is not, in and of itself, forgiveness. It is most often simply the decision to dedicate time and effort to the pursuit of forgiveness.

Actively Forgiving

The next stage of forgiveness is called the action stage. In the action stage we begin taking deliberate action to move in the direction of forgiveness. We might seek out the person we are trying to forgive to begin a process of reconciliation. We might seek help pursuing forgiveness from clergy or a therapist. We might read a book about forgiveness or pray for the wisdom to forgive. In some way, when we have entered the action stage, we do something active to begin generating forgiveness. This is different from sitting back and waiting passively for forgiveness to come to us. Again, forgiveness is unlikely to show up uninvited. It must, more often than not, be actively pursued. There is something about actively pursuing forgiveness that seems to almost literally involve a type of letting go. More than metaphorically, unforgiveness is often experienced as physically holding on to something and forgiveness is experienced as physically letting go of something. Letting go is a deliberate action. You must decide to let go, you must choose to let go, and then you must actually let go.

None of this is to say that our partners do not play an important role by honestly seeking forgiveness. There are things we can do when we have been hurtful to actively seek repair, reconciliation, and forgiveness. A heartfelt apology and efforts to make amends dramatically eases the path toward forgiveness. Apology and amends may even be essential if the ultimate goal is reconciliation. However, I want to be clear here that you do not have to be stuck in a state of unforgiveness just because the person who hurt you won't apologize. So much of forgiveness is about what *you* decide to do about it and it is possible to experience all the personal health benefits of forgiveness regardless of whether the other person cooperates or not. Although complete reconciliation may only be possible with the cooperation of the other, complete personal forgiveness is a power you hold for yourself.

Forgiving the Unforgivable

As a brief aside, outside of the context of long-term marriage, there are many circumstances in which forgiveness must be pursued without the cooperation of the offending party. When we have been the victim of a crime or assault, it is rare that the person who injured us will ever apologize or otherwise actively seek our forgiveness. At the same time, we are still fully capable of releasing ourselves from the prison of unforgiveness. We remain fully capable of genuinely forgiving and getting right with our lives again. As a case in point, consider the response of the Amish community in Pennsylvania to the senseless and brutal murder of so many of their daughters by a homicidal and suicidal stranger to their community in early October 2006. If there were ever an example of an event in which it would be understandable for people to hold on to unforgiveness forever, this tragedy provides it. Not only was the act easily unforgivable, but the person who committed it killed himself and was thus unavailable to express remorse and actively seek forgiveness. But the members of these shattered families almost immediately moved with strength and grace to actively and deliberately forgive. They seemed to know in a deep and authentic way what we are only waving words at here; that we each hold the power to forgive in our own hands. If we withhold it, we withhold it by personal choice. These families also seemed to know in a bone-deep way the power of forgiveness to free us and all those around us; free us to grieve, free us to support each other, free us to reconnect with each other and with God. In some deluded way, how much easier it would have been to suffocate under the weight of unforgiveness and yet how much more powerful to show up full-faced and broken-hearted to grant forgiveness.

Maintaining Forgiveness

The final stage of change is called the maintenance stage. In this stage we do what we have to do to maintain forgiveness. Once we have let go of unforgiveness, we may have to be careful not to pick it up again at some later date. Like a snowball rolling downhill, little bits of unforgiveness tend to accumulate other little bits of unforgiveness and grow over time into an enormous and heavy mass. Maintaining forgiveness and an atmosphere of forgiveness may require the regular practice of forgiveness, the regular practice of letting go of righteous hurt and not picking up scraps of unforgiveness that we can just as easily let lie.

Relapsing into Unforgiveness

The stages of change model also allows that even after we have been through a full cycle of change, we can at times relapse back into a state of unforgiveness. Sometimes a subsequent hurtful event can lead us back into a state of unforgiveness about something that we felt we had already forgiven. Sometimes we find ourselves stumbling into rumination about a previous hurt that leads back down the path of unforgiveness. Sometimes we might even find that something that happened to somebody else reminds us enough of that previous painful episode, that we find ourselves again feeling hurt and unforgiving. Regardless of the cause, the stages of change model regards relapse as normal and not at all shameful. Instead, relapse is regarded as simply another opportunity to practice change and the research suggests that with each cycle of change, the likelihood of lasting change improves. Thus, in terms of forgiveness, though we find ourselves cycling in and out of forgiveness and unforgiveness, if we continue to conscientiously practice the stages of forgiveness, we will eventually find the kind of forgiveness that lasts. It is at this last stage that we can say that we have truly escaped from unforgiveness.

THE STEPS OF FORGIVENESS

Deciding to Forgive

Given the stage model, forgiveness begins the moment we begin seriously considering forgiveness as an option. We might still be ambivalent about forgiveness; changing our mind back and forth between forgiveness and unforgiveness, but at least we have begun to entertain the possibility of living without bitterness.

The real momentum of forgiveness begins with the decision to forgive. Particularly in those instances when moving in the direction of forgiveness requires real effort. Again, it is rare that forgiveness sneaks up on us without our notice. Much more often than not we have to make a conscious decision to begin the process of forgiving. It is also clear that the decision to forgive is a beginning point; it is not forgiveness itself. We might have to make the decision to begin the process of forgiveness while still feeling unforgiving. This can be a difficult place to stand. It is like the moment of deciding to run a marathon. The decision makes the outcome possible, but there is still a long race to run.

The decision to forgive may begin when you notice that holding on to unforgiveness is making you sick and pinching you off from your partner and your life. As you begin to become aware that holding on to unforgiveness is dragging you down, you may also begin to notice that you hold the key to your own recovery.

Distress Tolerance

The next step in the forgiveness process involves distress tolerance. In order to move in the direction of forgiveness, we have to move in the direction of our hurt. Somehow at the moment this can seem counterintuitive. Everything in our whole experience is telling us to move away from our pain and the whole inbuilt rationale for unforgiveness is for us to minimize the possibility that we will ever be hurt again. Nevertheless, in order to move toward forgiveness we have to stop avoiding and running away and we have to start moving toward those feelings of hurt with compassion. If I am to forgive you for the hurt I feel I have suffered at your hands, I have to acknowledge the presence of that hurt without wishing it away, without demanding that you take it back from me, without holding it like a weapon or a shield. I must be open to tolerating my own distress. And tolerating my own distress means I must both hold it gently and own it as my own. Like a loudly crying child, my job at this point is to hold that hurt close, soothe it, and stand it back on its own two feet.

Continuing to move steadily through the process of forgiveness may also involve coming to accept that some residual feelings of hurt may never resolve. For example, after an affair both partners may always carry some hurt and shame. That doesn't mean that forgiveness is not occurring. It does mean that forgiveness can occur even when the hurt still hurts. In fact, depending on the severity of the injury, forgiveness may only be possible when one is willing to live with some residual hurt. Again, couples who have suffered an affair often find that that spot is always tender and sore, and they may both carry forward some sadness about that fact. Over time though, with forgiveness, the relationship regains its strength and stability, and what grows up that is healthy and warm vastly outweighs the twinges that remains from past hurt.

The point being that both the offender and offended may have to accept that some residual hurt may never resolve. Pursuing forgiveness sometimes requires that we learn to carry some residual hurt without turning it into sword and shield.

Empathy and Forgiveness

Forgiveness is an empathic act. When we have made the decision to forgive, when we have stopped running from our own pain, we can begin to feel for our partner again, seeing him or her as fully human, flawed and prone to stumbling. As we allow ourselves to empathize with our partner, we discover the true key to forgiveness, the empathic connection between two flawed beings. As we begin to feel with and for our partner, as we begin to stand inside his or her shoes, we find that our desire for revenge melts away and our passionate rejection of him or her shifts toward repair, reconciliation, and intimacy.

Forgiveness researchers Michael McCullough, Everett Worthington, and K. C. Rachal have begun to believe that empathy for the other person may play the central role in the process of forgiveness between partners. In fact, severing of the empathic connection between partners may be the central feature of unforgiveness. When we have been hurt and respond with unforgiveness, what had been close and interwoven is torn apart turning into great distance and separation. Empathy actively reweaves that connection with our partner and closes the distance created by unforgiveness.

Empathy involves two things. First it involves an act of imagination. It involves our conscious attempt to see the situation from our partner's perspective, to generously ask ourselves to imagine what the world looks like from inside our partner's skin. Granting our common humanity, we might ask ourselves, what mix of history and circumstance might lead me to stumble in the same way my partner has stumbled.

This does not mean that we justify hurtful behavior, but it does mean that we seek to understand with compassion how someone can find themselves acting hurtfully. Sometimes we refrain from our natural tendency toward empathy because we fear that to empathize with our partner is the same thing as saying that it is okay that he or she did something hurtful. We worry that we are saying that it is okay to hurt us again in the future and that it is okay to be careless with our feelings. However, that equation is not correct. It is possible to both empathize with you and state clearly that you crossed a line with me that it is not okay to cross. I can stand in your shoes and understand how a good and lovable person can get twisted and turned around and hurt someone he genuinely loves. I can empathize and forgive while still maintaining my personal integrity. Forgiveness is an act of strength and maturity, of clarity and courage.

The second part of empathy is an act of emotional resonance. Beyond imagining the world from our partner's perspective, we seek to feel what our partner is feeling as our own. When we find that we have hurt someone we love we experience a mix of feelings that can include shame, denial, protective self-righteousness, defensiveness, sorrow, grief, and the painful wish that we could snatch it back. Some parts of this complicated mix make us want to run away from our partner and hide (either physically or emotionally). Other parts make us want to rush to him or her and immediately make amends. Perhaps still others make us want to push our partner away as a way of denying our own mistake. If we can use our own experience of having been hurtful in the past to resonate with what our partner is feeling right now, then we might find ourselves quite naturally experiencing greater forgiveness and reweaving a strong connection. The regrowth of genuine trust may still have to wait awhile, but the experience of empathy-rooted forgiveness can happen now.

EMPATHY AND SEEKING FORGIVENESS

It's important to consider that forgiveness has both active and passive components. There are some things we have to do deliberately to facilitate forgiveness like deciding to forgive and practicing empathy. At the same time, the emotional experience of forgiveness is something that has to emerge on its own as a product of our actions and, many times, as a product of the actions of our partner.

We all know through experience that it is easier to forgive someone who has genuinely apologized and shown real remorse. In fact, true reconciliation may be impossible without a process of seeking forgiveness and actively making amends. You might be able to let go of unforgiveness even if the other person never seeks your forgiveness, but you may not be able to reconcile with that person without their active participation in the process of repair. It has been well established by forgiveness researchers that heartfelt apologies with open admissions of guilt have a powerful effect in terms of creating forgiveness. When we have been hurtful, seeking forgiveness often means expressing our softer emotions such as our genuine sorrow at having hurt our partner. Somehow the seeking of forgiveness has to convey the emotional message that we will be more careful with our partner's feelings in the future. An effective apology is much more than the simple words "I'm sorry." A genuine apology has to be reassuring. It has to be emotionally salient to your partner that you empathize with his or her hurt because empathy reassures your partner that you feel his or her hurt as keenly as your own.

WALKING THE PATH OF FORGIVENESS TOGETHER

Whether they are small acts of forgiveness for small injuries or large acts of forgiveness for large injuries, continuing to walk the path of forgiveness together means continuing to actively attend to the quality of your marital health. Remember that part of what makes a marriage susceptible to hurt is how healthy the marriage is in the first place. Even more so following a particularly painful period in a marriage, deliberately working on a strong and healthy foundation is essential to health and happiness. Spending quality time together, supporting each other's hopes and dreams and day-to-day struggles and joys, listening and being curious, reveling in your friendship and in your shared intimacies; all these things are necessary to building a healthy marriage and rebuilding through forgiveness.

HOW CAN YOU TELL IF YOU HAVE TRULY FORGIVEN?

Sometimes it can be difficult to tell if we have truly forgiven our partner for something hurtful he or she has done. You can tell the degree to which you have been able to forgive your partner by the degree to which you still experience the three signs of unforgiveness; namely (1) a desire to seek retaliation, (2) a desire to avoid your partner, and (3) a desire to withdraw when you are with your partner. Relationship scientists Frank Fincham of Florida State University, Steven Beach of the University of Georgia, and Joanne Davila of the State University of New York at Stony Brook (2004) found that when couples forgave each other they were less likely to use hostile statements about the incident in future conflict bouts. In other words, you will find that you aren't using your hurt as a weapon against your partner anymore, either overtly or covertly.

DEALING WITH THE HURT OF INFIDELITY

Forgiving infidelity may be the most difficult kind of forgiveness there is. Much has been written about repairing a marriage after an affair and it is a subject that in many ways deserves to be book length itself. Although the basic facts about forgiveness presented in this chapter remain true when applied to the special case of forgiving an affair, it is beyond the scope of this short chapter to do justice to the emotional complications of healing a marriage shattered by infidelity. Instead, I recommend a book by my colleagues Douglas Snyder, Donald Baucom, and Kristina Coop Gordon called *Getting Past the Affair: A Program to Help You Cope, Heal, and Move On—Together or Apart*. My team and I have reviewed many books on this topic as part of our work on the *Marriage Checkup*, and although there are many good books on the subject out there, this is the team's favorite by far. This book does an excellent job of addressing how to communicate, what is necessary on the part of both partners, self-care, and ways to rebuild trust and intimacy. It also addresses many different types of affairs including sexual, emotional, recent, and past affairs.

Recovering from an affair is difficult work and many couples do not reconcile. In fact, extramarital affairs remain the most commonly stated reason for seeking divorce. Thus, attempting to heal from the trauma of an affair is not the sort of thing that I recommend couples attempt to do on their own. When couples come in for a Marriage Checkup and we find that they are suffering from the effects of an extramarital affair, we uniformly recommend individual therapy for both partners and couples therapy for the marriage. Sometimes it may be best to start individual counseling first and then move into couples therapy once the initial work of individual therapy has begun. We tend to make this recommendation not because we think all couples should be in therapy, but because we know from the research how difficult it can be for couples to recover from an affair on their own.

SUMMARY

A healthy forgiveness system is essential to the long-term health and stability of your marriage. Research on the roll of forgiveness in healthy marriages is a burgeoning field in psychology, and a great deal has been learned about the vital role played by forgiveness in sustaining and maintaining marital health. A great deal has also been learned about the process of forgiveness and how to promote forgiveness on your own and through the help of counseling. In our marriages, we will all find ourselves needing to forgive as well as needing forgiveness. It is best to know this up front and to be prepared with a generous heart.

7

TEAM SPIRIT: MARRIAGE AS A SPIRITUAL JOURNEY

Recent research has begun to identify a shared sense of "being part of something greater than oneself" as a significant source of strength in some marriages. Discussed as a developing sense of marriage as a spiritual journey, this sense of nurturing the sacred in the ordinary has been found to be substantially health promoting. The goal of this chapter will be to help you assess the degree to which you conceive of your relationship as having a spiritual dimension. A discussion of the spiritual dimensions of marriage will be provided from a nondenominational perspective and suggestions and exercises will be provided for developing this aspect of a healthy marriage.

I want to note right up front that my discussion of spirituality in marriage is not limited to any specific religion or spiritual practice. The ability to experience your life and your marriage as a sacred or spiritual journey is available to anyone regardless of their religious or spiritual beliefs or lack thereof. If you practice a specific religion, then this chapter will be relevant to you. If you do not practice a particular religion, then this chapter is likely to be relevant to you as well. The ability to experience your marriage as sacred can take many forms and is certainly not limited to any particular practice

Table 7.1. MC Spiritual Intimacy Questionnaire

Definitely Something We Need to Improve 1	*Could Use Some Improvement* 2	*Neither a Strength nor Area for Improvement* 3	*Somewhat of a Strength* 4	*Definitely a Strength* 5

_____ 1. My partner plays a part in my spiritual life.
_____ 2. I play a part in my partner's spiritual life.
_____ 3. I am actively growing spiritually in my marriage.
_____ 4. My partner contributes to my spiritual growth.
_____ 5. I contribute to my partner's spiritual growth.
_____ 6. My partner supports my spiritual growth.
_____ 7. I support my partner's spiritual growth.
_____ 8. My marriage helps me feel like I am part of something bigger than just myself.
_____ 9. I experience my marriage as sacred.
_____ 10. I can talk intimately with my partner about my spiritual life.
_____ 11. My partner can talk intimately with me about his/her spiritual life.
_____ 12. There is a strong spiritual dimension to our marriage.
_____ 13. I live out my spiritual life through my marriage.
_____ 14. I consider my marriage holy, blessed, or sacred.

EXPLORING THE CONNECTION BETWEEN RELATIONAL INTIMACY AND SPIRITUAL INTIMACY

We will explore the available research and its implications later in this chapter. At this point, however, I want to start with what may be the heart of the matter. There appears to be a profound connection between the intimacy at the foundation of marital health and what we'll call here "spiritual intimacy."

What *is* the potential connection between spiritual intimacy and intimacy between you and your partner? The key may be vulnerability. Just as vulnerability is the key to intimacy between you and your partner, vulnerability may be the key to intimacy between you and the sacred. Moments of intimacy are achieved when we are able to put down the defenses that we have learned to reflexively hide behind. It is when we learn to stand completely unmasked in the world, completely naked before God, that we are most able to achieve authentic spiritual intimacy. It is when we are able to put down our walls and defenses with our partners that we are most able to achieve authentic interpersonal intimacy.

Both types of intimacy have in common that intimacy cannot be achieved without a leap of faith. The faith is that if you leap free of your defenses, you will find that you simply do not need them. When you hide your authentic self from your partner, you cut off intimacy and by cutting off intimacy you stunt your growth as a person and as a partner. When you hide from, deny, avoid, and run away from your vulnerability in the world then you stunt your personal and spiritual growth. It is only by authentically showing up without all the self-protective stories and habits accumulated over a lifetime that we are able to be truly intimate with our lives and with our partners. To the degree that you erect barriers between yourself and others, between you and your authentic experience, then you will be isolated and cut off from the sacred. It is this quest for spiritual intimacy that defines our active walking of the spiritual path. It is achieving spiritual intimacy that is the goal of all contemplative traditions from the Judeo-Christian to the Islamic, from the Hindu to the Buddhist.

Interpersonal intimacy follows a similar path in that we must show up as our true selves in order to allow for genuine intimacy. We avoid intimacy to exactly the same degree that we avoid authenticity and we avoid authenticity because authenticity necessarily involves being vulnerable and undefended. Stepping forward without our defenses allows intimacy to emerge. It may not guarantee it, but it firmly sets the stage for it. The sanctification of marriage allows both meanings of intimacy to be pursued together.

That being said, given the available research there is reason to suspect that spirituality must be actively lived, in other words, it must be a practice, in order for it to have its strongest effect on marital (and likely personal) health. Just as we must strive to keep ourselves open to our partners in order to maintain an intimate connection, we must actively practice remaining open to the sacred if we are to invite this dimension of intimacy into our lives and marriages.

THERE IS NO POLITICAL DIMENSION TO A MARRIAGE'S SPIRITUAL DIMENSION

There is a political left and there is a political right and there is the vast political middle. Regardless of a person's place on the political spectrum, all of us reading this book are interested in marriage and marital health and all of us reading this chapter are interested in spiritual health as well. What emerges from the research literature, however, appears to be entirely nonpartisan. A spirituality or religiousness actively lived confers strength and resilience to marriage. The how's and why's remain to be well answered, but the simplest results appear to be clear.

RECENT RESEARCH

Recently research has begun to explore in earnest the relationship between spiritual practice, spiritual connection, spiritual development, and marital and family health. This is another instance in which there is no separation between who you are as an individual and who you are in relation to others. Although not everyone actively engages in a spiritual practice or thinks about their married lives in spiritual terms, recent research suggests that those who do have a spiritual dimension to their marriages experience measurable marital health benefits. Shared spirituality, or perceiving a spiritual dimension to your marriage, appears to be something of a force multiplier. Its absence does not appear to make your marriage ill, but its presence does appear to add strength and resilience to your marriage.

SPIRITUALITY AND DIVORCE

Professor Annette Mahoney and her colleagues at Bowling Green State University conducted a recent review of the research on the association between religiousness and marital health. In their review of several decades of research they found remarkably consistent evidence for beneficial effects of shared spirituality in marriage. The original research in this area was quite limited in that it only examined whether people reported a religious affiliation or how frequently they reported attending religious services. These measures oversimplify an individual's spiritual practice, because whether we simply belong to a religion or go to church often, doesn't necessarily say anything directly about how deeply our personal spiritual practice is woven into our day-to-day lives. Nevertheless, research in this area has found repeated evidence that people who report a religious affiliation are less likely to divorce than those who do not (49 percent versus 62 percent). Further, similar research has found that 60 percent of infrequent churchgoers reported a history of divorce versus 44 percent of frequent churchgoers. Thus, in broad stroke terms, there is some admittedly messy evidence that a spiritual practice appears to make marriage more resilient against divorce.

At the same time, this research doesn't tell us why and we can all imagine both positive and negative reasons that religious practice might prevent divorce. The most negative reason being that people are more likely to stay in unhealthy and unhappy marriages simply because their religious beliefs prevent them from seeking a good divorce. Although it is likely that barriers to divorce imposed by particular religious beliefs do play a role in limiting the number of divorces among religious adherents, this factor does not appear to account for the entire effect. If imposed barriers to divorce were the most significant reason for this effect, we might expect to find a significantly larger number of unhappy marriages among the most religious because the less religious would be more likely to leave those unhappy marriages behind.

SPIRITUALITY, SATISFACTION, AND COMMITMENT

However, additional research finds a small but robust association between degree of personal religiousness (a measure of how important religion is in a person's life) and overall marital satisfaction. Thus, rather than finding more unhappy couples among the more deeply religious, research consistently finds a measurably higher degree of marital satisfaction among those who report that their religion is an important part of their personal lives.

Marital researchers have also found a modest association between personal religiousness and degree of commitment to marriage, with some additional evidence that people who report that religion is an important part of their lives are more willing to make personal sacrifices for the benefit of their marriage. In other words, the existing evidence is consistent with the idea that religiousness contributes to a person's greater commitment to, and willingness to sacrifice for, the long-term health of their marriage.

Greater commitment may confer health and stability through many potential avenues, including helping partners stay married during particularly dark times. Research has found that some unhappy couples who manage to hold their marriages together can, over time, recover into health and happiness. Knowing which couples might recover and which will remain perpetually miserable is, of course, still being actively studied, but the knowledge base continues to slowly and steadily grow.

Greater religiousness might also lead to a stronger sense of commitment because it adds an additional *type* of commitment to the marriage. If your marriage is a spiritual practice and your spiritual practice is personally important to you, then your commitment to your *practice* is likely to add to your commitment to your *partner* and to your marriage. In other words, you may be committed to your partner because you love him, he is a good person, you get along well together and you made a sincere promise to him. You might also be committed to your marriage because the institution of marriage is important to you; you take all of your commitments seriously, and maybe, because the barriers to leaving are high and risky. An additional level of commitment may be added by your commitment to your marriage as a spiritual practice or as a covenant with God (depending on your particular belief system). This additional type of commitment may confer greater or even unique benefits to marital health.

SPIRITUALITY AND COMMUNICATION

Researchers have also found evidence that greater self-reported religiousness is associated with more productive and less destructive marital communication. As I have pointed out before, if there is one area that has been meticulously studied in the marital area, it is clearly marital communication. There is more evidence for the powerful effects of marital communication quality on overall marital health than there is for any other aspect of marriage. There is also evidence that greater self-rated religiousness is associated with higher quality marital communication. In her own research Dr. Mahoney has found that (a) the degree to which couples reported engaging in religious activities together and (b) the degree to which they reported that they perceived their marriage as sacred were both related to their greater mutual collaboration when handling disagreements. In other words, such couples, on average, work better for the sake of the team during conflict.

Professor Mahoney and her colleagues conclude their review of the literature by noting that this is a new area of research that requires substantially more study. With that caution in mind, however, there is emerging evidence that greater religiousness and shared spiritual practice are associated with fewer divorces, a deeper sense of marital commitment, and overall happier marriages.

SPIRITUAL INTIMACY: WE, US, AND OURS VERSUS I, ME, AND MINE

Observational research, conducted by Professor John Gottman at the University of Washington, has demonstrated that couples who talk about the early trials and tribulations in their marriage with a shared sense of "we-ness" have healthier and more resilient marriages. These appear to be marriages in which partners tend to think in terms of we, us, and ours, versus thinking in terms of I, me, and mine. This sense of we-ness is likely experienced as being part of something bigger than yourself; a sense that your marriage is greater than the sum of its two parts.

Other research talks about this sense of "we-ness" in terms of what they call a relationship orientation versus an individual orientation. This research suggests that people who tend to think in relationship terms more so than individual terms tend to also report having healthier and happier marriages. Others, particularly theorists at the Stone Center at Wellesley College, talk about this way of being as "self-in-relation" versus the isolated self. The idea here is that some of us tend to think of ourselves more in terms of who we are in relation to others rather than in terms of who we are alone. Self-in-relation people tend to think of themselves in such relational terms as spouse, parent, sibling, child, friend, and partner. People with a more individual orientation tend to think of themselves in terms of what they do, what their goals are, what they own, or how successful they are. For those with a greater sense of self-in-relation, their sense of connectedness with others is a large part of their general sense of personal well-being. Regardless of how it is talked about, research from several different laboratories has been consistent in finding that this sense of interconnectedness to something greater than the individual self, when achieved within the context of an intimate relationship, contributes substantially to our overall and marital well-being.

It strikes me that this experience of we-ness is related in many ways to spiritual intimacy. For some, a sense of the self as part of something larger than the individuals in the marriage is experienced in largely spiritual terms. For others, spiritual practice may facilitate this sense of "we-ness" in their marriage. Either way, spiritual intimacy and we-ness may be cut from the same cloth.

THE SANCTIFICATION OF MARRIAGE

Returning to the work of Professor Mahoney and her colleagues, let's consider some of her current work studying a phenomenon they call the *sanctification* of marriage. Sanctification involves thinking about marriage in specifically spiritual terms. For example, a person might think of his marriage as holy, blessed, sacred, or as an embodiment of God (or a Higher Power or the Sacred). A person might see the sacred as present in her marriage and/or she might experience the sacred *through* her marriage. Professor Mahoney speculates that people who think of their marriages as sacred may be more forgiving of each other, more unconditionally accepting, more able to keep minor conflicts in perspective, and more likely to practice making positive attributions about their partners. For example, if your partner does something that is disappointing to you, a personal spiritual practice of forgiveness might provide greater motivation to let it go and to move in the direction of reconciliation. This, of course, wouldn't mean condoning hurtful or destructive behavior. It could, however, make actively addressing the issue with your partner more productive if a spirit of forgiveness and acceptance precedes that conversation. As I noted in a previous chapter, unforgiveness can accumulate a great deal of damage in a marriage.

SANCTIFICATION AND CONFLICT

Professor Mahoney also speculates that greater sanctification of marriage may help partners to move more actively and humbly to attend to moments of conflict. Such partners may also be more likely to use their spiritual practices as means of coping effectively with the emotional complexities of intimacy, marriage, and family life. For example, if humility is seen as a valued spiritual characteristic, then acknowledging one's own role in a problem or conceding one's own mistakes and mistaken views might come somewhat more easily and may smooth the road to recovery. In addition, if a person is committed to practicing his spirituality in his marriage, he may be less likely to let disgruntled feelings fester and may be more motivated to actively work toward reestablishing a sense of harmony. A person might also act out her valuing of unselfishness within her marriage, again facilitating greater harmony and a sense of loving-kindness. Finally, partners who actively strive to see God or the sacred as manifest in their marriage may also be more motivated to actively attend to the health of their marriage as a means of honoring their own connection to the sacred.

SANCTIFICATION AND FIDELITY

Professor Mahoney's theoretical work suggests that partners who are more actively committed to their spiritual lives are more likely to subscribe to teachings that emphasize the importance of sexual fidelity. Given that infidelity is the most commonly stated cause of divorce, greater personal motivation to practice fidelity should have a directly positive effect in terms of actively protecting marital health. Again, it is probably important here to note that there is a clear distinction here between proclaimed religiosity and personal commitment to one's own spiritual practice. Studies have indicated that lifetime prevalence rates of infidelity range from between 20 percent and 25 percent for women and between 20 percent and 40 percent for men. Given that infidelity is a remarkably common occurrence and that it is among the most destructive things that can occur to a marriage, any personal practice that might diminish its likelihood should significantly protect marital health.

SANCTIFICATION AND SEX

It is also possible that certain spiritual beliefs and practices may directly contribute to positive attitudes toward marital sex, potentially contributing to healthy and vibrant sexual relationships. Of course, the opposite may also be true of other religious beliefs and practices. However, many spiritual traditions clearly teach very sex positive attitudes within loving and committed long-term relationships. Such positive affirmations of a person's sexuality can have profound effects in terms of fostering healthy sexual authenticity.

A shared spiritual practice may also provide an avenue for partners to spend real quality time together engaged in genuinely intimate settings and conversations. Spiritual beliefs that are deeply held provide an opportunity for fostering intimacy through the direct sharing of something intensely personal and meaningful. Discussing spiritual beliefs together, praying or meditating together, and engaging together in spiritual community are all ways to nurture an ongoing connection between intimate partners.

SANCTIFICATION AND COPING

Spiritual practices may also provide direct means for coping with the challenges of marriage. For example, partners may pray for guidance or reach out for help from spiritual leaders or friends. More spiritually active partners may use spiritual practices to help them cope with their own destructive emotions and negative beliefs and cognitions. Greater access to social support from communities of fellow believers may contribute to the resilience of a couple's marriage. Shared spiritual practices may also provide partners with a common playbook from which to derive their shared marital and parenting philosophies and from which to derive mutually acceptable solutions to commonly encountered problems.

As an example, one couple I saw in therapy talked often about the foundational role that their faith life played in their marriage and family. During their darkest periods together, their faith kept them walking forward. Their faith community was available to them, in obvious and subtle ways, to support their struggle with each other. Their faith encouraged them toward humility, perseverance, tolerance of suffering and imperfection, and a willingness to put some things above personal ego. They worked for the sake of their marriage, and they sometimes worked for the sake of God when working for the sake of each other was particularly difficult. They were able to look for the face of the holy in each other even when the other was acting in ways that were deeply disappointing. By persevering they remained resilient to a moment in their lives which was their "perfect storm" and that could have easily undone many marriages. Again, it is unclear whether this couple would have survived if they didn't have access to a life of spiritual practice, but it *is* clear that these practices provided them with personal and marital resources that they would not have had otherwise.

SANCTIFICATION AND CARETAKING

Professors Kenneth Pargament and Annette Mahoney also note that research suggests that people are more likely to "invest more of themselves in the pursuit and care of those things that are sacred to them . . ." (Sacred Matters, 15). They note that people work harder to preserve and protect those things that they perceive as sacred. In particular, Professor Mahoney has found in her research that people who sanctify their marriages seem to treat their marriage and their partner with greater care and reverence. Her research has found that couples who report a greater sanctification of their marriage engaged in less hostile conflict, less conflict in general, and greater mutual collaboration and accommodation. Further, these couples reported greater overall marital satisfaction and reported feeling like they each simply got more out of their marriages. These researchers also note that particular emotions appear to be regularly associated with religious practice, perhaps becoming more prominent with deepening religious practice. These emotions include love, humility, gratitude, and an internally motivated sense of obligation. It is easy for all of us to see how cultivating such emotions in our marriages might add strength and richness.

SECULAR SANCTIFICATION

I think it is also important to reiterate here that all of the qualities and attitudes and practices that we are talking about here in specifically spiritual terms are advocated for and practiced within personal belief systems that are not considered religious by the people who practice them. Many acknowledged agnostics, atheists, and the simply more secular-minded have strongly advocated and practiced many, if not all, of these attributes. If the benefits of these types of practices are to be available to strengthen all marriages, then it is important for each of us to find our own ways to understand such practices within our personal belief systems. As I noted before, I believe that the qualities that we are discussing in this chapter are available to everyone, although those who are conscientiously dedicated to specific practices and practice communities may more conscientiously and regularly practice them.

IS THERE A DARK SIDE TO SANCTIFICATION?

Some research in this area suggests that people suffer more deeply when the things that they consider sacred are harmed or destroyed. Interestingly, research by Professor Mahoney following the September 11 terrorist attacks suggests that those who perceived the attack as a religious desecration reported a greater urge to seek revenge. Clearly, if these darker sides of lived spirituality generalize to marriage as well, then they could prove problematic.

Further, as I've noted before, intimacy is necessarily emotionally challenging and that emotional challenge may simply be too much for many. Having made themselves a little bit vulnerable, the consequent sensitivity drives many to retrench and redefend with vengeance and ferocity. Couples are often more defended and more tense with each other than with anyone else precisely because the emotional and personal demands of intimacy are too taxing for their existing emotion skills. I suspect there is a parallel in the pursuit of spiritual intimacy.

Nevertheless, a decent amount of research has been conducted in terms of the relationship between spiritual practice and marital and family life and the bulk of the research is quite consistent in finding an overall positive enhancement effect. That being said, this area of marital research is in its infancy and there is still a great deal to be learned about how spiritual practice specifically affects marital and family health and whether some practices are healthier than others.

CONCLUSION AND RECOMMENDATIONS

In the end, however, assessing the health of the spiritual dimension of your marriage appears to be worthwhile. If this is an area of your relationship that you consider a strength, then the most recent research suggests that this is adding substantially to the overall health of your marriage. If this is an area of your marriage that you consider to be a weakness and that you would like to engage more actively, then there are several options that you might pursue.

First, consider opening a dialogue between you and your partner about this area of your shared lives. This should not be a discussion about what you "should" do or "should" believe. Instead, it should be an openhearted exploration of what you each think and believe, what you each hold dear and sacred, and how you each perceive of yourselves in spiritual terms.

- What are your spiritual beliefs and practices?
- How do you see the sacred in your life?
- How do you see yourself in spiritual terms?
- What role does religion, spirituality, faith, or practice play in your personal life?
- How do you see this part of your life contributing to the health and well-being of your marriage and family?
- Are there aspects of this part of your life that you would like to practice more or less?
- Are there ways in which the two of you could share in or support each other in your spiritual lives?

Getting to know each other better in this way is a clear path to greater intimacy and may open up avenues for greater connectedness and strength that were not obviously available to you previously.

Second, consider engaging in some sort of spiritual practice together. This could be any spiritual practice that makes sense to both of you or that you are at least both willing to experiment with. This can include:

- attending a religious service together,
- reading religious or spiritual material together,
- praying together,

- practicing meditation or yoga together, or
- any other shared activity that touches on this aspect of your life.

Third, consider the practice of looking at each other and at your marriage as manifestations of the sacred. It is clear that there are elements of the mysterious in your marriage. As I've noted before, your partner is not who you think s/he is. In fact, neither are you. You are definitely not who you think you are. If cognitive psychology has taught us anything, it has taught us that our perceptions, schemas, projections, attributions, predictions, memories, constructions of self, and other are all faulty, biased, and full of holes. Whatever is going on, whoever we are, and whoever our partners are is a complete and utter mystery to us, despite how strongly convinced we are to the contrary. If this is not an aspect of the sacred, then nothing is. Can you practice looking for the presence of the sacred in your partner's face, in how he or she moves around in the world, in his or her moments of clarity as well as moments of suffering and confusion? Perceiving the sacred in your marriage is a deliberate practice and requires effort and determination. If, however, this is an area of your life that you would like to strengthen, then you might find this type of practice quite illuminating.

8

SEXUAL AUTHENTICITY: SHARING THE SACRED

The goal of this chapter is to help you assess the health of your sexual relationship as part of your overall marital health. Researchers and clinicians agree that if your relationship generally isn't going well, then you will see side effects of that ill-health in your sexual relationship. The reverse is also true. If your relationship is thriving across the various domains discussed so far, then it is also quite likely that you have a healthy and vibrant sex life.

Throughout this chapter we will be exploring the normal complexities of sexual relating within long-term intimate relationships and complex modern lives. We will also review some of the current evidence-based suggestions for improving the health of your sexual relationship. The main theme of this chapter, however, will be exploring the development of what we are calling "sexual authenticity. " We will explore what I mean by sexual authenticity throughout this chapter, but in short, think of it as your capacity to be completely present and completely yourself right in the moment that you are embodying your sexual relationship with your partner. Sexual authenticity refers to our capacity to show up fully and to allow our partner to show up fully in the sharing of our sexual relationship. Sexual authenticity develops as self-acceptance, partner acceptance, and genuine intimacy develop over the course of a long-term relationship. As with any health domain, small gains in sexual health can have significant long-term benefits. Similarly, the upper limits of sexual relationship health are vast, meaning that this is an area of growth that couples can continue to profitably explore throughout their lives together, if they so choose.

It will become obvious as we proceed that the previous chapters in which we explored issues of intimacy, acceptance, mindfulness, emotion skills, communication, and forgiveness all come together in the domain of sexual intimacy. The importance of each of these facets will become apparent as we explore the interconnectedness of sexual intimacy and marital health.

Table 8.1. MC Sexual Intimacy Questionnaire

Definitely Something We Need to Improve 1	*Could Use Some Improvement* 2	*Neither a Strength nor Area for Improvement* 3	*Somewhat of a Strength* 4	*Definitely a Strength* 5

_____ 1. My partner and I feel emotionally close to each other during and after sex (rather than more distant or lonely).
_____ 2. We're happy with our sex life.
_____ 3. I feel comfortable when my partner initiates sex with me.
_____ 4. Sex with my partner makes me feel close to him/her.
_____ 5. I feel comfortable initiating sex with my partner.
_____ 6. I don't find that I avoid having sex with my partner.
_____ 7. My partner and I communicate well during sex.
_____ 8. It feels like my partner really knows who I am sexually.
_____ 9. I feel like my partner accepts me sexually.
_____ 10. I do not keep parts of myself hidden when I'm having sex with my partner.
_____ 11. I do not often feel embarrassed during sex with my partner.
_____ 12. I do not often feel inadequate during sex with my partner.
_____ 13. I feel like I am really being myself when my partner and I are having sex.
_____ 14. Sex between us does not feel like it's just about "getting it over with."
_____ 15. My partner and I are really able to enjoy being sexual with each other, regardless of the outcome.
_____ 16. It doesn't feel like we are more focused on ourselves than on each other when we're having sex.
_____ 17. It feels like my partner and I are really there together when we're having sex.
_____ 18. It doesn't feel like we both go off into our own separate worlds during sex.

SEX, INTIMACY, AND FRIENDSHIP: THE MANY MEANINGS OF SEX

Your sexual relationship is a three-ring circus. At any one time, your sexual relationship involves (a) what is going on with you physically and psychologically, (b) what is going on with your partner physically and psychologically, and (c) what is going on between the two of you in terms of your relationship patterns and dynamics. Your sexual relationship is far from one-dimensional. In fact, it is quite remarkably multidimensional. What any one moment of sexual expression means to you today may be quite different from what it meant to you yesterday or what it will mean to you tomorrow. Today you may be expressing intimacy and affection; at other times you may be expressing fun and friendship. At still other times you may be pursuing escape and fantasy or adventure and daring. You may be engaged in self- or other-exploration and curiosity. Or you may be tuned into the spiritual and sacred dimensions of sexual relating. You might also simply be seeking comfort, reassurance, and soothing. In short, the individual and shared meaning of any particular sexual encounter is free to vary considerably within the same individual and most certainly between individuals. This is a rich and complicated area of adult life available to be explored with curiosity and joy. It means something different and multifaceted to every one of us. Some of that meaning is obvious to us and some of it is obscured and mysterious. The bottom line is that you can never really predict what combination of self, other, and relationship will emerge during any particular moment of sexual relating. Because of that fact, it is important to stay tuned in and willing to "go with the flow" in order to fully appreciate your capacity for sexual health.

Communication appears to be an enormously useful tool for fully realizing the potential within this broad area of our lives. This can sometimes be a difficult thing for partners to do with each other because talking about sex or, potentially even more anxiety provoking for some, talking *during* sex can feel embarrassing, shameful, like it "ruins the mood," or is simply too real or ordinary. Although verbal communication can be difficult for partners, research has found that both partner's satisfaction with their sexual relationship is associated with the degree to which they understand each other's always changing preferences. Studies have also found that helping couples to improve their sexual communication is associated with improvements in sexual and relationship satisfaction overall. Of course, not all communication is necessarily verbal; a great deal can be communicated between partners without using words at all. Although nonverbal communication is important and the mindfulness necessary to tune into each other during sex a vital underpinning of sexual authenticity, verbal communication before, during, and after sex is an essential and oft neglected element of optimal sexual health.

Openness, authenticity, and respectful acceptance of self and other appear to be the foundation of healthy exploration. Unfortunately these sexually healthy attitudes are also often quite challenging for partners because of the confluence of several factors. First, in general, we receive a very poor education about sex and sexuality. As a result we often know very little about what is healthy and normal, as well as very little about how our bodies work. Even more, we often know next to nothing about how our minds and emotions are involved in and intimately influence our sexuality and sexual expression. In the place of real knowledge, we most often substitute myths, superstition, things we've heard from other equally ill-informed people, and attitudes projected by the media and the sex industry. Second, we receive dramatically mixed signals about sex and sexuality from our culture. Our culture appears to be simultaneously both very open and very closed about sex and sexuality. Finally for these and perhaps many other reasons, sexual relationships are inherently emotionally complicated, involving the paradoxes of intimacy, communication, and acceptance. Fostering our own openness, authenticity and self- and other-acceptance with regard to our sexuality can be quite challenging under these circumstances. However, even small gains in these healthy attitudes are likely to have significant positive repercussions throughout your relationship.

Shame, hidden-ness, habit, myth, miscommunication, misunderstanding, exploitation, trauma, and ignorance appear to be the band of jailers that lock us away from this part of our lives. Shame and embarrassment make us hide in both obvious and subtle ways. Discomfort and lack of self-acceptance do the same. It is simply impossible to hide and be authentically present at the same time. We can also get lost behind habit, because habit is mindless and lacking presence. Myth and superstition trap us inside boundaries and hold us up to expectations that exist solely in our own minds. In short, anything that comes between us and being mindfully tuned in to our own experience of relating removes us from our lives and robs us of the richness and potential of these shared moments. Because sexual intimacy is a particularly complicated area of our lives, there are simply many ways to get lost and confused.

SEX AS A REFLECTION OF RELATIONSHIP HEALTH

How you and your partner relate to each other sexually is a reflection of how you relate to each other throughout the rest of your marriage. Just as importantly, it is also a reflection of how you each relate to yourselves.

If there are unhealthy patterns at work in your relationship, then those patterns are likely to also show up in your sexual relationship. For example, pursue-withdraw or pressure-resist patterns that characterize how you deal with issues of closeness, power, emotional support, or problem-solving are very likely to have predictable counterparts in your bedroom. For example, I saw a couple in therapy in which one of the major issues in their relationship was the sort of pattern in which one partner exerted substantially more influence in the relationship than the other. Malcolm had a big personality, a strong will, and a generalized sense of being entitled to the things he wanted. He was used to getting his way more often than not in the world and in his relationship and could be either charming or demanding in the pursuit of his goals. Paula on the other hand had difficulty knowing what she wanted at any particular time and even when she did know what she wanted she often didn't feel particularly entitled to it. She often felt like Malcolm's sidekick rather than his full and equal partner and in many ways she was comfortable with that role. At the same time, she had over the years built up a great deal of resentment toward Malcolm because, as she put it, "he always gets his way." Malcolm for his part saw little problem with the fact that he often gets what he wants and advocates for himself strongly. This hero-sidekick pattern pervaded much of their relationship together. However, this pattern had a distinct counterpart in their sexual relationship, because it was in this arena of their lives in particular where Paula asserted ultimate control. Malcolm could want and pursue sex with the same level of intensity and desire that he brought to all other domains of his life, but, as Paula put it, "my body is the one thing I am in complete control of." In other words, sex was the one place in their relationship where Malcolm could not prevail through the sheer force of his personality. Paula could preserve some sense of her own will and independence by simply refusing to give in to Malcolm's wanting. This counterpoint to the generally unhealthy pattern in their relationship had resulted in their sex life having completely stalled for over a year by the time they came to see me. This example shows how generally unhealthy patterns in the relationship can show up in the bedroom in both direct and indirect ways. The bottom line being that if your general relationship health has deteriorated; the health of your sexual relationship will be affected. In other words, it is rarely the case that problems you might be experiencing in your sexual relationship are confined to your sexual relationship alone.

SEX AS A REFLECTION OF EMOTIONAL MATURITY

Just as importantly, the health and quality of your sexual relationship is a reflection of how you relate to yourself. How comfortable you are with yourself will be reflected in how comfortable you are in sexual relation with another complicated human being. We all carry around emotionally complicated natures. We tend to tie ourselves in pretzel knots in order to force ourselves into acceptable shapes. We twist ourselves to be more acceptable to our own ideas about what we should and shouldn't be. We distort who we really are in order to make ourselves into what we hope will be more acceptable to others, particularly those others that we are most emotionally dependent on. Our relationship with ourselves can be less than accepting, compassionate, and loving. And to the degree that we are uncomfortable with ourselves, it is likely that we will act out that discomfort in our sexual relationship with our partner.

If we think back to the chapter on acceptance, it becomes clear that the health of our sexual relationship can be greatly affected by our capacity to accept ourselves and our partner warts and all. This type of acceptance includes acknowledging both what legitimately moves and excites us as well as what makes us nervous, uncomfortable, and confused. When we are better able to accept what is simply true about who we are and who our partner is, then we are in an infinitely better position to make honest decisions. We can deliberately decide which fears to lean into and which boundaries to protect. We can, as adults, with open eyes, make imperfect decisions and learn from our mistakes and successes. Our sexual relationships are genuinely an arena in which we live out who we really are, whether we like that fact or not. And as such, our sexual relationships with our partners can be a context in which we can explore how to become more fully accepting of ourselves in the act of relating to our partners. The bottom line being that how we feel about ourselves is a big part of how healthy our sexual life is.

Similarly, if we consider the previous chapter on emotion skills, we can see the important role that emotional maturity plays in our sexual health. How well we tolerate the sometimes emotionally complicated nature of a sexual relationship is predicated on how skillful we have learned to be in relation to our own emotional stew. Sex involves pleasure, lust, yearning, love, affection, intensity, joy, and playfulness. It also involves fear, worry, irritation, emotional hurt, aggression, resentment, frustration, spite, and doubt. To really embrace the richness of your sexual relationship, it helps to be intimate with your own emotional rollercoaster. When you are feeling angry with your spouse, acknowledge that you are feeling angry without necessarily expecting your spouse to make you feel better. Your anger is *your* anger. You can express it honestly to your partner. In fact, research suggests that your relationship will be better off in the long run if you do. However, expecting your partner to assume responsibility for your anger is simply asking for the kind of trouble that cannot be resolved. Ultimately you are responsible for holding your own anger with compassion and for moving in relation to others with integrity and respect. The same is true for feeling horny, lustful, attracted to, lonely, stressed out, and all the other emotions that come along for the sexual ride. Emotional maturity means owning these experiences as our own, expressing them with integrity and respect, and allowing our partners the freedom to respond in whatever way fits with their own personal integrity. Emotional maturity and a sexually healthy relationship simply go hand in hand.

CHAPTER 8

SEX AND INTIMACY: SEXUAL AUTHENTICITY

More about Intimacy Than Biology

More often than not when a couple is concerned about their sexual relationship the issue is more about intimacy than it is about biology. I do not want to wholly discount the very real possibility of biological complication, but even in cases of truly biologically based sexual functioning difficulties; issues of intimacy and erotic connection are at the heart of the matter. When partners become more concerned about the *outcome* of any particular sexual experience between them (e.g., orgasm), than they are about the quality of the process (i.e., failing to enjoy the ride for concern about the destination), then problems can emerge that can seem biologically based (such as "erectile dysfunction") or truly biologically based challenges (for example, paraplegia) can seem insurmountable. Almost all of the most common complaints about sex in marriage, such as premature ejaculation, getting and/or maintaining an erection, lack of sexual desire, painful intercourse, difficulty reaching orgasm, and simple sexual boredom can be blamed on biological or medical causes, but that blame is much more often than not at least partially misplaced. More often than not the culprits are psychological (e.g., anxiety, worry, low self-acceptance), relational (e.g., unhealthy relationship patterns, unresolved conflict), or a simple lack of proper knowledge (about how your body works and how your partner's body works). In other words, the bottom line is often about intimacy—intimacy between you and your partner, intimacy between you and your own psychological world, and intimacy between your and your partner's body. Again, considering the previous chapter on intimacy, notice how all the aspects of intimacy, both the bright side and the shadow side are present in each of these domains of sexual intimacy. Notice also how the complicated nature of intimacy can be at the root of many of our sexual issues.

Consider, for example, a couple I saw in therapy who complained about the wife's low libido. Both the husband and the wife were quite willing to locate the cause of their sexual dissatisfaction in the wife and what they had both identified as her disinterest in sex. She herself complained about not understanding the cause of her "low sex drive." During the interview with them they talked about the solutions they were actively considering including the wife getting more exercise (maybe she was just out of shape) or talking to her doctor about taking testosterone (they had heard this can increase a person's sex drive). It was clear that they had stumbled into a biological/medical explanation for the problems they were experiencing in their sexual relationship. For this couple, although it was true that the wife had little interest in sex with her husband, it turned out that the "real" cause was the steady buildup of resentment between them stemming from poor communication about work, coparenting, and the division of household labor. As they clarified with each other their thoughts, attitudes, fears, and concerns about each of these other areas of their relationship, they found that the pressure-resist pattern in their sexual relationship subsided and, lo and behold, the wife found herself mysteriously sexually attracted to her husband again without any increase in her testosterone levels.

SEXUAL INTIMACY

Willingness to risk vulnerability is necessary for open sexual communication and exploration, similarly a warm and emotionally accepting/supportive atmosphere is necessary for inviting and reinforcing that vulnerability and exploration. The goal here is to create the comfort and safety that support exploration and joy. Here is also where strength in vulnerability is perhaps most essential. As much in our sexual relationship as anywhere else is the lesson that you can be open and vulnerable, genuinely authentic and unhidden, and completely centered even in the midst of vulnerability unmet. Your partner might respond in ways that are wonderful or that are disappointing and you can still stay fully present, open, authentic, and vulnerable. Vulnerability unmet is an opportunity to experience your own strength and resiliency, your own capacity to stay engaged and fully present even in the face of another's stumbling, panic, withdrawal, or aggressive self-protection.

This is also the place to practice listening to your partner with your whole body, with all your attention and curiosity, empathy and compassion, humility and self-accepting confusion. You may not know where or when your partner is most vulnerably open, but with intention and attention you can learn. And this learning about our own vulnerabilities and those of our partners goes on and on. They are lessons that we learn again and again as we change, age, and mature.

Willingness to lean into vulnerability means willingness to trust your partner and allow him or her the utter humanity of both occasional success and occasional failure to meet us well in that vulnerable moment. It also means a willingness to trust yourself. To trust that if your partner succeeds in meeting you well in that vulnerable moment, you will not lose yourself and to trust that if your partner fails to meet you well in that moment that you will not be weakened or irreparably harmed.

Sexual intimacy also rests on a strong intention to watch and listen closely for moments of real vulnerability so that we can practice showing up in ways that provide support and stability. It means being as equally willing to try and yet fail, as we are to try and yet succeed. Even with the best of intentions, and we do not always have the best of intentions, it is inevitable that we will disappoint or misunderstand our partners from time to time. This is another form of vulnerability and affords another opportunity for fostering sexual intimacy. Are we courageous enough to unabashedly embody our natural human imperfection? Are we courageous enough to show up dressed as ourselves in our sexual relationship?

As I noted before, sexual intimacy involves both emotional nakedness and nonjudgmental acceptance. It also requires courage, resilience, humility, and emotional maturity. Although it is certainly possible to have sex without intimacy, I strongly suspect that it is quite impossible to have a truly healthy and vibrant sexual relationship that is not boldly intimate. Look back over the questionnaire at the beginning of this chapter for those items that deal with boldness and timidity and ask yourself if this is genuinely a strength in your marriage. If not, ask yourself if you are healthy enough for comfort at your current level of sexual intimacy, because you very well may be, even if you feel a little weak in this area. If you would like to try to strengthen this area of your marriage, then consider carefully the range of options presented at the end of this chapter.

THE SEXUAL INTIMACY PARADOX: THE SHADOW SIDE OF INTIMACY

Intimacy is not necessarily always soothing. Often it involves courageousness and self-acceptance in the face of our own insecurities. Genuine sexual intimacy requires the courage to take the emotional risks necessary to be fully authentic and unhidden with your sexual partner. Sex is often among the most difficult issues for us to be open about with others. What makes it even more challenging with our intimate partners is the fact that their opinions matter so much to us. The more someone means to you, the harder it can be to risk that person's rejection. If your partner's response didn't matter to you, then you most likely wouldn't hesitate to be completely open and uninhibited with your sexuality, enthusiastically following your emerging and changing desires in the moment. However, it is precisely because the process of intimacy results in our being most vulnerably exposed to our intimate partner that his or her negative responses hurt the most. This "shadow side" of sexual intimacy is what makes this area of our lives so emotionally complicated. Revealing yourself in your sexuality is undeniably emotionally risky. The better your partner knows you and the more his or her judgment matters to you, the riskier stepping out of your comfort zone can be. Thus, although intimacy is the key to optimal health within your sexual relationship, it is definitely not for the timid.

How does sexual intimacy develop its shadow side and how does that shadow side undermine our capacity for sexual authenticity? Intimacy theory posits that intimacy begins when we expose our vulnerability. That vulnerability itself is created in those places where we have learned that we are at risk of being judged, hurt, or punished. As we grow, our emerging sexuality may be one of the main areas of our lives where we learn that we are at risk of being judged, shamed, hurt, or punished. As we develop from childhood through adolescence, we learn from countless experiences that our sexuality is best kept hidden and is subject to significant censure. Most of us begin to develop sexual relationships in late adolescence or early adulthood under a cloud of risked disapproval and hidden-ness. It is little wonder that we develop enormous vulnerabilities associated with our sexuality and sexual behavior. It is also little wonder that that emotional vulnerability often follows us far into adulthood.

Intimacy, including sexual intimacy develops as we share these vulnerable, and therefore very private, aspects of ourselves with our partner and our partner responds with acceptance. The equation is fairly simple. The more accepting our partner proves to be, the more we share. The less accepting our partner proves to be, the less we share. As our partner gets to know us more deeply, we become more exposed and thus more vulnerable. The person who we allow closest to us becomes the person we are most vulnerable to. Because intimate partners are so emotionally exposed to each other and spend so much time in emotionally close proximity to each other, they are the most likely to hurt each other, both accidentally (e.g., grouchy before coffee) or on purpose (e.g., saying, "your just like your mother" during a fight). You hurt most deeply the people you are closest to. This is the intimacy paradox and is as true in the sexual domain as it is in other domains of your relationship. In fact, given the emotionally complicated and ambivalent nature of sexuality in most cultures, sexual intimacy can be the most emotionally complicated and vulnerable-making aspect of marriage. In short, it is perfectly normal for people to be skittish about being fully sexually authentic.

The main point here being that achieving sexual intimacy means having to courageously engage in aspects of your sexuality that you might be genuinely ambivalent about, aspects that have an approach-avoidance dilemma intertwined within them. Exploring sexual authenticity will mean confronting those aspects of your experience that are preventing you from being authentic. The way that sexuality normally develops in our culture is inevitably vulnerable making and the natural process of intimacy exposes those vulnerabilities and draws them up to our limit. As a result, it is normal for us to feel at least some degree of anxiety and hidden-ness. Having some trepidation about our developing sexuality is nothing, in and of itself, to be ashamed of. In fact, if we can forgive ourselves for this and begin to take it lightly that we carry with us certain emotional complications, we may be better able to lean into them with some degree of shared adventurousness.

One particular aspect to come to see as normal and to hold fairly lightly is that we are necessarily sensitive to our partners' reactions to us. We might even be particularly sensitive to what we *imagine* our partner's reaction might/could be. Rather than risk what we imagine might be a rejecting, offended, or judgmental reaction from our partner, we choose not to share our honestly held sexual desires with him or her. For example, we don't talk to each other while we're making love because we imagine the shock and surprise of our partner, or even possibly the anger and rejection, and we simply can't take that chance with something that feels so "high stakes" to us. Instead, we choose to stay within the safe boundaries that we have constructed together out of habit, no matter how tired and emotionally distant life within those boundaries has become. Because these are areas of our lives that are vulnerable and that we have learned to lean away from, we don't consider that our partner's reaction might be quite wonderful and exciting, even if we have to tolerate a certain period of awkwardness to get there.

We also tend to over-interpret our partner's reactions. This is true in general, but may be particularly true when it comes to something as potentially emotionally complicated as sex. In this domain, a moment's hesitation can be easily over-interpreted as a flat out and complete rejection. Imagine a moment in which you really want to try something new in bed, maybe a new sexual position. You make an initial move in that direction and because it is something new and different, your partner stiffens and looks puzzled. Instead of seeing this moment for what it might actually be, a moment of adjustment and a good time to communicate with your partner about something you would like to share, you over-interpret his or her puzzlement as rejection and withdraw, feeling a little resentful, back into your shared sexual "safety zone." Sometimes our partner (or we ourselves) will experience some ambivalence about what is happening in the moment and we will need the ability to tolerate that ambivalence in a generous way. Intimacy creates greater exposure and therefore it is necessary to acquire the emotion skills and emotional maturity required to stay generously engaged even in emotionally loaded situations.

The goal here in the Marriage Checkup is to help you to recognize if these "shadow sides" of intimacy have created real barriers to your sexual and marital health. If you recognize yourself as caught in this type of dilemma, the question becomes about how to use that recognition to get you and your partner cooperating again in a common and exciting direction. For some of you that will simply mean starting a conversation about what you would both like to explore in your shared sexual relationship. For others of you, it will mean agreeing to read a good book about the subject together as a means of getting the conversation started and joyfully entering a period of sexual trial and error. For some others of you, it will mean finding a qualified and talented marital or sexual therapist to help you both begin to recognize the blind spots and emotional tangles that are keeping you stuck and lost. The bottom line is to become activated about this issue. The key is to begin the process of doing *something* and trusting yourself and your partner, through the process of trial and error, to stumble into greater sexual and marital health.

AUTHENTICITY IS THE KEY

Authenticity is one of the keys to deepening intimacy. Genuine authenticity requires not abandoning anything that is true for the sake of anything else that is true. What do I mean by not abandoning something that is true for the sake of something else that is true? I mean that it is quite common for us to experience more than one emotion, thought, or impulse that can seem completely contradictory. For example, particularly when it comes to sexual relationships, we can often experience curiosity/excitement at the same time that we experience anxiety/hesitancy. Unfortunately, more often than not, we choose to abandon the truth of our curiosity and excitement for the sake of our anxiety and trepidation. What would it mean in this instance to stay true to both experiences—to be both excited and anxious? It would mean being able to have our anxiety without having to run away from it, defeat it, or pretend that it didn't exist. This in turn would mean that we would have to practice accepting wholeheartedly that anxiety is present. Accepting the anxiety that is present would mean allowing the feelings in the body that come with anxiety, again without trying to deny them or defeat them. It would mean tolerating those anxious thoughts and imaginations without necessarily believing them or fighting with them. It would mean allowing that anxious thoughts and feelings are present and floating by and practicing the emotion skill of letting them be without grabbing on to them or pushing them away.

By not abandoning the truth that anxiety is present you will be able to stay faithful to the truth that excitement and curiosity are also present. From this position you will have achieved greater clarity about who you really are in the moment, you will have become more intimate with *yourself*, and will be able to make choices based on that clarity. You will be in a position where you can fully embrace and experience that excitement and curiosity and choose to use it to guide you toward a genuinely sexually authentic experience with your partner.

Marriage provides a rich setting in which we can learn to be authentic in relation to others. It is difficult to learn to be authentic even when we are alone and have the protection of solitude and are away from the possible judgments of others. It is quite a bit more challenging to learn to be authentic in relation to others whose thoughts, feelings, and actions we cannot control. Others are always and without pause capable of responding in ways that we experience as validating or judgmental. In the spirit of not abandoning one truth to another, the question becomes can you stay faithful to your own authentic experience even in the face of someone else who is not responding well? Can you remain faithful to your experience even in the face of someone else who is responding differently than you wish? The committed long-term intimacy that can be available in marriage allows us the context in which to learn the sometimes difficult lessons of authenticity in relation.

This, again, is particularly true when it comes to your expression of sexuality in relation to your partner. Because sex that is really connected and really vibrant requires you to be fully present with your partner and not shut away inside your own head, it necessitates emotional vulnerability which in turn requires the emotional courage not to withdraw into yourself. You want to be able to express yourself sexually with your partner in a way that feels like it is really you, fully accepted and accepting. Your partner, of course, wants exactly the same thing. The key to sexual authenticity is that some significant portion of that acceptance will have to be self-acceptance in addition to the portion that is provided by your partner.

Sexual authenticity means being fully accepting of your own sexual experience as it is emerging in the moment. It means learning to become open and undefended about your experience of yourself as a sexual being. It means letting your sexuality and sensuality fully permeate your every fiber without apology or hesitation. It means letting yourself be completely at home in your own body. It means having your sexuality and sensuality with complete self-acceptance.

OWNING YOUR OWN SENSUALITY

From this perspective you are completely responsible for how you do and do not express your own naturally occurring sensuality. It is not up to your partner to tell you what your sexual experience should be. It is not up to your partner to make you feel comfortable with an aspect of your sexuality that you yourself are ambivalent about. You have to accept full responsibility for your own experience. That means you get to both have it fully, without denial, *and* you have to come to terms with your own anxieties, hesitations, and ambivalences on your own. Your responsibility for your sexual life lies solely with you. Although it is very tempting to place that responsibility on your partner, to put the ball in his or her court, whether you like it or not, the ball is always in your court.

For example, I worked with a couple in which the issue of who would initiate sex had become so anxiety provoking and embittering that they had simply stopped having sex altogether. As the years marched by, sex became easier to avoid and scarier and more embittering to approach. Part of taking personal responsibility involved each partner recognizing that leaning back into this area of their relationship was going to mean having to personally experience and tolerate the complicated emotional stew waiting for them there. All the things about sexuality in their marriage that they wanted to approach and all the things that they wanted to avoid would be there together in the same moment. Most critically, the other person would not be able to save them from those emotional experiences. In order to reignite their sexual relationship, each had to cope with feelings of resentment and trepidation that the other person had no access to. As it became clearer to each of them that responsibility for restarting their sex life was each partner's sole responsibility and could not be shared, they found that, paradoxically perhaps, they were both making more active moves to initiate sexual contact.

YOU AND YOUR PARTNER WANT DIFFERENT THINGS

You choose, with complete respect for your partner, how to live your sexuality while at the same time respecting your partner's right to be fully him- or herself, including his or her right to want something different than you do. That means you can want something sexually and your partner can want something completely different and that is both okay and perfectly normal. In fact it happens to you all the time. You might not know that it happens to you all the time because you don't communicate during sex. This is why sexual communication is so important. It is just as easy, if not easier to miscommunicate sexually as it is to miscommunicate in all the other areas of your life. You are both constantly "wanting" and "not wanting," completely independently of each other throughout every sexual encounter between you. If you aren't communicating with each other, then you are much more likely to lose contact with each other and resentments are bound to build. If you are actively communicating with each other during sex, then you are much more likely to have an intense and mutually satisfying sexual relationship. It is only through active communication that you can really get to know each other, even as you are both constantly changing.

This also includes really getting to know yourself as well as really getting to know your partner. It means not hiding who you are and what your experience is. Finally, and perhaps most importantly, it means being able to allow that things will not always go just exactly the way that you want. You will want one thing and your partner will want another. You will be vulnerable and your partner will miss it or be simply unavailable physically or emotionally. What is most important here is the experience of strength in vulnerability. You have to be able to allow for the "error" part of trial and error or you won't be able to fully explore your shared sexuality. Of course, this is easier said than done, but it is the only path to fully embracing your sexuality and to sexual authenticity.

SEXUALITY AND EMOTIONAL GROWTH

This means that you need your partner to be fully who he or she is, to be completely different and independent from you, so that you can learn to be completely who you are and to learn strength in vulnerability. Without a fully committed partner and a long-term relationship, this kind of emotional growth may be difficult, if not impossible. You need a fully committed partner for this kind of journey. It is the kind of journey that can take some time to begin in earnest, and because we are always changing, it is necessarily a lifetime's journey. Since sexual authenticity is about getting to know yourself and someone else fully, even as you both are changing, it cannot be achieved through a series of short-term relationships or in a long-term relationship in which both partners are constantly hiding themselves from each other or refusing to let themselves be seen and known.

This is an area within your relationship that genuinely has the potential to grow and keep growing. Contrary to what many couples believe, there are levels of joy and intimacy in sexuality that are really only available to partners who have been in an intimate relationship with each other for a long time. In other words, there is something about really knowing each other, really trusting each other, really feeling emotionally safe with each other that allows an experience of sexuality that is simply more profound and thoroughly enjoyable than that available to couples who know each other less well.

If you think about it for even a minute, this makes complete sense even to the most hard-nosed pragmatist. If your partner does not know you and know your wants and needs, your desires and preferences, even as those sexual impulses and preferences change from day to day and moment to moment, then clearly the quality of your sexual relationship is going to be compromised. Further this still by recognizing that the same can easily be said for you about yourself. You know on some level that you don't know your sexual self as well as you could. You have fallen into habits, even within your own expression and experience of sexuality, that are repetitive and outcome oriented. Like getting directions on the Web, you know how to get from point A to point B by "the shortest route possible," but you have not fully explored all of the scenic routes of your own body and sexual experience, much less those of your partner. If you have not fully and boldly explored your own sensuality and you have not fully and boldly explored your partner's sensuality, then clearly you are missing the full potential that is available to you in your healthy sexual relationship. Mainly, you and your partner simply have to face up to any feelings of awkwardness, shame, lack of self-acceptance, and lack of other acceptances that are getting in the way of fully and even playfully exploring all of the scenic routes available through your sexuality. If you are hesitating and hiding parts of yourself, then you are leaving a great deal of life unlived.

AUTHENTICITY AND ROADBLOCKS

Again, what does sexual authenticity mean? It means only being yourself. It means giving your body back to yourself and allowing your partner to do the same. It means being willing to explore the sensuality that is available to you fully, mindfully, and without apology. It means allowing yourself to have the feelings that you are having in the moment regardless of whether they make sense or are contradictory. It means being willing to lean into those areas of your own sexuality that make you hesitate and tighten up. It means learning how to accept the sometimes-complicated nature of sexuality with good humor and mutual compassion. If you can practice being completely present and completely yourself in every moment of your sexual expression and you can allow the same opportunity for your partner, then you open up endless dimensions of sensuality.

There may however be real and significant roadblocks in your way. Habits of body and mind are hard to even see much less purposefully shake off. For some of us these roadblocks are nothing more than the detritus left over from being raised in a sexually punitive culture. For others of us these roadblocks consist of histories of real abuse or neglect. For still others these roadblocks consist of overly judgmental notions of self-image and self-esteem. For yet others these roadblocks consist of simple and understandable ignorance, misinformation, and sexual superstition. Whatever your roadblocks consist of, they can be identified and if they can be identified then they can be made friends with.

SEXUAL INAUTHENTICITY

What is sexual inauthenticity? The main characteristic of inauthenticity is experiential avoidance and what motivates us to avoid our own truth and our own experience. Experiential avoidance is a term we use to describe all of those things that we do to avoid, deny, run from, or try to destroy whatever we happen to be experiencing in the moment. A simple example would be trying to deny that you are feeling sad. You might distract yourself from your own feelings by going to a movie, watching TV, reading a book, or getting into a conversation. You might convince yourself that the sadness you are feeling is really anger, because anger is a more comfortable emotion for you. You might drink or use drugs or simply by force of will shove any feelings of sadness away as illegitimate, unworthy, or shameful. We all do this to some degree with unpleasant feelings or thoughts or experiences. We also tend to do it with the absence of pleasant feelings. We might not be sad, but we're not happy or we don't feel content, so we try to smother, deny, or obliterate that experience as well. As noted in earlier chapters, psychological studies of emotions and thoughts have begun to make it clear that experiential avoidance does by far more harm than good. For the short-term gain of momentarily distracting ourselves, we make ourselves in the long run more thoroughly miserable.

OUTCOME- VERSUS PROCESS-FOCUS

Sexual experiential avoidance takes on many forms. Perhaps one of the most common involves becoming over-focused on the outcome of sex rather than on the process of sex. People often have sex with the sole goal of having or giving an orgasm, or of proving themselves as a sexual maestro or athlete or at the very least to assure themselves that they are "good at it." When you become focused on the outcome, you necessarily lose contact with the process. In other words, if you are focused on the outcome of sex, you aren't *having* sex. You are focused on what is or isn't over the horizon, you are focusing on the future and abandoning the present. You are simply unavailable to thoroughly enjoy your shared sexuality and sensuality because you are too focused on getting somewhere or proving something.

If instead, you can completely let go of any concern about where you are going, if or when you'll ever get there, and what it will be like when you do, then you can actually show up fully to the process of having sex *with* your partner. You'll be able to *really* enjoy it *as it is happening*. Otherwise, you are actually having sex with yourself and your own imagination about how it's going and where it's going. Your partner is really just a prop in your anxiety play.

One situation in which some couples sometimes find themselves over-focusing on the outcome is when they are trying to get pregnant. As "getting pregnant" becomes the focused upon outcome, partners can find that sex becomes emotionally complicated. I've seen couples in otherwise very healthy and satisfying marriages actually start avoiding sex that had become about getting pregnant. What is interesting about this example is that it so strongly demonstrates the basic idea that focusing on the outcome of sex, even an outcome that both partners may want very much, can undermine the quality of a couple's marital health.

Becoming outcome oriented steals you away from the moment of relating. This is also true about all the other ways that we disconnect and distance ourselves from the pure act of relating. Do we slip into unshared fantasies? Do we think about baseball or lists of things to do? Are we completely distracted by thoughts and feelings about other things in our lives? Are we caught up in acting out resentments and complications from other areas of our relationship? Are we acting out our own intimacy and self-acceptance issues in the bedroom? There are many, many ways that we can fail to show up mindfully and authentically and fully throw ourselves into a moment of sexual relating with our partner. When sex is an act of relating, an act of relationship, the enactment of fully being with and open to, when it is the relationship in process, then it can be transcendent. When it is about outcomes and expectations and performance and technique then it is compromised, smaller, darker, more pinched, hidden, and skittish. It is simply less.

SPECTATORING

A particularly pernicious form of being overly outcome oriented is called "spectatoring." We've all had this experience at various times in various areas of our lives. It is marked by the experience of watching yourself and your performance as if you were a spectator in the stands rather than a player on the field. You watch yourself like a sports or theater critic as you give your presentation at work, interview for a job, talk to new friends or business associates, or in any other situation where you can criticize your own performance. In particular, people tend to fall prey to spectatoring in bed. Because we have the tendency to become outcome oriented about our sex lives, we become self and other critical, we start to worry about our performance and critique it from the bleachers and before we know it we are completely distracted by what is going on in our own heads and completely unavailable to what is actually happening in the moment. We watch ourselves too closely and worry that something will "go wrong." We worry that we won't have an orgasm, or "keep it up," or that we'll have an orgasm "too soon," or that our partner won't enjoy him- or herself. We lose ourselves in our worry and our self-criticism rather than losing ourselves in the shared and intimate act of sensuality.

Spectatoring and outcome-focus rather than process-focus are two ways of removing yourself from the moment and becoming inauthentic.

TRYING TO PIN IT ALL ON YOUR PARTNER

Do you try to get your partner to make you feel better about those things you reject about yourself? Do you blame your partner for your own ambivalence about your sensuality? Do you blame your partner for your own sexual boredom or lack of interest in sex? Whatever the issue is that we are struggling with in our sexual relationship, it is a very common and very human move to place the blame squarely at the feet of our partner. Of course, this would be a fantastic move if it worked. We would remove any responsibility from ourselves, remain completely invulnerable, *and* our partner would do all the hard work of solving the problem on his or her own. It is a completely understandable move, because it can often feel like the only solution to an otherwise unsolvable problem. We at least get the relief of not having to struggle to solve the problem anymore. Unfortunately, this move never actually works. When we blame our partner, we completely give away all of our own power as we give away all of our responsibility. We fail to confront "the problem" authentically and to fully accept the consequences of decisions we make about our own sexuality. Completely blaming your partner never solves the problem. Believe me, I wish it did, but it doesn't.

Believe it or not, the solution always lies in the direction of accepting your own responsibility. This doesn't mean accepting responsibility for your partner and his or her behavior and choices. It does mean accepting full responsibility for your own decisions and behavior and the consequences of those decisions and that behavior. If you choose to initiate sex with a partner who isn't necessarily in the mood, then that is your grown-up decision. Embrace it and go for it and accept the consequences without blaming your partner. If you choose to avoid, deny, or suppress your partner's sexual initiations, then that is your grown-up decision. Embrace it and go for it and fully accept the consequences without blaming your partner. If your choose to limit your expression of sexuality to a relatively well-worn path, then again, embrace this as your completely deliberate choice with perhaps perfectly predictable consequences. This too is sexual authenticity. Inauthenticity would be denying that you are making grown-up decisions with grown-up consequences. Inauthenticity would be blaming the consequences of your choices on your partner.

Similarly, if you choose to be courageous about your sexuality and meet your partner as one independent adult meeting another independent adult, then that choice too will have consequences. Hints from the clinical and research literature suggest that this decision is more likely to result in positive consequences than the others.

EMBODYING SEXUAL AUTHENTICITY

What you actually do with your partner will flow from throwing yourself completely into the genuine connection between you. Mindful of the embodied connection between you and your partner, you can then let that connection lead you into what you actually do while making love. Allowing the process to unfold in this way creates a sensuality in which there are no techniques and no positions, there is no doing this to get to that, there is no possibility of success or failure, there is only the embodiment of relating and the living out of strength in intimacy. It is never about technique. It is never about outcomes like orgasm or praise or escape from judgment. If you are present and curious together, you will discover many things.

The basic question is can you really stand showing up? It can be difficult to really show up completely during sex. It makes many people anxious or uncomfortable to do something as seemingly simple as talk to each other during sex. This highlights how emotionally complicated sex can be. We are perfectly comfortable talking in almost any other context. In fact, for some of us it can be painfully uncomfortable not to talk when we are with someone else. However, for many, sex is different. Communicating during sex is taboo. It risks too much. It might "get in the way." It makes us nervous, embarrassed, or ashamed. Even more so when it comes to sexual desires or fantasies that we are hesitant to share or when it comes to making ourselves emotionally available in ways that may initially seem too real. Perhaps the most basic sexual skill is the ability to accept the full range of emotions and experiences that show up for us during sex. Accept without judgment, without seeking to escape or blame or fix. As simple as it might sound to tolerate our own experience and to keep moving in the direction of connectedness and health, it is clearly easier said than done.

One way we can talk about this is as mindful interconnection. Just as you can be mindful of the experience of eating an apple—aware of the color, the smell, the "pop" of teeth piercing peel, the flavor of juice and flesh—you can be aware of, and immerse yourself completely in the experience of mindfully interconnecting with your partner. For some partners this experience of deliberate and focused attention on the present moment during sex is quite wonderful. For others, this type of present centeredness is disconcerting, placing them in greater contact with aspects of themselves and their sexuality that make them uncomfortable and from which they usually find ways to distance themselves. Still, the route to sexual authenticity is through mindful present centeredness, which may require building tolerance for levels of experiencing that might be initially challenging.

The key is to stay present. It is only through staying completely present and attentive that we can learn how to be fully sexually authentic with our partner. As with all experiences that can be anxiety provoking, it is important to recognize that you do not have to do anything about the anxiety. You do not have to try to defeat it or ignore it, withdraw from it or smother it. You simply have to have it and let it be fully part of your experience. It is a mistake to think that you must first defeat your feelings of anxiety or awkwardness before really leaning into the experience of your sexuality. Setting out with the agenda of feeling perfectly comfortable first is clearly putting the cart before the horse. The more willing you are to have some uncomfortable feelings (shy, embarrassed, worried, frustrated) the more able you will be to be completely yourself and completely open when you are sharing sex with your partner.

Embodying sexual authenticity is about not hiding anything from yourself, not judging any part of your experience, communicating openly and maybe even playfully with your partner and living fully into your sexuality. It is to embrace the truth of your existence as a sexual being, to not cordon off your sexuality as dirty or shameful, but to let it be as much a legitimate part of who you are in the world as your eyes and hands. We are responsible for what we choose to do with our eyes and hands, but we never feel like we should have to apologize for *having* eyes and hands. I have my experience of my eyes. I have my experience of my hands. I have my experience of my sexuality. These are simple truths that we can legitimately embrace as fully functioning adults. Your experience and acceptance of yourself as a sexual being is a fundamentally important part of your overall mental, emotional, physical, and marital health. Fully accepting your partner as a sexual being is similarly central to that health. As complicated as our culture can make this for us, it is absolutely available to every one of us and fundamentally our birthright.

SEXUAL HEALTH AND MARITAL HEALTH

Satisfaction with your sex life is intimately tied to the overall health of your relationship. Research studies consistently reveal a large correlation between satisfaction with sexual intimacy and overall marital satisfaction. The association isn't so much about a "need" for sex as it is about one of the most fundamental expressions of intimacy within a thriving healthy relationship. Our sensuality and sexuality are a fundamental part of who we each are and if we do not feel authentic and satisfied with this fundamental quality of who we are, it is impossible to feel completely satisfied with our lives. As I hope to have communicated so far, sexual satisfaction also isn't about any of the goals or outcomes that partners sometimes become concerned about, like the frequency with which they are having sex or whether and when they have orgasms, or who got what up for how long and toward what end. Instead, it is about the natural and open expression of shared sensuality and fully expressed sexuality in the moment between two intimately connected partners.

More often than not, dissatisfaction with your sex life is a symptom of marital health issues, not physical or mental health issues. Although physical health issues can and do play a role both on the positive and negative side, much more often than not researchers and clinicians alike have found that improvements in marital health often relieve symptoms that were previously attributed to purely physical causes. Similarly, mental health issues like depression, anxiety, and others can have predictable negative effects on sexual satisfaction. Again, however, there is evidence from the psychotherapy research literature that improvements in marital health can have positive effects on mental health issues as well. If you find that you are struggling to feel free and happy in the expression of your sexual relationship, then marital research would suggest the first place you might want to look is into the quality of your marital health. Communication, intimacy, authenticity, mindfulness, time together, emotion skills, and forgiveness are all important to your overall marital and sexual relationship health. How are *you* doing on each of these dimensions in your marriage and how might you begin to walk deliberately in the direction of greater health?

It is similarly important to actively combat your own ignorance. Don't be afraid to read a good book or even a dozen good books. Even happy and healthy couples can benefit from more knowledge about sex and sexuality. Sexual education has left a great deal to be desired and we all walk away from it knowing only the smallest percentage of what we ultimately need to know. Similarly, pornography is a very poor teacher of sex and sexuality, not only teaching us very little, but many times making things more confused and outcome oriented. What we learn "on the street" or from our friends is only a reflection of the general ignorance of the culture at large and tends not to serve us as well as intended.

I would recommend the following books.

- *Rekindling Desire: A Step by Step Program to Help Low-Sex and No-Sex Marriages* by Barry W. McCarthy and Emily J. McCarthy
- *Sexual Awareness: Couple Sexuality for the Twenty-first Century* by Barry McCarthy and Emily McCarthy
- *Resurrecting Sex: Solving Sexual Problems and Revolutionizing Your Relationship* by David Schnarch, Ph.D.
- *The Sex-Starved Marriage: A Couple's Guide to Boosting Their Marriage Libido* by Michele Weiner-Davis

HOW YOU CAN FOSTER SEXUAL AUTHENTICITY

Encourage Yourself to Really Show Up

What does it mean to encourage yourself to really show up? It means encouraging yourself to deliberately lean toward greater connection with your partner during those moments when your instinct is to withdraw or to stay hidden. It also means leaning into those experiences of your sexuality and sexual expression that you tend to pull back from. Unapologetically and unhesitatingly embracing the entire experience of your sexuality in the moment can be very powerful. For many, it can be an overwhelming experience and subtly withdrawing from that experience behind mental and emotional barriers is an understandable way of limiting exposure to overwhelming feelings.

It can also be an experience that many of us don't quite feel entitled to, worthy of, or deserving of. It can be easy to feel that one is not good enough in some way to unabashedly claim legitimate entitlement to one's whole body, every inch of it, without shame or hesitation. So many of us feel that we are not good looking enough, not perfect enough, not healthy enough, not young enough, not lovable enough, not worthy enough of complete acceptance and not strong enough to handle anything short of complete acceptance and admiration.

Encouraging yourself to really show up can be done in many concrete ways. One way involves simply keeping your eyes open during sex with your partner. There may be nothing wrong with keeping your eyes closed in and of itself. However, keeping your eyes closed does lend itself to wandering away from the moment into fantasy or worry. Keeping your eyes open allows you to stay connected with your partner throughout the experience. Eyes closed during sex can be a very solitary and disconnected thing. Eyes open during sex is much more likely to involve really being with each other, experiencing a sexual partnership and a real and natural intimacy. As I noted before, this way of really engaging in an intimate sexual conversation with your partner can take on many forms from playful to serious, from superficial to deeply spiritual.

Eye contact during sex, a practice discussed by Dr. Schnarch in his book, is a particularly easy way to encourage yourself to show up. Again, if you are not used to this level of intimacy during sex, then it at first might feel awkward and distracting. However, again, the key to a richer experience is to wholeheartedly embrace the experience of awkwardness as an integral part of the moment and absolutely necessary in terms of stretching toward greater health. After awhile, you will get comfortable with this level of intimacy and you may be glad for having tolerated a little bit of awkwardness to get there.

Another simple way to encourage yourself to really show up is to talk, to use your words to communicate with your partner while you are making love. Communicate about what feels good. Communicate about how you are feeling and how you are feeling about your partner. Smile at him. Tell her you love her. Make noise to communicate how you are feeling, what feels good, how good it feels, and to let your partner share in your experience of the moment.

I want to particularly encourage you to communicate with words because for many people this is the most awkward way to communicate during sex, and so probably needs the most encouragement. Communicating with words may be the most powerful way of really showing up just as yourself, really as yourself, as the you who has fully integrated her or his sexuality into his or her whole being, rather than as the very isolated you who only shows up during sex and who is completely cut off from the rest of who you are in your day-to-day life. Since talking is so ordinary and everyday and yet so often missing from our sex lives, it can serve as a powerful bridge between these different dimensions of yourself, creating a much greater sense of sexual authenticity and thus a much richer and more powerful shared sexual experience. Again, if you are not used to this level of intimacy, it will be awkward at first. Again, the payoff of tolerating and working through the awkwardness may be well worth the extra effort in the long run.

Of course there are also many and varied ways to communicate nonverbally during sex and ultimately these are all available to be explored between you and your partner. Nonverbal communication is an important way of showing up in an authentic way.

EVERYDAY SENSUALITY

Another way to encourage yourself to really show up during sex is to let parts of your sexuality show up between you are your partner during other ordinary parts of the day. Since sexuality and sensuality are about process and not outcome, it is available to you and your partner to share moments of sexual connection during the day that are just about being alive and connected and that don't necessarily carry with them any obligations or promised outcomes. For many couples, any kind of sexual or sensual touching during the day can be fraught with feelings of frustration or pressure. It can become part of an ongoing tug-of-war and as such become completely unavailable to partners as a source of intimacy, connection, and eroticism. If this tug-of-war has moved into your relationship in a way that is blocking real connection between you and your partner, you may be able to work it loose yourself using good communication strategies and emotion skills or you may want to take advantage of a well-qualified couples therapist to help you free yourselves from its clutches. If you and your partner can appreciate your shared sexuality during your regular day-to-day lives, then you may find yourselves feeling more thoroughly integrated and better able to be sexually authentic.

Another way of encouraging yourself toward greater sexual authenticity is to practice thinking of yourself as a sexual being. Pay attention to what else shows up for you when you think of yourself as a sexual and sensual person. Do you feel unworthy of fully claiming your own sexuality, of actually living all the way into your own body? Do you feel somehow not good enough or not deserving? Do you feel your sexuality is somehow shameful or maybe even dangerous? Do you worry that the truth that you are a sexual being is unacceptable to others? Do you worry that you may need the acceptance of others or perhaps the permission of others in order to fully claim your sexuality? Sexual authenticity is not necessarily uncomplicated for any of us. The practice of thinking of yourself as a sexual being can help you to usefully explore those ways in which you have learned to deny yourself your full humanity. Again, this particular type of challenge can become easier as we get older and more comfortable with ourselves. However, even age and maturity do not always accomplish this spontaneously. What comes up for you when you practice thinking of yourself as a sexual being while you are brushing your teeth? While you are getting dressed for the day? While you are drinking your coffee? While you are making the children's lunch? While you are driving to work or to run errands? While you are in a meeting with colleagues? While you are eating lunch? While you are arguing with your spouse? If you can practice letting yourself have and own your sexuality/sensuality throughout the day, then you will learn that you can trust yourself with this aspect of who you are, that you can trust yourself to act in a mature and responsible way without having to deny or withdraw from your own authentic experience. As you become more fully integrated with your sexuality, you will find that when you actually do choose to express that sexuality openly it can be a much more profound and authentic experience.

Challenge yourself to explore authenticity and you will find that this practice enriches your life in all areas. Sexual authenticity is just one type of authenticity and you may want to explore what it means to show up authentically in other areas of your life as well. We'll leave a thorough discussion of that, however, for another time.

Encourage Your Partner to Really Show Up

You can help to encourage your partner to really show up by using the techniques I described in the previous section. Remember to be gentle, forgiving, and accepting because this may be as or even more awkward and daunting for your partner than it is for you. Encourage, but don't demand, that your partner open his or her eyes during sex. If he or she does, smile and welcome him or her in a natural and friendly way. Similarly with eye contact and talking, encourage, don't push, and be completely accepting and friendly. As with all intimacy, vulnerability must be met in a way that encourages a sense of safety and strength in vulnerability. If you both talk with each other about trying these things during sex, about sexual authenticity and what it might mean to both of you, then you will be better prepared to be good partners to each other (and to yourselves) while you both explore showing up for this part of your shared lives. The key is to be inviting and willing to lovingly accept having your invitation go unanswered from time to time. Do your best not to succumb to any temptation to push and demand or be anything but accepting of where your partner is today. Any pushing or pulling is likely to result in the type of tug-of-war that can be extremely difficult to resolve on your own.

MINDFUL HUGGING AND SNUGGLING

Another way to practice moving toward a greater capacity for sexual authenticity involves holding each other mindfully. We talk about this as mindful hugging or mindful snuggling. Many times the things that get in the way of our showing up completely during sex will show up in some form while we are simply holding each other past the point where we usually find ourselves wanting to break contact and disconnect. Some sex therapists talk about this as hugging until relaxed and use it as a way of treating issues that manifest as anxiety or tension during sex. David Schnarch notes that many people discover to their surprise that they resist being held for extended periods of time or, alternatively, resist holding someone else for extended periods of time. That sort of resistance can show up in ways that severely limit our capacity for authenticity. Hugging or snuggling until relaxed can serve as context for learning where and how we might be getting stuck and for actively working through those areas so they no longer shackle us into old and tired patterns. Try it and see what happens.

Stand comfortably in front of your partner and enter into a simple hug. Pay attention to your experience of yourself in your own body. Pay attention to your breathing and let it become natural and unforced. Notice the thoughts that drift through your head and let them go by naturally without grappling with them. Just let them show up and disappear of their own accord. Pay attention to the experience of connection between you and your partner. Feel your partner's breathing and the warmth of his or her body. Let him or her enter your senses completely and without hesitation or comment. Shift around a bit if you need to in order to stay physically comfortable, but maintain the hug until you feel yourself spontaneously relax and until you feel your partner spontaneously relax. You might have to tolerate a good bit of awkwardness, tension, and other mental, emotional, and physical obstacles prior to the experience of spontaneous relaxation, but that is the whole point. This is about learning more about yourself and how you hold yourself back from real connection.

Discuss with each other what this exercise was like for each of you in a spirit of nonjudgmental acceptance of both yourself and your partner. There are no wrong or bad experiences here. Whatever you and your partner experienced is something to learn about and learn from.

Focus on the Process, Not the Outcome; This Moment, Not That Moment

As I've noted several times already, the key to a healthy sexual relationship is to focus on becoming process oriented rather than outcome oriented. A process orientation means that you are focused on enjoying the ride and simply couldn't care less about the destination. A process orientation is about *this* moment not *that* moment. It is fully entering into a journey with your partner that has absolutely no destination, no goal, no outcome, no place to go, and no time to be there.

Let Go with Both Hands

A great deal of difficulty that couples experience in their sex lives stems from trying too hard to control every aspect of the experience. Partners try to control their orgasms, their erections, whether the sex is "good" for the other partner, their thoughts, their feelings. So much effort is put into trying to establish and maintain control that there is very little room left to simply enjoy the experience of sharing sex with their partner. To let go with both hands means to relinquish the effort to control and instead to simply focus on and enjoy what is actually happening. Letting go with both hands means practicing acceptance of everything that happens as it is happening. This means accepting sex that is good, bad, and mediocre. When you let go of having to control outcomes, when you focus more exclusively on process, sometimes you find that you are having "great sex"; sometimes you will find that you are having "bad" sex, and sometimes you will find that you are having "mediocre" sex. Recognize that these labels are essentially meaningless if you are truly focused on connecting in the moment. Although you will inevitably label your experience, the experience is what it is and the label is what it is and the two only connect when you connect them. Letting go with both hands means noticing when you are trying too hard to control your sexual experience or to control the sexual experience of your partner and then simply letting go of that effort to control.

Follow your sense of interconnectedness. Notice that the metaphor here is about following something and not about leading. When we are trying too hard to control, we have the cart before the horse. We are trying to lead our sexual experience. If I do x, then y should follow. If I touch her like this, then she should like it. If I think about this, then I should enjoy myself more. If I don't distract him, then he should maintain his erection. Again, this drive to control completely interferes with our ability to really appreciate and enjoy our sexual relationship. Rather than trying to lead our experience, if we simply pay attention to our experience of connection and get behind it so we can follow its lead, then we invite a greater sense of aliveness into our sexual relationships.

Explore your shared sexuality with curiosity and playfulness. Again, this emerges out of a sense of following our experience rather than leading it. Rather than setting out to find something specific, we set out to find whatever is actually there with real curiosity and openness. We explore our shared sexuality rather than trying to force it into some predetermined mold reflecting what it "should" be, how it "should" feel, where it "should" lead. Shared curiosity, shared playfulness, shared openness to experience have the potential to help you reawaken that spark in your sexual relationship because they are the antithesis of monotony and boredom. Even if you travel the same path every day, if you walk that path with curiosity and let go enough to let the path lead you, then you will experience it as new, alive, and vibrant. You may also be more likely to notice side paths, alternate paths, shade trees, and bird songs that you never noticed before.

Learn as much as you can about each other's constantly changing sexual experience and about sexuality in general, but don't create more "shoulds" to live up to. Genuine curious exploration will inevitably result in your knowing a great deal more than you did before each trip. Be cautious however about our natural human tendency to turn what we have learned into rules that we then end up following the next time. The trouble with following rules like this too closely is that they tend to get in the way of experience and limit our ability to learn new things and to adapt to changing circumstances. Who you are today sexually (and in general) is not who you will be tomorrow. If you follow rules you developed today then you are unlikely to discover who you are in the process of becoming tomorrow. The same, of course, is equally true for your partner. If it is true that we are all constantly changing in both obvious and subtle ways, then where is there room for boredom? If you are bored, you aren't paying attention.

IN CONCLUSION

The point of this chapter is to provide an opportunity for you to think about the state of your marital health within the specific domain of your shared sexual relationship. The questionnaire at the beginning can be used to help ask yourself some questions about where your strengths and weaknesses are in this domain of your marriage. It is clear from the marital research that the healthy expression of your sexuality and your marital health are intimately connected. In this chapter I have tried to focus on the psychological dimensions of sexuality, focusing particularly on what seems to me to be the central message coming out of the research and clinical field about sexual health. The bottom line is simple. Sexual health flows out of a process orientation to sexual expression rooted in a strong sense of self- and partner-acceptance. Sexual ill-health, on the other hand, tends to grow from a focus on outcomes, control, "shoulds," a judgmental attitude toward self and partner, and withdrawal from and avoidance of your own sexual experience.

At the same time, as I mentioned briefly earlier, real physical and mental health issues can have predictable and treatable sexual side effects. Physical health issues need to be taken seriously and if you suspect that physical health issues are interfering with your sexual health, then explore those questions with your physician. Similarly, if you suspect that mental health issues such as depression or anxiety are interfering with your sexual health, then explore those questions with your mental health provider. Even in such cases, however, the psychological dimensions of sexuality discussed in this issue remain foundational to sexual health and I would encourage you to consider them seriously when giving your marriage its regular checkup.

9

MONEY: SPENDERS, SAVERS, AND THE DELICATE BALANCE

Conflict about money is one of the most common areas of serious disagreement between partners and the patterns of those disagreements are surprisingly similar across relationships. This chapter will help you assess the health of your financial partnership with your spouse and determine whether you and your partner play roles in the most common spender-saver pattern. The spender-saver pattern will be described and I will offer some general guidelines for how you might cope more gracefully with this very common difference.

MONEY TROUBLE

Almost all couples argue about money. They may not begin their first date fighting about money, but money becomes a source of friction in marriage with surprising regularity. Relationship scientists have found that arguments about money are among the most frequent sources of marital conflict. In my work as a couple's therapist, most partners I see are having some unresolved conflict about money. It may not be the main reason they are seeking counseling, but it is very often in the mix somewhere. There are many patterns that partners can fall into concerning money and the emotional meanings and implications of money issues are varied. However, more often than not, what I find is that when money is a relationship issue, generally one partner is more of a spender and the other partner more of a saver. In your relationship, which one are you?

SELF-ASSESSMENT OF THE SPENDER-SAVER PATTERN

For each of the descriptions below, rate yourself and your partner on the provided 5-point scale in terms of how well the portrayal generally describes you.

Description of a Saver

I tend to be a reluctant spender. Generally, I am not an impulse buyer. I often think a lot about something I want to buy before I buy it. In general, I would rather save money than spend it. Having a lot of debt makes me nervous. It is important to me to save money. I don't really feel comfortable unless I have enough money put away for a rainy day and for emergencies. I will happily go out of my way to save money on a purchase. I am willing to put up with some inconvenience to save money. If I have extra money, I would rather save it than spend it. I find that I do not really enjoy spending a lot of money on things. There aren't many things that I would be willing to go into debt for. I tend to be good at saving money. I consider myself frugal. Spending a lot of money on something makes me feel uneasy. I do not see any point to spending money just because you have it.

1	2	3	4	5
Not like me	A little like me	Moderately like me	More like me than not	A lot like me

Description of a Spender

I enjoy spending money. I am sometimes prone to impulse buying. I would rather spend money than save it for a rainy day that might not ever come. I am willing to go into debt to get something I really want.

Although I'll do it, I don't really *enjoy* putting money away to save for a rainy day or for emergencies. Spending a lot of money on something can be a lot of fun. I think you work hard to make money so you can spend it enjoying life. If I see something that I want and I have the money to get it, I usually buy it as soon as I can. I would rather save time than money. I am not likely to go out of my way just to save a little bit of money. I am not often willing to put up with much inconvenience just to save a little money. Although I know that having savings is important, I would rather not save any more money than I have to. If I have extra money, I would rather spend it than save it. I do not generally consider myself frugal. I am not very good at saving money. Saving too much money makes me feel uneasy. I don't see any point to denying yourself something you can afford.

1	2	3	4	5
Not like me	A little like me	Moderately like me	More like me than not	A lot like me

THE BEHAVIOR OF SAVERS AND SPENDERS

Within most couples I have met, one partner is usually more of a spender and the other is more of saver. For some reason, these two types of people find each other irresistible. As you can tell from the descriptions above, spenders and savers have quite different styles of handling money. In fact, rather than *styles*, it is probably better to think of them as different *emotional relationships* with money.

Although most people tend to think about money as a topic for rational discussion involving spreadsheets and budgets calculations, arithmetic and maybe some simple algebra, the fact of the matter is that far from a purely rational subject, money in the context of marriage is, at its root, a fundamentally *emotional* issue. No matter how many times couples create budgets and spreadsheets and lists of priorities; no matter how many times they have the same argument over and again at different volumes and pitches; no matter how many agreements they enter into and break, the issue continues to emerge in just the same way again and again. The most trouble I see spender-saver couples get into is trying to discuss and resolve their money issues completely rationally, while leaving unacknowledged and unaddressed the underlying emotional meaning that money has for each of them.

Spender-saver couples can have long, exhausting, and even bitter discussions about money that end with feelings of frustration and dissatisfaction. And the reason they walk away dissatisfied is because while they have spent all their time and energy addressing the issues as if they were rational math problems, they have spent little to no time talking about and dealing with the underlying emotional meanings.

WHAT IT'S LIKE TO BE A SAVER

For savers, the underlying emotional issues have to do with feelings of safety and security versus feelings of threat and anxiety. People who fall closer to the saver end of the spectrum simply cannot feel safe and secure in the world unless they know that they have a solid financial cushion to fall back on in case of emergencies. Again, this is not a wholly rational experience, but instead to a large extent an emotional experience about what it takes to feel comfortable in the world and able to relax and enjoy life. If a saver feels like he or she does not have a comfortable financial cushion socked away somewhere for safekeeping, then he or she will have a very hard time feeling safe and relaxed. Savers want to be able to know that they have a solid financial base that they can count on and that they can touch base with when they feel anxious. If that sound financial base is there, then a saver feels safe and secure. If that sound financial base is not there, then there is simply no way that a saver will ever feel entirely okay in the world.

The actual size of that financial base can be somewhat beside the point. Again, because this is a basic emotional necessity and not a rationally arrived at number, that financial base has to *feel* right. Whether that financial base ultimately feels right can be a function of several factors including overall levels of stress or any feelings of instability arising from other areas of life The main point is that the saver's financial base has to *feel* stable, secure, safe, unassailable, and guaranteed.

Because for a saver the goal of money is to have it as a source of safety against an unpredictable world, spending money is rarely a pure and unadulterated joy. For savers, spending money is almost never just good old-fashioned fun. It is almost always at least a little emotionally taxing because spending money means taking away from the safety net. Again, remember, and I'll keep reminding you of this because it is so easy to lose sight of, this is not a *rational* thing, it is an *emotional* experience.

Imagine as an analogy that you are performing a high-wire act several hundred feet off the ground and the only thing between you and certain death are the thin strands of rope woven together into your safety net. Obviously the better the net, the more comfortable you are going to feel doing your act and the more you are going to be able to stay focused on putting one well-balanced foot in front of the other. The flimsier the net, the more anxious you are going to feel and the harder time you are going to have focusing on the demanding task of staying balanced on the wire.

Now, to stretch the analogy, imagine that to get what you need for day-to-day survival on the wire you have to "spend" strands of the rope that make up your safety net. Every act of pulling out a rope and trading it in for something you need is going to entail a certain sense of threat to your overall safety. If you know you have plenty of net to spare, you can feel somewhat more comfortable, but if you feel like the net is a little thin for your tastes, then every act of spending comes at an emotional cost to your overall sense of safety and well-being.

So, for savers, family finances are emotionally complicated. Not only do they have to spend parts of their safety net themselves, but now they have partners who spend parts of their safety net as well. And their partners' spending is out of the saver's personal control. Now, it is bad enough having to spend your own safety net to meet the needs of yourself and your family, it is even more crazy-making to be standing on that high wire looking down at your partner yanking out strands of your safety net and seemingly spending them without a care in the world.

This is where many arguments start for spender-saver couples. The saver begins to feel threatened by his or her partner's spending and says or does something to confront that sense of threat. As a saver, you might come home to find that your partner has made a new purchase that you didn't know about and your first emotional reaction is a sort of clenching tension that comes from feeling one of your safety strands snatched away. This is your, "What the hell! Where did that come from!?" moment which is often the most proximal trigger for the ensuing argument.

CHAPTER 9

WHAT IT'S LIKE TO BE A SPENDER

In contrast to the saver, the spender's emotional experience of family finances is quite different. For spenders, the underlying emotional issues have to do with feelings of freedom and autonomy versus feelings of scarcity, deprivation, and despair.

For someone who falls more on the spender side of the spectrum, money is to be enjoyed and savored for what can be done with it. Rather than live to work, the spender works to live. Although spenders realize intellectually that savings are necessary for things like retirement, putting the kids through college, and as a financial safety net, the emotional experience of *needing* a safety net is nowhere near as palpable as it is for a saver. Almost all of the emotional experience is on the other side of the balance sheet, on the side that is about using money to freely enjoy an autonomous life.

Many, but not all, spenders have personal histories of deprivation. Histories in which money was scarce and they regularly felt the pinch of not having enough and not having as much as their peers. Although this is not always the case, spenders who grew up with the experience of scarcity develop as adults a sense that they no longer want to live a life of constant denial and that they don't want their own children to experience the same humiliations that they did when they were growing up. Thus, when a spender considers a purchase that they know they can afford, the experience is one of finally having the *freedom* to no longer have to do without.

By way of analogy, imagine that you have been kept in a too small dungeon for much of your life in a setting where you were able to peer out of a small window at the world of other peoples' freedom. Maybe you were even able to interact with those people through your tiny window, knowing that at the end of the day they could always go back to their freedom, leaving you in your tiny cell.

Now imagine that you have finally been given a reprieve from that cell, along with a vague, Kafkaesque, threat that you might be hauled back into it at some unspecified time in the future. Although that threat might gnaw at the back of your mind, every act of your new freedom would be an experience of joy and redemption. Why would you ever voluntarily choose any form of deprivation again? Just the memory of that cell would be nauseating.

For the spender, using money to enjoy life is that emotional experience of joy and redemption. Furthermore, any act of denial or restraint would come with at least a whiff of that old cell, even in those instances when you know that restraint is the wisest choice, the emotional experience would still be decidedly unpleasant. Again, remember that this isn't a rational process, but an emotional one. You may know rationally that the generic potato chips are just as good as the name-brand, but somehow voluntarily choosing the generic *feels* like giving in to your jailers and buying the more expensive name brand feels like a celebration of autonomy. The experience is even stronger when it comes to spending money on your children.

THE SAVER AND SPENDER GET MARRIED

Now, for whatever reason, savers and spenders find each other irresistible and are forever falling in love and getting married. Sometimes they recognize their differences and luckily stumble into ways of coping with them that leave neither partner feeling threatened or diminished. Other times they unluckily stumble into ways of reacting to each other that lead to polarization and corrode the foundation of their marriage.

Of course if you consider the two analogies presented as describing the worldviews of spenders versus savers, it is easy to imagine how those two ways of living in the world of money are destined to clash in significant ways. Any act of spending has a significantly different meaning to each partner. To one partner, it is an expression of freedom. To the other partner a weakening of the safety net. Similarly, any act of saving has different meanings to each partner. To one partner it is the creation of safety and security. To the other partner it is the slamming of the dungeon gate.

POLARIZATION

I suspect that many partners who end up struggling with the spender-saver theme in their marriage did not start out their marriage as polarized as they eventually become. It appears that partners enter their relationships with natural set points for how much saving or spending they require to feel comfortable. However, interacting with a partner who has a different money style seems to pull people into more extreme positions. To the degree that the spender begins to feel constrained by the behavior of the saver, he may feel almost compelled to assert his need for freedom even more dynamically. Similarly, to the degree that the saver feels her safety net threatened by the behavior of the spender, she may feel equally compelled to defend that safety net even more vigorously. After some time, the saver ends up feeling that she is struggling to maintain a more fiscally constrained lifestyle than even she is completely comfortable with and the spender ends up feeling that he is struggling to experience that sense of freedom more and more desperately.

Tropical Fish

For example, one partner I know recalls an incident in which she was on her way out of the mall after shopping for a much-needed pair of work pants, when she passed a gorgeous display of tropical fish. She and her husband shared a tropical fish tank that they both loved, but because finances were tight they had argued about buying any more fish. After their last argument ended, it felt like they wouldn't be buying any more fish anytime soon. As she walked through the mall, she recalled not particularly even wanting a new fish as she passed the pet store display. However, as she turned the corner on the way out she started to think, "Who the hell is he to tell me I can't buy a fish if I want to." So, even though she hadn't wanted to buy a new fish initially, the onrushing feeling of being constrained made her feel that the only way to reassert her freedom was to go back and buy that damn fish. At the time, she recalls knowing in her head that they really couldn't afford a new addition to their tank, but the decision at that moment was not about what was rational, but about what felt right. She knew as soon as she bought the fish that it was going to lead to a major argument, and yet she felt compelled to assert her autonomy.

Notice that the polarization process between her and her husband resulted in her spending more money than even she was comfortable with. Sure enough, just as she had predicted, she and her husband had a major argument about the fish later that evening. As they recalled it later, it became clear to them that the argument touched on just about every topic in their relationship except the underlying emotional issues really at stake. They didn't avoid those important emotional underpinnings purposefully. They simply had no idea how to put words on the emotional processes that were really driving their conflict. As they came to recognize those underlying emotional processes, it became clear that, in some ways, the husband himself wanted to spend money acquiring new fish for their tank (they both shared a love for the hobby), but felt constrained by his wife's spending to be even more frugal than he would have been otherwise. Because each was constantly reacting to the other, they were trapped in a vicious cycle in which they ended up completely polarized around an issue that they actually shared; their mutual love of tropical fish. Not only did both of them enjoy their shared hobby and want to buy new fish for it, but they both wanted to buy the very same kind of fish. Nevertheless because he was just a little more hesitant about spending the money and she was just a little bit more enthusiastic, they eventually found themselves in completely opposite corners, locked into opposing each other over something they both actually agreed about. This, as it turns out, is a very common type of event for couples locked in a spender-saver pattern in their marriage.

As I've noted before, most couples try to resolve these disagreements by talking about the money that they do or do not have in what sound like rational terms. One argues that they shouldn't spend the money because of several very practical sounding reasons and the other argues that they should spend the money because of several equally practical sounding reasons. The discussion then heats up and becomes an argument, ending with both partners feeling upset, dissatisfied and more isolated and lonely than before. The dissatisfaction and loneliness ultimately stem from the fact that the discussion they are having does not address his fears about his safety net and her fears about living a life of deprivation.

RECOMMENDATIONS FOR HOW TO COPE EFFECTIVELY WITH THE SPENDER-SAVER PATTERN

Acceptance of the Fundamental Difference

The first thing to keep in mind when determining to cope more effectively with a spender-saver pattern in your marriage is to accept that this difference between you and your spouse is deeply rooted and unlikely to simply go away. It is, in other words, what relationship scientists refer to as a *fundamental difference*, one that actually defines who you are as a couple. I sometimes refer to these as "naturally occurring flaws in the fabric," after the tag manufacturers place on leather coats and briefcases. The tag says that some flaws are a natural part of the fabric and are to be expected because leather is an organic material. Marriages are also organic—living things with their own naturally occurring flaws.

Professor John Gottman of the University of Washington has studied long-term marriages—those couples who have made it to their 50th wedding anniversary. When these couples are asked about the major areas of disagreement in their marriages, they are all able to list a handful of issues that followed them throughout their marriage. What I find most interesting about these studies is that when these couples are asked when these issues first emerged in their relationship, almost all of them report that the main areas of friction between them emerged very early in their relationship, sometimes before they were even married.

What this suggests to me and to the relationship scientists who conducted these studies is that all couples have "perpetual issues" that will follow them from the day they are married to their 50th wedding anniversary. What distinguishes those partners who make it to their 50th wedding anniversary from those who do not is the quality of their interactions around their perpetual issues. Those couples who make it discover ways of "arguing" about their perpetual issues that result in feeling like they have struggled with it *together* and have reached a temporary understanding that feels hopeful to them both. Despite the perpetual nature of the particular problem, they are able to struggle with it in a basically empathic, cooperative, and respectful way. More often than not, both partners walk away from these discussions feeling closer to each other and better understood. They carry their baggage together as teammates rather than enemies.

Those couples who do not make it to their 50th wedding anniversary, rather than facing their perpetual issues together, let those issues come between them. They place the blame for the issue squarely *within* the other partner and then struggle to defeat that partner rather than struggling to cope with a shared concern. For example, with an issue like money, the couples who make it recognize their fundamental differences and *accept* each other and their relationship for having those differences. Although it is a source of irritation for them, they do not seek to tear each other apart in a vain attempt to solve the issue forever. They know, at some level, that this issue is going to follow them for the rest of their lives and that if they are going to cope with it effectively and have a strong and loving relationship, then they are going to have to be gentle with each other when they confront the issue, because any real damage they do will remain a part of them for the rest of their lives.

At the same time, they do not ignore or withdraw from the issue. They recognize that those issues that are the touchiest demand regular attention and care in order to prevent them from silently corroding the foundation of the marriage. In other words, they join together around their perpetual issues regularly as a way of touching base with each other and getting back on the same page with a shared understanding of each other's perspective.

Unhealthy couples blame each other bitterly for being a spender or a saver. They attack each other verbally and use strong-arm tactics to try to force change. They are critical and belligerent toward each other. Or even worse, they withdraw from each other and refuse to grapple with the issue at all, until it blows up in their faces. Because the issue emerges as something that must be destroyed, and because partners often place the blame for the issue squarely inside the other, they do not approach the issue gently. Instead, they approach the issue as forcefully and aggressively as they can, hoping that if they hit it hard enough, they will never have to confront it again. Unfortunately, since "it" is located within the other, then those efforts to destroy the issue end up doing significant damage to the marriage. The couple ends up walking away from these interactions feeling lonelier, less well understood, and more embattled than they did before. Before long, the foundation of the marriage has corroded to such an extent that it will no longer hold the weight and the couple ends up either filing for divorce or living in a loveless marriage.

Again, the solution here is to begin to recognize that these are simple and fundamental differences. Perpetual issues are a simple product of the "chemical reaction" between two different and complicated people. They are not something broken inside the marriage or inside either one of you individually. If you can accept that all marriages have their perpetual issues and that this "money thing" is just one of yours, then you are in a much better position to forgive your marriage and your partner for not being unattainably perfect. You are also in a much better position to regularly and gently put your hands on this issue in a way that builds compassionate understanding and wise action rather than bitterness and distrust.

Acceptance is the key. Accept that your partner has a different emotional relationship with money than you do and that your partner's relationship with money is just as legitimate as your own and that it is *never going away*. Part of loving your partner in a deep and intimate way is accepting him or her fully for this difference and finding a way in your own heart to give him the room he needs to be different in this way and still be loved by you. To the degree that you reject this difference, you reject your partner and your marriage. There is not a hair's breadth of difference.

Accept also that *you* are different from your partner. Accept that your emotional relationship with money is what it is and is as legitimate and worthy of respect and care as your partner's. Also accept that it is an *emotional* relationship and not a wholly rational one. That means that when you and your partner talk about this issue, you must talk about how you are *feeling* and you must work to empathize with your partner's feelings as well. Fifty-year marriages arrive there *with* their perpetual issues, but they tend to talk about them in hope-building rather than hope-dashing ways.

In sum, acceptance means accepting that (1) this is a normal difference between you and your partner; (2) this difference is going to be a perpetual issue between you; and (3) this issue must not be ignored, but must be cared for regularly and gently. You *can* make it to your 50th wedding anniversary intact, but you will make it, if you do, with your perpetual issues in tow.

PRACTICING A HEALTHY WAY OF DISCUSSING THE ISSUE

How should you talk about this issue in a way that makes you feel closer to each other rather than further apart? Start by acknowledging the issue regularly. The worst thing you can do is ignore it or withdraw from each other in the face of it. The second worst thing you can do is confront it in an attacking, critical, or demeaning way. Instead, seek to love your partner for this difference and give him or her the room he or she needs to be different from you in this way. Try to recognize that the goal of these discussions is to find some common understanding of each other such that you both feel understood and made room for. Neither of you have to "win," but instead you should both feel made room for. As much as the rational aspects of money have to be dealt with, remember that perhaps the most fundamental aspect you need to deal with for the health of your marriage is the emotional part. A saver needs to feel that his need for a safety net and his worries about weakening that safety net have been heard, acknowledged, and valued by his partner. Similarly, a spender needs to feel that his need to *enjoy* the fruits of his labor and feel at least somewhat free from lack and scarcity have been heard, acknowledged, and valued. If these emotional needs have not been met in the conversation, then you will inevitably walk away feeling frustrated and unhappy.

My suggestion is, if it appears that you and your partner are suffering from a spender-saver pattern in your marriage, practice noticing that pattern as a *pattern* that emerges from the combination of your two styles. It often helps to give the pattern a name that you can both recognize. You can call it "spender-saver," "our money thing," or "Bob." Whatever you call it, being able to name the pattern is a giant step toward marital health. In our own research, we have found that couples who can begin to talk *about* their patterns rather than simply engaging in those patterns show increases in marital health and satisfaction.

If you can recognize and talk about your patterns, then you are in a better position to have three things happen. First, you can become better able to recognize a "spender-saver" argument after it is over. Recognizing the pattern after it has run its course helps couples to "let it go" and seek reconnection and repair easier than when the pattern goes unrecognized. It is easier to say, "I guess we just did our spender-saver dance" as a step toward reconciliation than to re-enter the fray from exactly the same perspective that caused the argument in the first place. Relationship scientists call this "meta-communication," which means being able to take a perspective from which you and your partner can talk about how you have been talking. It allows you to shift to a different level and approach the issue from a broader point of view. Entering the argument at the level of a spender who is trying to defeat a saver is entering at the level of the argument itself and virtually guarantees that you'll end up beating your head against the very same wall that just gave you a marital concussion. Entering the argument at the "meta-level" of partners who just happen to have a "spender-saver" pattern gives you both a perspective from which you can come together in relation to the pattern and commiserate, and maybe even laugh about your shared perpetual issue. The emphasis here is on finding a perspective that allows you both to move to the same side of the issue ("we stand in relation to the pattern") versus remaining stuck in a perspective that divides you ("I stand opposed to you").

The second positive thing that happens when you begin to recognize and talk about your patterns is that you sometimes "wake up" in the middle of a spender-saver argument and short-circuit it before it runs its full destructive course. You might find that halfway through your usual spender-saver argument you realize that the pattern is running on autopilot and instead of continuing to play along, you might say, "hey honey, I know what's happening here, we're doing our spender-saver thing, let's eat ice-cream instead." Recognizing a pattern as it is happening can help you derail an argument in its tracks and put you both back on a track that is healthier and more productive.

The third positive thing that can come from recognizing and naming your spender-saver pattern is that you might be able to head off your typical argument altogether. As the spender, you might come home to find a new purchase in the house and have your knee-jerk "What the . . . !" reaction, but instead of approaching your partner at that particular level, you might instead recognize, "Oh yeah, I'm having my typical 'saver' reaction," and wait until the "reaction" passes so that you are in a better position to respond in a healthy way rather than react in a less healthy way. If you can enter the conversation at the level where you are recognizing and naming the pattern, the odds are much better that it will progress in a way that leaves you both feeling more satisfied and better able to compromise. You might say something like, "I'm having my 'saver' reaction to your new golf clubs. Can we talk about it?"

As the spender, you might notice your impulse to buy something you can't afford or don't really need and say to yourself, "I'm having my 'spender' reaction," and again wait for the reaction to pass so you are in a better position to respond in a relationship healthy way. You might also notice yourself reacting to your partner's impulse to save and put words on that reaction like, "This is our 'spender-saver' thing. I'm noticing the more you want to save, the more I want to 'spend' to make sure we aren't depriving ourselves unnecessarily." Discussions that start with a recognition of the pattern are much less likely to devolve into destructive arguments and much more likely to lead to resolutions that feel right to both of you.

Ultimately, recognizing and being able to name the spender-saver pattern will help you to avoid more arguments, to shorten the arguments that you do have, and to reconcile more quickly following arguments that run their full course.

PUTTING YOURSELF IN YOUR PARTNER'S SHOES

Perhaps the main point here is developing empathy for your partner's emotional relationship with money and compassion for your shared "spender-saver" dilemma. As a spender, it is important to empathize with your saver partner's need for an emotional *process* to occur before he or she can feel okay about purchases. You'll notice that savers often approach and then walk away from things they want to buy several times before they finally (often somewhat reluctantly) buy them. I worked with a couple whose saver partner "shopped" for a camera that he wanted to buy for close to a year before he finally screwed up the emotional resources to buy it. And even then, it was an emotionally mixed bag for him. On the one hand, he was glad to have the camera and enjoyed using it. On the other hand, he felt bad about spending the money on it for months.

For spenders, it is also important to acknowledge and empathize with a saver's need to have a financial safety net that *feels* sufficiently invulnerable. Perhaps the most important thing to keep in mind is that what feels right to a saver is only partially related to what might objectively be considered a sufficient safety net. The real issue is about being able to soothe nagging anxieties about money by being able to touch base with a palpably sound financial safety net.

Finally, for spenders, it is important to recognize and empathize with the saver's automatic flinch every time a strand is spent from her accumulated safety net. It is easy to take that flinch personally and it may even at times be personally directed, but ultimately it is not about you, but about the saver's underlying emotional relationship with money. That flinch is not likely to ever go away and it is not a pleasant experience for the saver. A little empathy and compassion from you can go a long way toward soothing him or her and will ultimately solidify the strength of the foundation of your marriage.

For savers, it is important to empathize with your spender partner's fear of the deprivation dungeon and the need to feel like money is being used to live life as fully as possible without unnecessary deprivation. For a spender, perhaps the worst curse would be a life wasted saving money that could have been used for a more joyous and liberated life. It is important to savers to understand that spenders need to feel that "earned freedom" every once in a while without the guilt and shame that plagues the lifelong saver. Savers need to find ways to nurture that joy for their partner on a relatively regular basis, otherwise their partners will begin to feel suffocated and deeply unhappy. This doesn't mean that the two of you need to sacrifice your legitimate need for a rationally determined safety net, but it does mean that within your means, you, as a saver, need to "let it go" every so often and allow your partner some guilt-free spending.

Finally, it will be important for you both to practice mutual compassion. Mutual compassion means practicing compassion for both yourself and your partner at the same time. Recognize both your own fears and needs and your partner's fears and needs and take both of you into account in a gentle and loving way when it comes to your dealings with money. This type of mutual compassion will create greater health and resilience in your marriage and you will both feel stronger, healthier, happier, and more fulfilled by your partnership.

SEEING AN ACCOUNTANT

I sometimes recommend that couples who suffer from a shared "spender-saver" pattern see a good accountant together. We have to acknowledge that it is difficult to maintain perspective on our own emotional relationship with money and despite our own best intentions, it is surprisingly easy to find ourselves back inside that pattern, beating our heads against that same unbreakable wall. A neutral third party, well trained in financial matters and able to bring a more wholly objective perspective to your finances can help you both meet your shared goals while managing your irrational fears. A good financial advisor or accountant will take both of your perspectives into account and will allow for both saving what is necessary *and* enjoying the fruits of your labor. A good accountant will help you both do the rational work that you need to do. At the same time, don't expect your accountant to help you manage the emotional work that you both need to do.

REGULAR TIME GOING OVER THE FINANCES TOGETHER

I also often recommend that partners struggling with a spender-saver pattern sit down together regularly to talk about money. This is often most easily accomplished by sitting down to do the bills together. The reason that I often recommend this is because so many couples suffering from this particular problem try to resolve it by ignoring it and avoiding the subject altogether. This type of avoidance is perhaps the worst way of coping with this issue, both because it is unhealthy for your marriage and because it can be unhealthy for your family finances as well. Family finances have to be dealt with reasonably and frequently. Avoiding that necessity can only lead to trouble. Although it can be difficult to confront this perpetual issue on a regular basis, the more practiced you get at it, the healthier your marriage will be over the long run.

For many couples avoiding each other in order to avoid conflict about finances leads to a more pervasive withdrawal from the relationship. For these couples, it is often most beneficial for them to schedule relatively frequent meetings to discuss financial matters. Regular practice will allow partners to learn how to be effective financial teammates and improve the level of compassionate understanding in the relationship as a whole.

WHEN TO SEEK THERAPY

If you find that it is difficult to acknowledge and name your pattern and that you cannot help but slip into destructive arguments about money over and over again, or that you simply can't bring the topic up in a healthy way, then it is probably time to schedule a few sessions with a good couple therapist. Again, it can be exceedingly difficult for us to see our own blind spots and the help of a well trained and more objective third party can do a world of good in a relatively short period of time. You might want to think of this more as enlisting the help of a good coach than "seeking therapy." For some people the negative connotations of seeking therapy can be enough of a barrier to keep them from getting easily available help to improve marital health. Try to think of seeing a couple therapist as no more shameful than seeing a dentist or calling a plumber. Getting the help that you need when you need it and before it is too late is never a bad idea. It is infinitely better to seek help and find out that you really didn't need it than to not seek help and find out later that you really did need it. The saddest cases that I see in my practice are those couples who don't get to therapy until it is too late to save their marriage and they both acknowledge that if they had sought therapy earlier, it might have saved them and their children from the pain of divorce. It is always better safe than sorry. So, if after reading this chapter together and trying on your own to cope more gracefully with your spender-saver pattern, you find that you continue to feel lonelier rather than closer, then please don't hesitate to give therapy a try. It could make all the difference in the world.

ADDITIONAL READING

Pybrum, S. (1996). *Money and marriage: Making it work together–a guide to smart money management and harmonious communications.* Exton, PA, Abundance Publishing.

Rich, J. (2003). *The couple's guide to love and money.* New York, NY, New Harbinger.

Collins, V. F., & Brown, S. B. (1998). *Couples and money: A couples' guide updated for the new millennium.* Sherman Oaks, CA, Gabriel Publications.

10

COPARENTING: COMRADES IN ARMS

The quality of a couple's intimate relationship and the quality of their coparenting are related but not identical phenomenon. The goal of this chapter will be to help you assess the quality of your coparenting across a range of parenting domains. You will also be introduced to the most interesting aspects of the theory and research that has been conducted in this area including concepts such as "gatekeeping" and the unique effects of marital distress on male withdrawal from effective coparenting. The chapter will also provide evidence- and theory-based recommendations for strengthening the quality of your coparenting in the service of both the health of your marriage and the health of your family as a whole. In this chapter, we will explore how parenting can go right and how parenting can go wrong in ways that can undermine the very foundations of our marriages.

COPARENTING IN MODERN MARRIAGES

Coparenting, raising children together as a couple, is perhaps one of the most challenging aspects of modern marriage. Coparenting is challenging for all couples and can be made even more challenging as our lives become busier and the availability of extended family networks

Table 10.1. MC Coparenting Questionnaire

Definitely Something We Need to Improve 1	Could Use Some Improvement 2	Neither a Strength nor Area for Improvement 3	Somewhat of a Strength 4	Definitely a Strength 5

_____ 1. I feel like my partner and I are "in it together" when it comes to parenting.
_____ 2. We are good parenting partners.
_____ 3. I am supportive of how my partner parents and my partner is supportive of how I parent.
_____ 4. We don't struggle against each other as parents.
_____ 5. I have positive feelings toward my partner as a parent.
_____ 6. We both actively participate in our children's lives.
_____ 7. We both "get down on the floor" with our children.
_____ 8. We both engage in conversation with our children.
_____ 9. We are both actively engaged in steering our children toward those things that are good and healthy and away from those things that are bad and unhealthy.
_____ 10. We both actively engage in "hands-on" parenting.
_____ 11. We are both capable parents. Neither of us is more of an expert.
_____ 12. We almost never actively oppose each other as parents.
_____ 13. We rarely step on each other's toes when it comes to parenting.
_____ 14. We tend to agree more than disagree about parenting.
_____ 15. We both feel appreciated and supported by each other as parents.
_____ 16. The division of childcare labor feels fair to me.
_____ 17. The division of childcare labor feels fair to my partner.
_____ 18. When I make a mistake as a parent, I feel emotionally supported by my partner.
_____ 19. When my partner makes a mistake as a parent, he or she feels emotionally supported by me.
_____ 20. We don't put our marriage on the backburner.
_____ 21. We keep our marriage a priority even given the demands of work and parenting.

becomes thinner. For so many couples, most if not all of the work involved in raising their children is shouldered by them and them alone. However, even when parents have plenty of help from family and community, the sometimes delicate and unspoken negotiations around our sharing of the parenting role is often a source of real challenge and struggle. During the transition to parenthood, so much of who we are and what we care about is suddenly on the line as we try on this new part of our lives. It can often feel like we were just getting our legs under us as adults and partners when we were suddenly thrust into this new role of "mom" or "dad". From this new perspective our relationship to ourselves has changed, our relationship with our new baby is rapidly expanding, and our relationship with our loving partner has suddenly become something quite dramatically different. Our relationship with our partner not only becomes different, but different in ways that we didn't, and possibly couldn't, anticipate.

THE TRANSITION TO PARENTHOOD

Researchers have repeatedly found that the transition to parenthood is associated with predictable declines in marital satisfaction for most couples. Thus, for many of us, the extraordinary demands of becoming new parents not only stress us physically and emotionally, but maritally. At the same time, researchers have found that becoming parents also strengthens the bond between partners, making them more committed to each other and to their shared lives together. So, at the same time that sleep deprivation and the many new demands of caring for a newborn are stressing us out physically, emotionally, and maritally, we are also more often than not immersed in a greater sense of connectedness and shared purpose with our partner.

Although it is a cliché, it is a cliché for a good reason. Almost nothing changes your life quite as radically as becoming new parents. Few of us are as prepared for becoming parents as we would like and we almost all struggle through the transition to parenthood. Those first heady days following the birth of our first child pass by in a blur of sleeplessness, elation, exhaustion, fear, and worry. I can remember being amazed that the doctors and nurses just let us walk out of the hospital with this very brand new, very fragile little human being. I'm not sure I've ever felt like more of an imposter in my life. Here I was pretending that I knew what I was doing, pretending I had every confidence in us as new parents, and fully expecting someone to show up at any moment and demand proof of our qualifications to parent this child.

Why is the transition to parenthood consistently associated with declines in marital satisfaction at the same time that it is associated with increases in marital stability? First and foremost, the transition to new parenthood is simply and unavoidably stressful. The word "stress" has become so common now that in some ways it hardly adequately captures the experience of becoming new parents. In many ways we are being just as newly born into the world as new parents as our child has been born into the world as a new human being.

When we first become parents we have a great deal to learn and we have to learn it very quickly and "on the job." To top it off, as it turns out, babies are very demanding. Demanding of time and energy and emotional resources. Newborn babies interfere with our sleep until they learn how to sleep through the night on their own, and research tells us that few things are as stressful as sleep deprivation. In addition, as we'll see later, patterns often quickly emerge between new parents that are, in and of themselves, very stressful.

Unfortunately, one of the most predictable effects of chronic stress is that it lowers our tolerance threshold for everything else in our lives. We become more easily irritated and annoyed by both big and little things and our resources for remaining emotionally centered are stretched thin. So, between you and your partner, you'll find that little things that you used to be able to tolerate just fine are suddenly astonishingly grating, charming quirks can become like fingernails on a chalkboard. Minor disagreements that would previously have gone by without much fuss suddenly become the seeds for genuinely heated arguments. In short, all the small and large imperfections of our marriages become magnified by the stress of becoming new parents.

Even more, many new categories of conflict emerge directly from our efforts to fit into our new skin as parents and to learn how to parent effectively together as a team. Who's getting up when with the baby, who's responsible for what, what is the best way to handle—take your pick—crying babies, diaper rash, play time, dressing baby, fussy baby, feeding baby, sleeping baby, sick baby, etc.

Second, a great deal of the time, energy, and emotion that is now being devoted to caring for your new child is taken directly from time, energy, and emotion that you used to devote to nurturing and enjoying your marriage. So many of us, maybe all of us, borrow heavily from the time and energy we used to devote to our marriage and reallocate those resources to childrearing and work. In essence, we put our marriages on the backburner in order to focus on the baby and the job. We assume that the marriage can take it and that it is a noble sacrifice without realizing that the health of the marriage is the basic foundation of the whole family. We stop taking care of the health of the marriage and inevitably the marriage gets sick, and when the marriage gets sick every other domain of the family gets sick too.

It is not all doom and gloom however. First of all, some couples actually thrive through the transition to parenthood. Those who do thrive through the transition are those whose marriages were strongest to begin with. By strong I don't simply mean that they felt happy with each other and in love, but that they had strong and healthy communication skills and patterns, effective and regularly used problem-solving skills, healthy and mature emotion skills, rich resources to draw from in terms of life skills and family and community support, and a rich and vibrant intimate connection. Similarly, even for couples who do struggle through the transition to parenthood, the rewards and richness of the experience are often the most salient part of that experience. It is a period in our lives full of love and growth, and a deeply rooted sense of meaning and entering into something much larger and deeper than before. Even when we struggle, we are aware that we are blessed.

WHAT IS "COPARENTING?"

Who Does What?

Researchers have consistently found that healthy coparenting is associated with both greater marital health and greater child health. Professor James McHale, formerly of Clark University and currently at the University of South Florida, is one of the originators of the scientific study of coparenting. According to Professor McHale, coparenting can be thought of as that part of our relationship that involves how we coordinate our shared responsibility for taking care of and raising our children together. Perhaps the main component of coparenting involves the division of childcare responsibilities. In other words, the first part of coparenting is about the "who does what" of parenting, the day-to-day hands-on tasks that have to be taken care of like feeding, changing, and bathing. The division of childcare is a major concern to most parents. At the same time, childcare is very rarely divided perfectly equally. Much more often than not, in all cultures around the world, mothers assume the primary responsibility for day-to-day childcare. That being said, it is equally true that the vast majority of fathers are significantly involved in, and make regular major contributions to, the care and upbringing of their children. Some couples try to share all childcare tasks equally. Other partners work to take on different domains of childcare. Finally, in some couples, one parent takes on the primary role of childcare provider while the other parent contributes in more of a breadwinner role.

WE-NESS

Professor McHale makes a point of letting us know that although coparenting does primarily involve carrying out the day-to-day tasks of hands-on childcare, it also involves several other components. First among those other components is the degree to which partners feel a sense of "we-ness" when it comes to parenting. In other words, regardless of who changes more diapers, do you and your partner feel that you are "in it together" when it comes to parenting? Many partners, even if the division of childcare is far from objectively equal, feel strongly that they are on the same team and that they have a loving and committed parenting partner. Other partners, however, feel less like a united team and more like competitive opponents, with each vying to parent their own way despite the opposition of the other parent. This "solidarity/support" dimension of coparenting can be thought of as falling on a continuum from feeling that you and your partner are a solid team that supports each other's parenting well to feeling that you and your partner oppose and undermine each other as parents more often than not. The main question here being how supported by your partner do you feel in your role as a parent?

NEGATIVE VERSUS POSITIVE FEELINGS

Second among the additional coparenting components is how much partners struggle with each other as parents and how much that struggle is characterized by negative feelings toward the other parent. When you consider how you feel about your partner as a parent, is that feeling mostly positive or mostly negative or some mix of the two. If you feel like you struggle with your partner a lot as a parent and that he or she regularly steps on your toes in your role as a parent, then you likely feel mostly negatively toward him or her. If, on the other hand, you feel that you and your partner are most commonly on the same page with each other and that your partner "has your back" as a parent, then you most likely feel very positively toward her or him as a coparent.

GETTING "DOWN ON THE FLOOR"

The final additional coparenting component involves how actively both partners engage with their child and take part in directing the child in positive ways. This part of coparenting concerns the extent to which you both literally and figuratively "get down on the floor" with your children, engage in conversation with your children, and otherwise actively participate in their lives. It also involves the degree to which you and your partner actively engage in steering your children toward those things that are good and healthy and away from those things that are bad and unhealthy. When it feels that you are both actively engaged in hands-on parenting, then that feeling of "we-ness" and of being partners and teammates is much deeper and more reassuring. Again, you feel more like part of something larger than yourself and less lonely in your work as a parent.

In short, coparenting involves many aspects of our relationship with our partners as parents. This includes the actual day-to-day chores of parenting as well as how united we feel as parents, how positively we feel toward each other as parents, and how actively engaged we both are in the day-to-day lives of our children.

When coparenting works well it can bring partners together in ways that few other things can. In fact, there is some evidence that a good coparenting alliance can significantly enhance the quality of a couple's relationship. This may even be true for some couples who are otherwise struggling in their marriage. On the other hand, a coparenting alliance that is unhealthy and conflict-ridden can easily undermine an otherwise healthy marriage and can even diminish the parenting effectiveness of partners who might otherwise be very capable parents. In short, there is a strong relationship between the quality of marital health and the quality of our coparenting, with each affecting the other in equal measures.

CHAPTER 10

COPARENTING TRAP #1: PATTERNS MOVE INTO OUR MARRIAGE

As I noted earlier, the transition to parenthood is perhaps among the most challenging periods in any couples marriage. It is also among the most predictable. The research that has been done studying couples across the transition to parenthood has found that for most couples their marital satisfaction deteriorates to some greater or lesser degree during this transition. At the same time, partners' commitment to each other and to their family increases. The transition to parenthood is unique in this effect because satisfaction with your marriage and commitment to your marriage much more often than not go hand in hand. It is really only during that period when we are becoming new parents that satisfaction and commitment move in opposite directions from each other for many couples, with commitment increasing at the very time that satisfaction is diminishing.

That being said, not all couples suffer a decline in how happy they are with their marriages during the transition to parenthood. For a smaller subset of couples, the transition to parenthood does not affect their satisfaction with their marriage, and for some couples their satisfaction with their marriage actually improves. Although it is not perfectly clear what helps some couples to weather the transition to parenthood better than others, the research does provide a few clues. For example, there is some suggestion that couples whose relationships are already very healthy prior to becoming pregnant and having a child are the most likely to remain healthy and satisfied with their marriages even as they struggle to adjust to being new parents. On the other hand, those couples who were already suffering from some of the common relationship corroding problems, such as those discussed in this book, and whose marriages were already beginning to show signs of ill-health, appear to be the most likely to see their satisfaction with their marriages deteriorate during the transition to parenthood.

In other words, and this will come as no surprise to those of you who are parents, adapting to parenthood is stressful, time consuming, sleep depriving, and priority shifting. Any problems that already existed in your relationship are only going to get worse as you struggle with the stresses of becoming new parents. Further, it appears to be quite common that those changes that occur in your marital relationship, whether positive or negative, are likely to remain over time. Unlike many stressful periods, relationships do not seem to easily spontaneously recover from the patterns that get set in place during the transition to parenthood. This is most likely the case because as we create new patterns, as we adapt to being new parents, those new patterns become part of who we are together. As these patterns become set in stone, they are unlikely to change unless the circumstances of our lives change radically enough to force us to adapt yet again.

Research on Training Parents

All is not lost, however. We can, with conscientious attention, improve the health of our coparenting and simultaneously improve the overall health of our marriages even if we have stumbled into patterns that are making us struggle harder than we have to. Research on what is called "parent training" consistently shows that parenting dynamics can be improved with practice. This research also shows that as parenting dynamics improve, so does overall marital health and child well-being. For example, Oriana Linares and her colleagues at the NYU School of Medicine found that good coparenting training resulted in "significant gains in positive parenting and collaborative coparenting for both biological and foster parents at the end of the intervention. At follow-up, intervention parents sustained greater improvement in positive parenting, showed gains in clear expectations, and reported a trend for fewer child externalizing problems" (Linares et al., 2006). Additionally, William Doherty and colleagues at Georgia State University (2006) found that "a relatively brief intervention during the transition to parenthood can improve fathering." In short, if we have found that we are indeed stuck in coparenting patterns that are making our burdens heavier and joys fewer and further between, then many times a simple and short course in parent training (think of it as parent coaching) can do our lives a world of good. Sometimes we can get that parent coaching straight from a good book on the subject (recommendations will be made later in the chapter) and sometimes we find that employing a professional is our most effective tool.

For many couples, however, one of the most common experiences of the transition to parenthood is a sense that things are not turning out quite the way we had hoped and patterns are emerging between us that are frustrating and discouraging.

COPARENTING TRAP #2: THE ARRIVAL OF THE GATEKEEPER

The truth is, for all of us, we start the lessons of becoming parents essentially from scratch. When we head home from the hospital neither we nor our partners know much beyond the basics about parenting and much of what we do know we know in theory only and not in practice. Even something as simple a diapering is awkward and time consuming at first for both parents. We have to learn through the experience of trial and error how to interpret our baby's cries, the earthy dance of feeding and burping, the heartbreak of diaper rash, and how to care for a sick child. We learn through trial and error how to comfort a baby who is uncomfortable, tired, angry, scared, hungry, or just plain bored. The learning curve is steep and the lessons are constantly changing. The very early stages of the transition to parenthood can either set the stage for shared parenting or for "gate-keeping" and role polarization.

For almost all couples, both partners start out in just the same place. Both just as lost at sea and both learning just as fast how to navigate the open waters of new parenthood. Soon, however, one partner will take the lead over the other. This can happen because our culture tells us fairly explicitly that mothers are supposed to be the primary parent and so we tend to begin behaving in accord with that bias fairly quickly. This also often happens simply as the result of one parent returning to work before the other. When mom stays home with the baby she naturally engages in more of the regular trial-and-error learning that teaches us how to be effective parents. Since it is practice that makes perfect, the parent who stays home gets more practice and starts to simply know more about how to care for this particular child. When dad returns from work after that first day back, he is suddenly a whole day behind in the trial-and-error homework of parenting. Days away from home accumulate quickly and soon enough one parent emerges as the expert and the other as the novice.

New mothers are also much more likely than new fathers to seek advice (or just get advice) from other, more experienced parents in their circle of family and friends. In other words, a lot of parenting advisors show up in the form of grandparents, sisters, aunts, cousins, and friends. New mothers quickly take advantage of this available expertise to help them better navigate the early trial-and-error period of parenting. Since new fathers are much less likely to take advantage of (or be granted access to) this torrent of free advice, this is another factor in their wives' quickly taking the lead as the new parenting expert.

The emergence of expert and novice is often at the heart of partners' coparenting challenges. It is simply very hard to feel like co-equal partners in parenting when one partner feels like the parenting expert and the other feels like a parenting novice. There is a well-researched phenomenon known in the literature as "gate-keeping" that often emerges out of this imbalance and serves to perpetuate it. Gate-keeping refers to those times when the person who is seen as the primary parent essentially oversees or manages all contact or interactions between the child and the other parent. For example, when the other parent changes a diaper, the "expert" parent critiques the quality of the work. When the "novice" parent feeds the child, the "expert" sets the standard for what is and isn't acceptable in terms of what, when, and how the child eats. In other words, when one parent is gate-keeping it often looks like that parent is the parenting "manager" and the other parent is a parenting "employee."

This sort of pattern is very common and actually quite difficult to avoid. It's difficult to avoid because of the process I just described where circumstances conspire such that one partner gets much more trial-and-error practice at parenting than the other. This pattern is also very dissatisfying in many ways for both partners. Most commonly partners experience it as a chronic source of frustration. For the partner who is emerging as the "expert", he or she begins to feel exhausted by the demands of parenting, but ends up feeling like he or she simply cannot take a complete break because even when she does she has to make sure that the other parent is "doing it right" (which essentially means doing it the way the expert would do it). The primary parent often ends up feeling like "it's impossible to get good help these days" or just as commonly that her partner is "just like another child in the house." This is obviously not the sort of pattern that lends itself to deep feelings of connection and alliance.

The "employee" for his or her part, often feels belittled, shut out, mistrusted, and frustrated at not being able to develop his or her own sense of expertise and comfort parenting. He or she begins to see the other parent as "the boss" and all the associated resentments of being "bossed around" quickly move into the space between them, gnawing away at their sense of connectedness and intimacy.

Notice, however, the subtle way in which the boss-employee pattern creeps into the mix here. The "boss" has a "helper," but explicitly does NOT have a *partner*. The language of the helper and the helped is exceptionally sticky and once partners are caught up in it, is can be very difficult to shake off. This sort of pattern is a shame because the emerging "expert parent" really wants a partner, not an employee and the "novice parent" wants to feel like a full-fledged co-equal and competent adult parent. The tragedy of gate-keeping, however, is that the gatekeeper does just as much to maintain the pattern as does the other partner. It can be exceptionally difficult to let go of the expert role and genuinely let the other parent learn from his or her own experience of trial-and-error parenting. However, it is only by allowing the other parent to make mistakes and learn from them that the couple can ever develop a sense of *partnership* in parenting.

Equally, it can be very difficult to step out of the "employee" role and begin actively engaging in the trial-and-error learning necessary to develop your own expertise. The errors can sometimes feel awful and it is so tempting to let the live-in expert take over when things get confusing and difficult. Nevertheless, stepping up into that space to actively learn through experience is essential to squeezing the gate-keeping pattern out from between us so that we can reestablish our connection as loving coparents.

COPARENTING TRAP #3: FATHER'S RETREAT

As I've already noted, the gate-keeping pattern is equally frustrating for the emerging "novice parent." He or she gets stuck in a role of implied incompetence that is virtually impossible to get out from under. As one parent takes on the role of expert, the other, usually the father, often simply retreats from his parenting role and into his role as "employee" to a greater or lesser extent. Feeling incompetent and judged poorly by his partner, he finds himself holding back and interacting less and less with his new baby and also interacting less and less with his wife. The center of the family starts to move to revolve around mother and child, leaving the father feeling like he is on the outside looking in.

This process of fathers beginning to move to the sidelines is rarely obvious to partners when it first starts. In fact, it is quite subtle and most partners do not recognize it is happening until it has created such a large rift between them that it is impossible to miss. Even at that point, although it will be obvious to both partners that *something* has gone wrong and that neither of them are feeling well-centered as parents, it is often still unclear exactly what is causing the problem or even exactly what the problem is. The new mom continues to learn more and more about being an effective parent both through trial and error and through the help and advice of other parents. As she becomes more expert, she wants to share what she has learned with her partner. The challenge at this point is that without space for trial-and-error learning, advice doesn't really contribute to learning through experience. The benefit that the primary parent has is that her advisors all (usually) go home and leave her to incorporate that advice into her own trial-and-error learning. The handicap that the "novice" parent has to cope with is that the local expert never goes away and allows him room to incorporate that advice into his own trail-and-error experience.

What happens then is that when things get tricky with the baby, it is simply too tempting for both partners to have him simply turn the baby over to his wife. For example, consider the first time the baby catches a cold and is feeling sick and throwing up. Not knowing exactly what to do, not having a source of good "coaching" advice, and not being at all comfortable simply not knowing exactly what to do and learning through trial and error, both partners come together in a way that drives him to hand the baby off to her and retreat to the sidelines. Once this pattern has set in, it easily gains and maintains its own momentum.

At the same time, the wife as emerging expert often simply moves in to take over during these challenging moments, asserting her place as "expert" and unintentionally squeezing her partner into a role as novice parent and incapable bungler. This happens despite his natural ability to learn to function effectively as a parent, and often despite his desire and intention to do so. Each of these moments of anxious "not knowing" presents another opportunity for her to assert her status as emerging expert and for him to retreat into his status as outsider.

The upside to this role is that the "novice" parent is able to duck a lot of responsibility for childcare. The downside is that it can play havoc with marital health and can leave the "novice" parent feeling chronically judged, incompetent, less influential, and less connected to his or her children. The parent in this role also contributes to maintaining the boss-employee pattern by deferring to the "expert" parent whenever he experiences the "error" side of the trial-and-error learning process. Rather than fully experiencing the error and learning from it how to be a more effective parent, he will reinforce the unfortunate "boss-employee" pattern by simply giving up and letting the other parent take over.

This pattern tends to not only diminish the health and quality of partners' parenting; it also diminishes the quality of their relationship health as well. Particularly for fathers, retreat from parenting is also retreat from his relationship with his wife. When marital satisfaction declines, research has shown that husbands tend to withdraw from parenting as well. When marital health is strong, husbands tend to be more engaged fathers. In other words, parenting and partnering tend to go hand in hand and any pattern that diminishes one diminishes them both.

Leading researchers in the area have begun to recommend that new parents pay particular attention to the probability of slipping into this type of gate-keeping or "employer-employee" pattern and make arrangements to help minimize its likelihood. For example, both parents might consider taking extra time off from work if at all possible during the crucial first few weeks so that they both get started on equal footing as competent parents learning from the same trial-and-error period.

Repairing Father's Retreat

Notice the Pattern

If this pattern has already emerged in your marriage, there is every possibility that you can actively manage it for the better. For example, for many couples, simply knowing the pattern is in place and how it perpetuates itself can help them figure out how to limit the negative effect it has on their relationship. For example, being able to see the pattern and being able to call it by name helps you to orient toward it in a much more productive way. In contrast, when the pattern is in place but you can't see it and don't know what to call it, then it is the pattern that is in the driver's seat rather than you and your partner.

Finding No Fault

It is also helpful to simply acknowledge that this type of pattern can be very sticky and difficult to get back under the control of your partnership. It is clear that in these patterns neither partner is "at fault" and that the pattern essentially moves into your relationship uninvited. Although it is not unusual for partners to blame each other for the unpleasant effects of patterns such as these, it is equally clear that blaming each other will not be even a little bit helpful. It is also helpful to talk to each other about the pattern in a non-blaming and non-defensive way, and to openly acknowledge to each other that this type of deeply set pattern is unlikely to change radically overnight. It will take diligent and loving attention from both partners to begin the process of building in new and healthier habits. Even then, it is likely that bits and pieces of this pattern will continue to show up in your relationship from time to time for quite awhile after you become determined to change it.

Trial-and-Error Learning

Perhaps the most active approach to taking control of this pattern involves both partners dedicating themselves to kick-starting the natural trial-and-error learning process. First, the "expert" parent tries to "make room" for the other parent to try, fail, try again, fail again, try again, and eventually learn his or her own style of effective parenting. This doesn't necessarily mean to abandon all the expertise acquired by the "expert" parent, but it does mean that that parent can take a real break during the time that the other parent is learning by trial and error.

Second, the partner who has found himself in the "novice" or "employee" role can actively seek out opportunities to parent completely on his or her own, without being under the direct supervision of the other parent. In other words, that parent can begin the trail-and-error learning process again by actively seeking out opportunities to try, fail, try again, fail again, try again, and eventually learn his or her own style of effective parenting. Again, that doesn't mean abandoning the benefits of all that the other partner has learned, but it does mean seeking and taking that advice only in service to the on-the-job training of frontline parenting.

COPARENTING TRAP #4: HOSTILE-COMPETITIVE COPARENTING

Another negative pattern that can sometimes emerge between partners is one in which they start to actively oppose each other as parents. This opposition can occur while both parents are present (e.g., "You're being ridiculous. Let him eat wherever he wants"). It can also occur when the other parent isn't around (e.g., "You know how your mother is. Don't even tell her about it."). When parents are actively opposing each other, even people who might otherwise be very good and effective parents can find that opposing each other has made them ineffective. Even more so, when parents begin to hostilely compete with each other, the children suffer.

Yvonne Caldera and Eric Lindsey (2006) from Texas Tech University found that "competitive coparenting was associated with mothers' and fathers' perception of a less secure parent-child attachment relationship," meaning that parents who were more likely to compete with each other as parents, as opposed to cooperate, were also more likely to have children who felt less securely attached to their parents. Or, as the authors put it, "Thus, it appears that parents who vie with each other for their child's attention and work against one another when playing with their child may undermine their child's sense of confidence or security in his or her relationship with each parent." In other words, the children pick up on the inconsistency and competitive conflict between the parents and don't know how to resolve it. Instead, they simply end up feeling confused and anxious.

Melissa Sturge-Apple and Patrick Davies at the University of Rochester and Mark Cummings at the University of Notre Dame in a 2006 study found that when partners become detached from each other because of issues in their marriage, they appeared to simultaneously become more detached from their children. These researchers suggested that it may be important for parents to recognize that hostile arguing and hostile withdrawal from your partner has a measurably negative effect on your ability to be responsive and loving parents. They suggest that if we as parents can attend more conscientiously to active engagement in healthy communication and problem solving, rather than succumbing to the temptation to withdraw when angry, then our parenting is as likely to benefit as our marital health in general.

Finally, James McHale and Jeffrey Rasmussen (1998) found that high parental hostility and competitiveness, low family harmony, and high parenting discrepancies observed while parents played with their 8- to 11-month-old infants were predictive of greater child anxiety and higher child aggression as rated by teachers *three years later*. I think this is a particularly noteworthy study because it shows the long-lasting effects of hostile-competitive parenting and that those effects are easily noticeable by other people, including the child's preschool teachers.

If you are finding that your interactions with your partner around your child are more often than not characterized by tension and jousting between the two of you, then this is a pattern that the research would suggest is important for you to actively address. Later in this chapter I make recommendations for parenting books that can be helpful to read together as partners in the spirit of becoming more collaborative teammates. I also make other suggestions that might help you disengage from this type of destructive pattern.

COPARENTING TRAP #5: COMPETING PARENTING GOALS AND PHILOSOPHIES

It is quite common for partners to have philosophical and stylistic differences when it comes to parenting. For example, one partner might emphasize the importance of preparing children to be independent and competitive, while the other partner might emphasize guiding children toward creativity and compassion. Although these different parenting philosophies can be compatible, it is just as likely that partners can find themselves in opposition to each other because of these differing philosophies.

The research literature on coparenting suggests that it is not uncommon for partners to have quite different parenting philosophies and yet still coparent effectively to their children's benefit. Effectively coparenting around different parenting philosophies appears to be more about how partners talk about their differences, and their style of working toward common ground, than it is about how different their parenting philosophies are.

Conflict and polarization around parenting differences is unfortunately common. What makes these issues particularly susceptible to friction has to do with the depth to which we all learn our approaches to parenting. We all appear to learn our parenting styles through a combination of (a) modeling how our parents parented us, (b) any early practice we may have had caring for others, and (c) our own efforts to deliberately learn and practice specific parenting skills. Because most of our instincts about parenting were learned from our own parents, we tend to internalize those parenting instincts at a "bone-deep" level. That means that our responses as parents are to a large degree automatic. The degree to which we actually parent differently than we ourselves were parented requires conscious and deliberate effort on our part. In other words, we adopt the parenting philosophies of our parents or other influential models, unless we are consciously working to adopt a different philosophy. Because our parenting styles are so deeply embedded, when our partner has a noticeably different style, the contrast can be jarring. It is very easy to see that different style as "wrong" because it so intensely *feels* wrong given our own deeply held perspective. The bottom line is that it is common for partners to have different, and deeply held, parenting styles and that it is almost inevitable that that difference will become a source of recurring friction between partners.

Again, the research suggests that it is how couples approach this common friction point, rather than the existence of the friction point per se, that determines how well they co-parent and thus how well their children benefit from that coparenting. Partners who can nonjudgmentally acknowledge their philosophical and stylistic differences and work collaboratively and actively toward compromise tend to be more satisfied with their coparenting and more effective at it. Partners who are judgmental about their partner's style and who stumble into competing with each other about who is "right" become dissatisfied with their coparenting and co-parent substantially less effectively.

One of the keys to coparenting effectively when you have different parenting philosophies is frequent and open communication about parenting values and goals.

DRAWING ON YOUR STRENGTHS TO CREATE A HEALTHY COPARENTING RELATIONSHIP

Solidarity and Support

What does healthy coparenting look like? How can you tell if your coparenting is healthy? The first sign of healthy coparenting according to my colleague James McHale is a feeling of "solidarity and support" between parents. In other words, when your coparenting is functioning well it should feel like you have a good partner, teammate, and ally when it comes to your shared role as parents. Although we want to be cautious about setting up expectations for perfection, because no genuinely human endeavor is perfect, it is important to emphasize that the more you and your partner feel like genuine allies when it comes to parenting, the healthier everyone is going to be. Healthy coparenting is essential for a healthy marriage and is equally important to the physical and emotional health of the children.

As important as a feeling of solidarity is, feeling like you and your partner actively support each other in your individual efforts as parents is equally important. As much as parenting is a joint activity, it is also an individual activity. Much of the work we do as parents we do on our own, without our partner's immediate involvement. It is important for both partners to feel that their spouse supports their parenting efforts and decisions. When the coparenting system isn't working well, partners often undermine each other's parenting either directly or indirectly. The degree to which you feel like your partner "has your back" as a parent is a fairly accurate gauge for how well you are both functioning as coparents.

BALANCE ACTIVE INVOLVEMENT

The second sign of healthy coparenting is both partners' active and balanced involvement in parenting the children. Again, this may not mean that both parents are involved in exactly the same ways or for equivalent amounts of time. It does mean that both parents are *actively* involved in the down-to-earth processes of parenting. When the coparenting system has begun to break down one of the main symptoms is that one or the other parent will begin to drift away from actively engaging with the children. Research has found that this may be most likely to happen to men when the marital relationship has begun to deteriorate. For many men it is their relationship with their wives that goes hand-in-glove with their relationship with their children. If the marital relationship becomes ill, so will his parenting relationship. This appears to be less common with women in that a deteriorating marital relationship does not necessarily have an immediate impact on how actively involved she is with her children.

What active involvement looks like will be different from parent to parent and from marriage to marriage. It can include all the aspects of caring for children's well-being including feeding, bathing, playing, talking, dressing, providing for, decision making, monitoring, laughing with, telling stories to, correcting and reprimanding, communicating expectations, demonstrating love and affection, taking to the doctor, helping with homework, praising, and all the other variations on the theme. Some parents will do more of one thing than another, but the main point is that both partners have a genuine sense of regular connection with each of their children *as parents*.

LIMIT CONFLICT ABOUT THE CHILDREN

The third sign of healthy coparenting is that there is little child related coparental conflict. In other words, how much you and your partner fight about the children and how you are caring for and raising them is an indicator of how healthy your coparenting is. Signs of health in this area include a sense that more often than not you and your partner are on the same page as parents and that when you aren't on the same page you have a healthy process of accommodating those differences. Do you tend to agree more than disagree about parenting? Do you feel that your basic parenting values are more often similar than different? Do you tend to agree on how to discipline the children? Does it often feel like the children actually create conflict between you? Do you both tend to decide together what the rules are for your children or at least usually agree about what those rules should be? Do you tend to see eye-to-eye more often than not when it comes to things your children want from you like money, gifts, and privileges?

GRACEFUL COORDINATION

The fourth sign of healthy coparenting is a sense of graceful coordination of caring for and raising your children. Does it feel like your coparenting partnership runs as smoothly as can be expected from complicated human beings? Do you and your spouse communicate regularly enough and well enough to effectively coordinate both the big things and the little things that make up the practice of parenting? Does it feel like you both have important roles to play in the care and raising of your children and do you both feel appreciated and supported in those roles? Coparenting is a team sport and graceful coordination counts.

Next, does the division of childcare labor feel fair to both of you? Division of childcare can be a tricky thing. Different couples divide up the responsibilities of childcare in different ways. Some couples adopt a style that is very traditional with one spouse working full-time outside of the home and the other working full-time as the primary caretaker. Other couples try to share all the childcare responsibilities equally. Still others divide up childcare into "domains of expertise" with some responsibilities belonging fairly exclusively to one partner and other responsibilities fairly exclusively to the other partner. Most of the imaginable ways of dividing up the childcare pie have the potential to be perfectly healthy. The key according to the latest research appears to be whether or not that division *feels* fair to both partners. How fair any particular setup feels is probably determined by each partner's expectations and by the quality of their communication about those expectations and about their ongoing needs. There is some sense in the literature that this feeling of fairness has to do with how appreciated and "shown concern" each partner feels with regard to their parenting efforts and how supported they feel in their moments of great failure.

CHAPTER 10

ONGOING COMMUNICATION

All approaches to dividing up childcare responsibilities will require ongoing, open, and active communication in order to assure that regular minor course corrections are always in progress. Again, like the driving analogy. If you both keep your parental hands on the steering wheel through regular communication about your life together as parents then you will be able to easily and smoothly steer through the predictably bumpy obstacle course that is modern parenting. If, however, you are not keeping your hands on the steering wheel; if you are not communicating about parenting and simply crossing your fingers and hoping you get through it okay, then you are virtually guaranteed to have a very bumpy ride.

Healthy parenting also involves *shared* parenting, including allowing room for each parent to have his or her own style and make his or her own mistakes. Each of you will bring your own strengths and weaknesses to parenting your children. Each of you will come to parenting with your own bag of tools as well as your own baggage. Each of you will learn "on the job" slightly different lessons. Because you will each develop your own styles as parents, you will both have to give your partner room to be, to try, to fail, and to learn. At the same time you will have to chat often about your different parenting experiences, allow for those differences to be okay, and to continue coordinating gracefully.

It may be necessary for you and your partner to have regular "management meetings" that help you stay on the same page with regard to your parenting goals and how you both want to handle different parenting challenges. When we *react* to crises, we are less creative and less able to make wise decisions consistent with our parenting values. When we take the time to anticipate parenting issues before they become problems, then we are in a better position to think creatively and to make deliberate value-consistent parenting decisions. Value-consistent parenting decisions are those decisions we make when we have taken the time to consider exactly what it is we are trying to accomplish as parents and why we believe those shared goals and philosophies are important. If we are both clear about our shared parenting philosophy, then when important parenting decisions need to be made, we can make those decision based on our shared values. For example, you might want your children to learn how to make their own decisions and how to defend those decisions against peer pressure. Given that goal, you might provide your children with opportunities to make some of their own decisions on a regular basis and you might be careful to praise those decisions that are different from their peers, and maybe even sometimes different from your own.

Much of coparenting involves our own efforts to parent in ways that are consistent with our most deeply held parenting values and it is very common for these to be at odds with our "knee-jerk" parenting reactions. In other words, we almost all struggle to some extent to cope with some of the ways that we tend to *react* as parents that we know are inconsistent with our values. Coparenting can be a rich resource for helping us to approach parenting mindfully. If both partners are cooperating in terms of a shared parenting approach, then each can be a support to the other's efforts to parent in ways that are consistent with his or her parenting values.

DON'T BACKBURNER YOUR MARRIAGE

The transition to parenthood also involves learning how to take care of our marriage and how to take care of each other as parents, even as we are taking on all the new responsibilities of parenthood. Unfortunately for many of us, learning how to be good caretakers of our marriages in this new parenting context is a task that often falls through the cracks. We fail to recognize that caring for our marriage is the best gift that we can give to our children. We "backburner" our marital health at great risk to the basic foundations of virtually everything else that we care about.

In my practice of couple therapy and in my work conducting Marriage Checkups, I have seen so many couples who have put their marriages on the backburner (in order to focus on taking care of their children and managing the demands of full-time work), that I suspect it may be more the norm than the exception. Many couples end up behaving as though they believe that the marriage should be able to take a certain amount of neglect, should be able to sustain itself on its own merits, and should not need any special attention to survive. They begin treating their marriages like a desert cactus, something that should ideally be able to go for long stretches of time with little to no active nurturing. Even those couples who know they should be taking better and more active care of their marriages tell themselves that they'll focus on each other and on the quality of their marriage when they "get around to it." They hope to be able to count on "found time" to spend together nurturing their love, intimacy, and friendship. The sad truth is, however, that no one ever "finds time" amidst the demands of parenting and work.

As partners and parents we have to make time to spend nurturing and enjoying our marriages. I suspect one of the keys is recognizing that the health of your marriage is the cornerstone of the health of the entire family. Time has to be conscientiously scheduled. A healthy marriage is a living and breathing thing requiring regular attention to be healthy. It is far from indulgent to take the health of our marriages seriously. We need to recognize that the best way to keep our children healthy is to keep our coparenting healthy, to keep ourselves healthy, and to conscientiously and lovingly keep our marriages healthy. In fact, this might be a good time for you to take out your calendar and schedule some time for you and your partner to look forward to spending together. Go ahead. I'll wait.

OPTIONS FOR ADDRESSING COPARENTING ISSUES

If, now that you have taken the coparenting questionnaire and read this chapter, you think this area of your relationship might need a little extra attention, you might consider implementing one of the following options.

Option #1: Consider reading one or two parenting books together as a means of starting an ongoing conversation about collaborative coparenting. The idea is to use the reading-club model to explore in a nonjudgmental way your similarities and differences, as well as to play together with some of the ideas of the parenting experts. Our suggested reading list includes only books from well-established parenting researchers and experts:

- *Charting the Bumpy Road of Coparenthood: Understanding the Challenges of Family Life* by James P. McHale. (Washington, DC, Zero to Three Press, 2007).

- *The Incredible Years: A Troubleshooting Guide for Parents of Children Aged 2–8 Years* by Carolyn Webster-Stratton, (Toronto, Canada: Umbrella Press) and based upon her research. You can check out her website at: http://www.incredibleyears.com/
- *Parenting the Strong-Willed Child (2–6 year olds)* by Rex Forehand and Nicholas Long, (New York, NY, McGraw-Hill, 2002).
- *SOS: Help for Parents* by Lynn Clark, (Berkeley, CA, Parents Press).
- *Parent Management Training* by Alan Kazdin, (New York, NY, Oxford University Press, 2008).
- *The Power of Positive Parenting* by Glenn Latham, (Mumbia, India, P&T Ink, 1999).

Option #2: Consider seeking out a parenting workshop offered by professionals in the field that you can attend together as yet another way of starting an ongoing conversation about collaborative coparenting and to explore in a non-judgmental way your similarities and differences, as well as to play together with some of the ideas of the parenting experts.

Option #3: Consider signing up for a limited number of couples counseling sessions around issues of effective coparenting. The goal here would be similar to the recommendations above in terms of using therapy as a context for starting an ongoing conversation about collaborative coparenting. Sometimes the patterns we get stuck in as couples can be difficult to find our way out of on our own and a good couples therapist can help us to see the forest for the trees.

11

AND THE COURAGE TO CHANGE: PROBLEM SOLVING AND CHANGE

The main point of this chapter will be to help readers assess the quality of their relationship problem solving and how effectively they and their partners' advocate for necessary change. The chapter will discuss the common pitfalls that partners encounter when they push for change and what the literature has begun to suggest are the most effective strategies for pursuing change. For example, theory and research have begun to coalesce around recommending strategies in which problems are presented in ways that are both direct and reassuring to the partner. This work also recommends responding to a partner's complaints with curiosity and generosity, while acknowledging the urge to self-defend. We also include in this chapter exercises and recommendations for practicing healthy problem-solving techniques and for recovering from problem discussions that go awry. Take the following quiz to evaluate whether problem solving in your marriage is seen as a strength or as an area in need of some improvement.

WHY ARE PROBLEM-SOLVING SKILLS IMPORTANT TO MY MARITAL HEALTH?

What is effective problem solving? It is your ability to function as a team to effectively address both individual and shared problems. Big

Table 11.1. Marriage Checkup Problem Solving Questionnaire

Definitely Something We Need to Improve 1	Could Use Some Improvement 2	Neither a Strength nor Area for Improvement 3	Somewhat of a Strength 4	Definitely a Strength 5

_____ 1. When we argue, we try not to hurt each other.
_____ 2. We're good at making up after a fight.
_____ 3. When one of has been hurt, we are good at forgiving each other.
_____ 4. We function as a team to effectively address both individual and shared problems.
_____ 5. We don't slip into problem solving when the other person really needs emotional support.
_____ 6. My partner and I are good at raising issues with each other.
_____ 7. We don't sweep our problems under the rug.
_____ 8. We rarely fall into destructive communication patterns like "pursue-withdraw."
_____ 9. We don't get stuck in unproductive arguments.
_____ 10. Our arguments don't escalate.
_____ 11. We tend to raise issues gently.
_____ 12. My partner and I usually go along with one another's wishes.
_____ 13. Even during disagreements, we tend to validate each other's feelings.
_____ 14. We tend to give each other the benefit of the doubt.
_____ 15. Neither of us withdraws from the other during conflict.
_____ 18. We tend to simply complain rather than criticize.
_____ 19. Even when disagreeing, we communicate respect rather than contempt for each other.
_____ 20. We tend not to be too defensive with each other.
_____ 21. We tend to have many more positive than negative interactions.

and little problems are a normal and expected part of life. In fact, calling them problems is probably not as helpful as calling them puzzles or challenges. I want to convey here that energetically engaging in these puzzles and challenges isn't just an inconvenient part of our lives. In many ways it is the very fabric of our lives and, as such, is one of our richest sources of joy and happiness. This may not be the usual way we think about "life's problems," but it is certainly a way of thinking that is available to us and that is much more conducive to our health and happiness than the pervasive "life will get better when I solve all my problems" story that we usually carry around.

Given that life and love are in many ways "made of" puzzles and challenges, how skillfully we engage those puzzles and challenges determines our capacity for love and happiness. Every domain of our lives that we choose to care about will be made of its own puzzles and challenges. This is as much, if not more, true of marriage and family as it is true of all the other domains of life.

PUZZLE-SOLVING SKILLS AND PROVIDING EMOTIONAL SUPPORT ARE NOT THE SAME

Good research by my colleague Donald Baucom and his collaborators at the University of North Carolina has found that good puzzle solving and emotional support both contribute uniquely to overall marital health. This is an important finding because, partners often confuse times when they are seeking emotional support and times when they are seeking help with puzzle solving. I'm sure you can remember a time when your partner shared a problem with you and you found yourself offering all kinds of well-intentioned suggestions about how to solve the problem, only to have the conversation go rapidly off the rails. This experience of the conversation becoming tense and dissatisfying is almost always a sign that we have mistakenly started puzzle solving in a situation calling instead for emotional support. Thus, one of the first and most important puzzle-solving skills is being able to accurately determine whether a situation brought to us by our partner calls for good emotional support (see the empathic listening section in the communication skills chapter) or good puzzle-solving support.

In truth, good problem solving generally involves both skillful emotional support *and* skillful puzzle solving. Most times when we are struggling with a relationship problem, the struggle is more about being clearly heard and empathized with than about a concrete solution to the problem. It can seem like we are fighting for some resolution to the problem when we are really fighting to be understood and cared about. We want our partners to recognize that we are in pain or maybe that we are just really uncomfortable. When we are in that spot we are looking for empathy and maybe a few words of encouragement.

Unfortunately, it is often easier for us to talk about the problem than to talk about the feelings "the problem" is rooted in. For example, consider Rose and Jeremy. One of their biggest recurring fights was about whether to move or stay in their current house. Jeremy and Rose had both been previously divorced and met each other relatively soon after their respective divorces had been finalized. After they had dated for about a year, Rose moved into Jeremy's house. Unfortunately, this was the same house he had lived in with his ex-wife. At the time it was a matter of convenience for Rose and comfort for Jeremy. Two years after the wedding, however, Rose continued to feel uncomfortable living in the same house Jeremy had shared with his former wife. Although she had hoped she would begin to feel more "at home" in the house, for whatever reason it just wasn't happening for her. For his part, Jeremy could see the light at the end of the mortgage tunnel and had been looking forward to being able to retire and buy a summer home.

Unfortunately, when the issue came up between them, Rose and Jeremy immediately started trying to persuade each other to their own position, trying to "solve the problem" by changing the other person's mind. This was a sticky enough problem for them to begin with, but the fact that they had never taken the time to really understand where the other person was coming from and recognize and validate each other's underlying feelings, had made the problem genuinely irresolvable. Neither of them could budge toward genuine problem solving because neither of them felt understood by the other. Jeremy didn't really know about Rose's "not feeling at home" and Rose for her part didn't really know about Jeremy's hopes and dreams for retirement. Without that more thorough understanding, a route toward effective problem solving just wasn't available to them.

Later we will discuss in more detail how to make sure that you and your partner are skillfully providing each other with both good emotional support and good puzzle-solving support when you team up to grapple with these types of particularly sticky challenges.

GOOD PROBLEM-SOLVING SKILLS ARE ESSENTIAL TO MARITAL HEALTH

Although not all problems lend themselves to concrete solutions, they all must be addressed with courage and a spirit of collaboration. When problems are hidden they create spaces between us that isolate us from each other. Although we may not solve all of our issues—there will always be points of friction between us—if we know how to step forward as partners into those spots that pinch, we will better maintain that connection that sustains our marital health.

More research has been done on couples' problem solving than on any other area of marital research. As a result, there is a great deal of evidence linking how we problem solve with each other to all other areas of our marital, mental, and physical health. Take for example the studies conducted by Dr. Janice Kiecolt-Glaser at the Ohio State University Medical Center showing that highly conflictual problem solving actually weakens our immune system. In these studies Dr. Kiecolt-Glaser uses a standard problem-solving interaction setup in which partners sit across from each other and are asked to work toward some resolution of one of the main areas of disagreement between them.

The innovation of Dr. Kiecolt-Glaser's research has been to add to this standard problem-solving task a procedure for monitoring immune system functioning throughout the course of the couples' interactions. She uses an IV to draw blood at regular intervals throughout the couple's interaction and then later in the lab, analyzes the strength of each partner's cellular immune system functioning at each of those intervals. What she has found is that partners who engage in respectful problem-solving discussions have immune systems that aggressively respond to signs of infection. In contrast, partners who engage in hostile or hostile-withdrawn styles of problem solving have immune systems that respond more weakly to signs of infection. The implication being that these hostile partners are therefore more susceptible to illness, likely stay sick longer, and heal more slowly from the everyday scrapes and bruises of life precisely because of the poor state of their *marital* health.

Dr. Kiecolt-Glaser's research is just one example of the vast amount of research that has repeatedly found strong associations between couples' problem-solving skills and the overall health of their bodies, their marriages, and their children. The bottom line is that something as simple and common as how we speak to each other when we are disagreeing has both immediate and long-lasting effects on every health dimension of our lives and the lives of those we love.

PROBLEM-SOLVING PATTERNS

Professor Andrew Christensen and his colleagues at UCLA have extensively studied couples' problem solving and have argued that destructive problem solving tends to fall into several characteristic patterns. Of those patterns, perhaps the most common is called "pursue-withdraw." A pursue-withdraw pattern is characterized by an approach to problem-solving disagreements in which one partner pursues the issue and the other partner simply withdraws from the whole interaction (e.g., Sheila: "I needed you home to watch the kids so I could make my meeting but you had to stay at work to take care of some "emergency" there instead. I need you to take my obligations seriously." Jose: "Whatever! I can't talk to you when you're so upset"). The pattern escalates because the withdrawal almost literally *pulls* Sheila into pursuing at least some acknowledgement that she has a legitimate issue. In this case, Sheila might begin to demand a response (e.g., "You can't just walk away from me every time I bring this up!"). In response, Jose withdraws even further (e.g., "I'm going out. I can't even be around you when you're like this"). Even if Jose doesn't physically leave, he can still withdraw into himself by refusing to engage the issue with Sheila. This pattern will run its course such that each partner will continue to pursue or withdraw until they have both spent all the time or energy they have available. These types of patterns can be so powerful that they actually seem to drive themselves and simply drag the partners along behind. Both partners exit from this type of pattern feeling awful and isolated from each other. It can even be difficult for partners to figure out how to set things right between them after the fact without falling into the pattern all over again.

We tend to talk about patterns like these as "uninvited guests" that sweep into your lives and wrest control of your marriage away from you. Each partner comes into the marriage susceptible to some of these patterns given his or her own personal history, but it is the interaction of both partners' susceptibilities that ultimately gives life to any particular pattern. In other words, destructive communication patterns are neither partner's individual "fault," but are instead a product of how the partners come together as a couple (much like sodium and chloride coming together to form salt). Although these patterns move into the relationship uninvited by either partner, it is possible for the *couple* to overcome their destructive effects if they can recognize the pattern when it is occurring and deliberately apply more constructive puzzle-solving skills. We will discuss those skills in detail later in this chapter.

There are many other patterns that can invade your relationship. For example, "mutual avoidance" is a pattern in which both partners collude to avoid discussing problematic issues in their relationship. Another is "mutual criticism" in which partners take turns lobbing random criticisms at each other, often wandering far away from the original issue. A third pattern is "criticize-defend" in which one partner criticizes the other (e.g., "I can't believe how selfish you can be") and the other defends without trying to understand (e.g., "I'm not being selfish. I've been busy"). A fourth pattern is "emotional-rational" in which one partner engages the issue at the emotional level and the other partner engages the issue at the rational level. For example, "I can't help feeling jealous when you talk to your ex-wife." "You have no reason to feel that way. You know I would never get back together with her." Another pattern is "escalate-capitulate" in which one partner escalates the conflict and the other partner simply backs down. Escalation can take many forms from simply pushing the issue with more intensity than the other partner can stand, to becoming hostile, threatening, or violent. Capitulation itself can range from a mild feeling of "go along to get along" to an intense feeling of being forced or coerced.

MORE SYMPTOMS OF DYSFUNCTIONAL PROBLEM SOLVING AND THEIR FUNCTIONAL ALTERNATIVES

In addition to the negative patterns discussed above, there are several additional symptoms of unhealthy problem solving that have been discovered by marital researchers. In this section I will introduce you to a few of these processes and also discuss functional alternatives.

Negative Escalation

The first of these destructive processes is negative escalation. Negative escalation simply refers to those arguments in which both partners continue to exchange negative comments with each other until they essentially run out of steam. Complaints are met with complaints, criticisms are met with counter-criticisms, insults with insults, defensiveness with defensiveness, and on and on, with each negative move countered by an equally negative move by the other partner. These cycles appear to gain so much momentum that partners keep at them until they simply cannot continue.

Even more worrisome these cycles can escalate in intensity from 0 to 60 in nothing flat. One minute the couple is arguing about work schedules and the next minute they are threatening divorce. Both partners tend to walk away from these exchanges stunned by how quickly the argument went thermonuclear. Perhaps the worst thing about escalating conflict is that absolutely nothing we say during these fights can ever be unsaid. We escalate to injure the one person in the world that it is actually easiest for us to hurt.

Soft Start-Up

The healthy alternatives to negative escalation are soft start-up and accepting influence. John Gottman of the University of Washington describes soft start-up as the efforts that partners make to be gentle with each other when they bring up a problematic issue. No one is ever thrilled to have her partner come to her with a complaint about her behavior. Yet openness to such complaints is absolutely essential to the long-term health of every marriage. Because receiving complaints is unavoidably emotionally challenging, even the most skillfully delivered are by their very nature difficult to hear. Emotionally skillful partners understand this fact intuitively and therefore use their love and empathy for their partner to raise problematic issues in as gentle a manner as possible. This is a particularly advanced relationship skill in that it requires us to do two things simultaneously. First we have to respect ourselves by courageously bringing up issues that would otherwise fester. Second, we have to respect our partner by being lovingly careful about *how* we bring the issue up. In our own research we have referred to this as the "spoonful of honey" that helps the medicine go down.

Think about some complaint you would like to address with your partner. For example, maybe you've been putting your sexual relationship on the backburner and want to say something about it to your partner. If you wait until you're feeling particularly upset about it to bring it up, odds are you won't complain in a way that is easy to hear. You might say something like, "Why don't you ever make a pass at me anymore? Have you just given up on sex?" or some other accusatory shot to the gut. If, however, you resolve to bring up the issue when you aren't particularly upset about it and with the intention of being gentle with your partner, you might say instead something like, "I've been thinking about how much I enjoy our sexual relationship and thought maybe we could think together a bit about how we might make more room for it in our lives. What do you think?" Again, although there is no perfect way to complain, it is clear from the research that a soft start-up can go a long way toward getting a puzzle-solving discussion off on the right foot.

Accepting Influence

Similarly, "accepting influence" refers to our willingness and ability to accommodate our partner's wants and needs. Whereas escalation essentially works to dismiss or stifle our partner's bids for accommodation, accepting influence allows that a spirit of compromise is more often than not the strongest and healthiest response. This is not simply capitulating and saying "yes, dear" to every demand, reasonable or unreasonable, that our partner makes of us. It is instead conscientiously allowing that our partner's wants and needs are legitimately felt and that more times than not there is room for compromise and accommodation. Accepting influence can involve everything from going with your partner to see her choice of movie to moving to another town to accommodate your partner's career. Accepting influence allows that there will always be some wants and even some needs that are difficult, costly, or simply impossible to accommodate. Those are likely, however, to be relatively rare. Actively loving someone means making room for him or her in your life. In research conducted with my graduate student Amy Meade in my lab, we have found that a greater willingness to accept influence is associated with several dimensions of marital health for both men and women, including greater satisfaction and intimacy.

Most interestingly, we also found that the manner in which we *reject* influence has a substantial additional effect on our marital health. In other words, the most satisfied couples both accepted and rejected influence. However, when healthy couples reject influence, they did so with kindness and compassion. This research suggests that in addition to accepting influence, it is also important for us to be able to reject bids for accommodation as long as we can do so with kindness. For example, you might say, "I know you want me to go with you to visit your sister, but I'm really not up for it right now," as opposed to, "Stop pressuring me, you know I can't stand visiting her."

Invalidation

An invalidating response is one that dismisses our empathic connection with our partner. Given an opportunity for empathic connection, we choose instead to defend ourselves and reject our partners. So, for example, imagine a partner who complains, "Why do you always have to come home so late?" An invalidating response would be one without any hint of empathy for the partner, such as, "I don't *always* come home so late. I have a demanding job. So sue me." A more validating response would include some empathy for the partner, such as, "I *have* been coming home late a lot lately, haven't I? I'm sorry. I know you don't like it. Things are a little out of control at work right now."

Invalidation is often a form of defensiveness. We feel criticized by our partner's complaint and our knee-jerk reaction is to defend ourselves before we even have a chance to hear our partner out. Oftentimes the easiest way to defend ourselves is to simply dismiss our partner's complaints or worries as completely illegitimate. In the above example you might feel like there is nothing you can do about what is going on at work, that you are also stressed out, and that you would like to be able to relax and recuperate with your partner rather than being on the receiving end of a complaint. In response, your reaction is to invalidate your partner, which, unfortunately, makes the whole situation worse.

As I've noted before, we often fail to validate our partners because doing so feels like we're losing, giving in, or somehow agreeing that we're "bad" and have to change to meet our partners' demands. Genuine validation has none of these implications. It is perfectly possible for me to validate your being upset and worried without necessarily agreeing about how best to resolve the issue. I can empathize with you and let you know that I genuinely care, even if it is not entirely clear to me exactly what to do about it.

Withdrawal and Avoidance

Withdrawal and avoidance prevent problem solving. There is simply no way to successfully address an issue by withdrawing from it. Although withdrawal and avoidance may limit conflict in the short run, we always pay the price in the long run. Withdrawal and avoidance are almost always in the service of avoiding conflict and, of course, this makes sense in the short run because conflict is really unpleasant and no one engages in conflict with their spouse because they enjoy it. On the other hand, as I've mentioned before, conflict is not only inevitable, it is actually essential to the long-term health of your marriage. Withdrawal undermines our ability to distinguish resolvable from irresolvable problems and the resolvable problems pile up.

Do you tend to withdraw when certain issues come up in your relationship? Or perhaps you simply do your best to try to avoid those issues altogether. If so, the first healthy step involves simply noticing what you are doing. Notice when you are withdrawing and the thoughts and feelings you are experiencing. Just noticing can provide the perspective that you need to begin moving in the direction of your most deeply held values and commitments. If you can feel yourself beginning to withdraw and also recognize that withdrawing will harm your marriage in the long run, then you can talk yourself into remaining engaged. What is the alternative to withdrawal and avoidance? The simple answer is engagement, simple, honest, trial-and-error engagement.

The metaphor I often use with couples is about when I first learned to ski. I remember quite vividly that my first instinct was to lean backward, which only caused me to completely lose control. Clearly I was convinced that when falling down a mountain on slippery sticks, leaning backward was the only sensible thing to do. In that spot I had to talk myself into doing exactly the opposite of what my instincts were telling me. I had to lean downhill despite the fact that it *felt* like exactly the wrong thing to do. Once I was able to talk myself into it though, I immediately gained greater control over the situation. Then followed the inevitable trial-and-error period in which I continued to fall a lot, but from that first moment of leaning forward I knew that this was the direction of learning how to master this skill. If I had, instead, continued to follow my natural instinct to lean backward, not only would I have never learned how to ski, but I would have almost certainly hurt myself in the process.

Learning how to "lean into" a problem discussion when your instinct is screaming at you to run away is just the same kind of process. If you continue follow your instinct to withdraw or avoid, you lose all control over the situation and you will inevitably cause a great deal of harm. If, however, you can talk yourself into leaning forward in that spot, even though you don't know exactly what to do or say or how to do or say it, you will find that you are retaking control of the long-term health of your marriage and family.

It is important to recognize, however, that this initial "leaning forward" is only the beginning of a trial-and-error period during which you will continue to "fall down" a lot while you continue to master good conflict engagement and puzzle-solving skills. If both you and your partner recognize that you are entering a trial-and-error period and can treat each other gently and give each other the benefit of the doubt and the necessary emotional support, then eventually you will learn how to skillfully keep your marriage healthy and a source of real joy.

PROBLEM-SOLVING SKILLS

The skills for effective problem solving are a tried-and-true part of the marital literature and have been effectively taught for decades to couples at all stages from premarital preparation to full-blown marital therapy. There is good evidence, both clinical and empirical, that these problem-solving skills are effective for couples and their marital health.

One thing to recognize is that not all problems are solvable in the way that we usually think about solutions. For the most part, when we think of solving a problem we imagine a scenario in which once the problem is solved it simply ceases to exist. For example, if the problem is that I would like you to start helping more with the laundry and after we talk about it we start sharing equal responsibility, then the problem is solved in the traditional sense that it simply ceases to be a problem. On the other hand, as we talked about in the chapter on acceptance, some problems simply aren't available for this type of solution and are best thought of as requiring some degree of acceptance. For example, if I am a bit scattered and absent-minded and that drives you around the bend, this is probably not going to be completely solved no matter how skillful we both are at problem solving. We might be able to manage and cope with this natural flaw in the fabric of our marriage, but the true problem solution here will involve a large helping of acceptance on both our parts.

That being said, let's spend some time reviewing the basic ingredients of good problem-solving skills.

Breaking the Problem in Two

The first, and perhaps most important, step in good problem solving involves making a clean break between the two goals of problem solving. *The first goal is to ban all problem solving.* We almost all jump into problem solving much, much too quickly and as a result immediately bog down in a hopeless quagmire. By jumping too quickly into problem solving, we skip past the absolutely essential step of making sure that the problem has been clearly understood from both partners' perspectives. If the two of you haven't clearly heard and understood each other, any attempts at productive problem solving will be completely wasted energy.

Why is this a crucial step? Because more often than not (1) you are not both seeing the nature of the problem eye to eye and thus are trying to solve two (or three or four) different problems simultaneously, and (2) you yourself are probably less than crystal clear about what exactly the problem is. You might clearly know that you are upset and that you have a strong desire for something to change to make you feel better, but the specifics may be unclear or your initial hunch may be imperfect.

Additionally, and perhaps surprisingly, more often than not, the real problem is that you simply don't understand each other well and, as a result, you aren't functioning well as partners. Many couples find that once they have sat down and set out as their goal simply making sure that they both feel empathically understood, they discover that there really is no specific problem to solve. In a very real sense, the problem that needed solving was that they needed to have a good talk.

In those instances when there genuinely is a problem that must be identified and solved, spending the necessary time reaching an empathic understanding of each other insures that you are in a better position to find the best available solution. Two heads are better than one. When you can join together as a team and work cooperatively and productively together as partners, then problem solving really does become puzzle solving and the experience can be much more positive and rewarding.

Look back over the communication chapter and take those recommendations as your starting point for any serious problem solving that you need to do in your relationship. This is particularly true for those spots where you find you have become particularly stuck. Problems that are easily identified and resolved don't really need the structure and conscientiously applied skills described here. The easy stuff isn't really the issue for any of us. It is those puzzles that have proven themselves to be particularly challenging for us where we will find these specific problem-solving skills most useful.

After you and your partner have had a good discussion and you both feel that you have been clearly and empathically heard by the other, then you are in a position to move on the second part of problem solving.

THE STEPS FOR GENERATING GOOD SOLUTIONS

Setting the Agenda

The first step for generating good solutions is generating a good problem. The best type of problem is one that is specific and concrete. The easier it is to get your head around the problem, the easier it is going to be to find a workable solution. The fuzzier the problem, the more it is going to resist your attempts to solve it. You might also find that you need to break a big and complex problem down into simpler pieces and problem solve each of those components one at a time.

For example, maybe the problem involves household chores and one partner's complaint that the division of responsibilities just doesn't feel fair. Following problem discussion and having reached a sense that they understand where each of them is coming from, the couple's next task is to decide which aspect of the puzzle they are going to try to solve first. The entire puzzle of household chores may be too complicated for one problem-solving session, so the couple might decide to first address the main chores that have to be done at the end of the day when they are both tired: cooking, dirty dishes, helping with the kids' homework, and putting the kids to bed. The key here is that both partners agree that this is the part of the greater puzzle that they want to address at this point. If you have difficulty reaching consensus about the agenda, you might want to step back into the problem discussion phase to make sure you've understood each other well enough to find common ground.

Brainstorming

Once the agenda has been set, the next step is brainstorming. The goal of brainstorming is to come up with as many ideas as possible; good, bad, and ugly. The key insight that gives brainstorming its power as a problem-solving skill is that creativity and evaluation should be two completely separate steps. Generating ideas and critiquing ideas at the same time severely hampers your ability to discover the best solution. Brainstorming allows you to think as freely and creatively as possible without the constraints of instant criticism. If you know you'll be able to come back later and really think deeply about all the possible solutions you've generated, then you can feel freer to let loose with all the ideas that cross your mind. The goal here is to generate a long list of possible solutions without worrying at all about how good any of the ideas are. In fact, it is often best if you approach brainstorming with a real sense of humor and try to include as many silly solutions as you can think of as well.

So, for example, given the agenda of "evening chores," the couple might generate the following list.

1. Hire a chef, maid, and nanny.
2. Bob does all the chores while Anne naps.
3. Kids do all the chores while parents nap.
4. Switch to paper plates and plastic spoons.
5. Order out every night.

6. Anne and Bob take turns at each of the chores.
7. Bob cooks, Anne helps with homework, and they both take turns doing dishes and putting the kids to bed.

Consensus

Once you have generated a list with every idea you can think of, then the goal is to go over the list and cross out all the ideas that are just plain silly or clearly unworkable. You both should agree about which ideas to cross off. If either one of you votes to keep an idea on the list, it stays for further discussion.

After you have pared down the list, the task is to discuss each of the remaining ideas and to try to come to some consensus about which ideas you both like the best. When you have narrowed the list to just those ideas that you both agree have some potential, then it is simply a matter of picking one of those ideas to try out first. The thing to keep in mind at this point is that you are going to try out the solution you pick for a period to time and that you will both have a chance to reevaluate how well it is working before finally settling into it.

Reevaluation

The final step is to decide over what period of time you are going to try out the new solution. In this case, the couple decided to try solution #7 for two weeks and then to sit down again and reevaluate how they both felt about it. The key is to be conscientious about holding the reevaluation meeting because these issues can often be emotionally complicated enough to make you reluctant to sit down and talk about it again. If upon reevaluation you both decide that the solution is working well, then you can settle into it for the time being, with the understanding that either partner can bring the issue up again in the future if necessary. This allows for the possibility that circumstances change and a good solution today may not be a good solution a year from now. If, on the other hand, at reevaluation the couple decides that the chosen solution isn't working well, then another problem-solving session can be scheduled and they can take another run at generating a workable solution. Some particularly tricky problems may require more than one attempt at problem solving.

IRRESOLVABLE PROBLEMS: BACK TO ACCEPTANCE

It will always be the case that some problems, no matter how clearly stated, will simply continue to defy easy, concrete solutions. These are the sorts of things in your relationship that aren't so much puzzles to be solved as those natural flaws in the fabric that characterize all relationships. For these sorts of perpetual issues, communication and acceptance appear to provide couples with the greatest health benefits. Suffice it to say that problem-solving skills are essential tools for maintaining the health of your marriage. At the same time, they are only one set of tools and an optimally healthy marriage has many other types of tools at its disposal.

12

ATTACHMENT STYLES: ESTABLISHING A SECURE BASE

BUILDING ATTACHMENT HEALTH AND FITNESS

What Is an Attachment Style?

Your attachment style is the way that you have learned how to act in relation to close others when you are feeling afraid, sad, worried, confused, or in some other way upset or off balance. We learn our attachment styles from our early interactions with caretakers and close others, particularly during times when we are emotionally upset or hurt. Some of us learn that we can count on others to be there for us, and it is therefore relatively easy for us to reach out to others for help and comfort. Others of us learn that it is foolish to count on others to be there when we are upset and we find that we are very reluctant, or even opposed to reaching out for help and comfort. Still others of us learn that it is almost impossible to predict whether others will be there for us when we need them. As a result, we find that we need lots of reassurance from those we are closest to and cling tightly to them to make sure that help and comfort will be there when we need it. Although there are many variations on these three simple themes, the bottom line is that we all learn different lessons about what to do when life has upset our balance. Some of us move toward others, some of us move away, some of us simply keep to ourselves as much as possible, and some of us cling to others as tightly as we can.

Scientists tell us that from the moment we are born we are engaged in the process of seeking attachment with others. As human beings, we are born into the world in an astonishingly vulnerable state. We simply cannot survive without the attentive care of others. Because it is essential to our survival, from birth we begin learning an intricate and challenging dance with those who care for us; a dance involving the myriad forms of call and response involved in needing, seeking, and giving care. At first, we cry and squirm, coo and smile, gaze and snuggle, all as ways of reaching out for the caring attention that sustains and comforts us. In turn, the people who have gathered around us respond to our reach. How our caretakers respond to our reach teaches us what we can expect from those who are closest to us in our times of need.

Our attachment style is a reflection of what we learned as children about whether or not and under what circumstances others could be counted on to come to our aid, to notice and care when we are upset and out-of-sorts. Our attachment style is the way we have learned to interact with significant others at those times in our life when we are feeling out of balance.

The purpose of this chapter is to help you consider the blend of attachment styles that best describe you. My hope is that consideration of your attachment styles may provide you with insight that you can use to the benefit of a healthy and happy marriage. In the next section, I provide a guide for thinking about attachment styles and some suggestions for interpreting that information.

Before going on, however, it is important to note that although attachment styles are often presented in terms of categories, it is best if we think about them as behavioral tendencies or strong habits or patterns. None of us fall squarely into any one category, but instead show blends of more than one pattern or style. It is also important to note that attachment styles can and do change under the right conditions. The questionnaire below is inspired by one of the original measures of adult attachment and is only intended to give you a place to start thinking about your attachment style.

WHAT ARE MY ATTACHMENT STYLES?

Read each of the following paragraphs and rate on the corresponding scale how well you would say the paragraph describes you. You will likely recognize yourself in more than one description and that is to be expected. You are unlikely to fit any description perfectly and your personal style may a combination of more than one. You might want to photocopy these pages so you can complete the questions again at a later time.

Attachment Style #1 (Dismissive Avoidant)

When I am upset (sad, confused, lonely, worried, frustrated, ill, or otherwise out-of-balance), I usually keep it to myself. I believe that I can handle upsetting things best if I handle them myself. Most other people can't really be counted on to be helpful to me and sharing what is upsetting to me with them just isn't worth it. I consider myself the sort of person who can handle just about anything on my own. It makes me uncomfortable when others come to me for comforting. I would rather they dealt with it on their own.

1	2	3	4	5
Not like me	A little like me	Moderately like me	More like me than not	A lot like me

Attachment Style #2 (Fearful Avoidant)

When I am upset, I usually keep it to myself and try not to let other people see that I'm upset. I don't like to burden other people with my problems. I generally like to be seen by others as cheerful, calm, likeable, or helpful. I am often at least a little uncomfortable around others, especially when I'm upset. I tend to pull away from others when I'm upset and prefer to handle what is upsetting me in private.

1	2	3	4	5
Not like me	A little like me	Moderately like me	More like me than not	A lot like me

Attachment Style #3 (Anxious/Ambivalent or Preoccupied)

When I am upset, I usually turn to significant others fairly quickly for comfort and support. It is not always easy for them to comfort me and I tend to need a lot of attention to feel better. I find that it is hard for me to really trust that other people will always be there for me. I tend to need and seek a lot of reassurance. I sometimes worry that I'm not good enough for the significant people in my life. I try pretty hard to get and keep the approval of significant others. I tend to think that the people I'm closest to don't want to be as close to me as I want to be to them. Sometimes it feels like I smother the people I love or cling to them too tightly. I tend to feel fairly anxious about my relationships and think and worry about them a lot. It's not uncommon for me to get mad at someone I'm close to because it feels like they aren't paying enough attention to me.

1	2	3	4	5
Not like me	A little like me	Moderately like me	More like me than not	A lot like me

Attachment Style #4 (Secure)

When I'm upset, it is usually fairly easy for me to lean on others for support, to talk to others about what I'm upset about, or to ask for help. It is fairly easy for me to feel close to other people. It is also fairly easy for others to feel close to me. I don't really mind depending on others. I don't really mind when other people depend on me. I tend to find the people who I'm closest to comforting to me when I'm upset. It's also fairly easy for me to be comforting to the people who I'm closest to when they are upset.

1	2	3	4	5
Not like me	A little like me	Moderately like me	More like me than not	A lot like me

THE ROLE OF ATTACHMENT STYLE IN MARITAL HEALTH: WHAT DO RELATIONSHIP SCIENTISTS KNOW?

Before I describe in more detail each of the styles that you rated, there are several points that I should clarify so that we don't take those labels too seriously, or at least more seriously than they deserve to be taken. First, as I just noted, you should try not to pigeonhole yourself within one and only one style and you should definitely not pigeonhole your partner (people tend not to like it when other people label them).

Something else to keep in mind is that attachment styles can change with time. It is relatively easy to hear descriptions of attachment styles as something we are stuck with. On the one hand, there is good evidence that the attachment styles that we form in childhood can follow us into our adult relationships. On the other hand, it is also the case that a sizeable percentage of people with insecure styles ultimately develop more secure attachment styles as adults. Currently, the conventional wisdom among relationship scientist is that healthy adult relationships help people develop more secure attachment styles. The bottom line is that if you have rated yourself somewhat highly on one or more of the insecure styles, don't worry too much. Not only is it possible to cope effectively with insecure attachment styles, but with time and loving attention, it is also possible to develop a more secure style.

THE MOSTLY SECURE ATTACHMENT STYLE

Attachment style #4 is a description of a secure attachment style. I call it "mostly" secure in the heading because nobody is perfect and I don't want to set perfection up as the goal. Secure attachment styles are formed in childhood when parents are more often than not attentive and responsive to our attachment bids. Again, attachment bids are all those ways that we reach out for care and comfort, including crying, calling, smiling, cooing, reaching, and gazing. Over time, the ways that we make attachment bids change from those of an infant to those of a child, then to those of an adolescent, and finally to those of an adult. Regardless of life stage, however, attachment bids all have in common that they are ways of reaching out for caring and comfort, particularly in times of stress. If our primary attachment figures were attentive and responsive, and tended to respond to our attachment bids in nurturing and soothing ways, then we likely developed a secure attachment style.

So, you might ask yourself the following question. When I was a child and I was scared or sad or lonely or worried or confused or anxious or hurt; for example if I woke from a really bad nightmare or a pet that I loved died or my best friend moved away or I fell and hurt myself, who could I go to for comforting, how comfortable did I feel going to that person, and how did that person usually respond to me in that moment. Try to think of specific and detailed examples of things that happened to you as a child that you can base your answers on. If you only have a general sense and can't think of any specific examples, then note that because we'll talk specifically about that later.

Now, if in response to this question you can think of several times in your childhood when you were upset, hurt, or otherwise out-of-balance and you reached out and were met by your primary caretaker in a warm, nurturing, and soothing way, then your Secure attachment style rating is likely fairly high. These two feelings: (1) that others are dependable, caring, and comforting, and (2) that we ourselves are worthy of caring and comforting and are comfortable seeking such, are the hallmarks of a secure attachment style. Children raised with attentive and responsive caretakers learn that they can trust the world of close others to support them when they are unbalanced by circumstances and as a result they tend to be self-confident, creative, inquisitive, and more assertively independent.

Secure adults are comfortable with intimacy and easily trust intimate others. They are both comfortable seeking comfort and providing comfort when it is asked for. They are not clingy in a relationship because they trust it as solid. Because they have learned that they can trust others to be there for them, secure individuals are both comfortable with emotional closeness and comfortable with their own independence. Just like the secure children they once were, secure adults tend to be curious and confident in their interactions with the world, specifically because they know in their bones that intimate others will be there to support them when they need it.

At the same time, secure individuals tend not to tolerate a lot of relationship dysfunction. Although they are generally tolerant of a partner's expected imperfections, they also know exactly what a healthy attachment relationship looks like and are unlikely to tolerate for long a relationship that has become chronically unhealthy.

THE ANXIOUS-AMBIVALENT (OR PREOCCUPIED) ATTACHMENT STYLE

Attachment style #3 describes an anxious-ambivalent or preoccupied adult attachment style. It is epitomized by a profound sense that relying on close others is tricky business because you can never be certain if they are going to be there for you when you need them. Because the world of close others seems unpredictable, people with an ambivalent attachment style tend to monitor their intimate relationships very closely and can often seem clingy and demanding. They are often anxious about their close relationships and can be difficult to soothe and comfort.

When you think back on those times when you were a child and you felt worried or scared or sad—what I have been calling feeling off balance—what do you remember about how your parents' typically responded? Do you remember having to work fairly hard to get their attention? Did you have to be somewhat demanding in order to get your parents to take care of your needs? When you needed them, did it feel like you could never be quite sure if they would really be there for you?

The experience of the typical anxious-ambivalent child is of parents who were sometimes terrific, who were there and soothing, and wonderful and, on the other hand, who could also be neglectful, out-of-touch, distracted by their own issues, or punitive and overly demanding. They may have been the type of parents who seemed difficult to please, but who were there for you enough to keep you from completely giving up on them. You may also remember being frequently frustrated and angry with them for disappointing you, ignoring you, pushing you away, or otherwise failing to comfort you when you were upset. You may find that now as an adult, you still have a complicated and somewhat emotionally turbulent relationship with them (one or both of them).

It appears that children who grow up with an inconsistently attentive caregiver learn that getting care and attention requires a lot of work. Children naturally want to explore the world they live in and play with all of the interesting things that they see. Fundamentally this is how we learn virtually everything that we need to know as we grow up. However, one of the unavoidable results of that free exploration is that we frequently stumble into things that hurt, scare, frustrate, or upset us and before we can continue exploring we need to be comforted, reassured, and set right. Imagine you are toddling around in your little toddler world and you fall down, or get bit by an ant or pinched by a cousin or scared by the neighbor's dog, so you run to your mother for reassurance and she simply is not "there" enough to be comforting. Maybe she's on the phone or doing laundry or watching TV or depressed or anxious herself and simply can't meet your need for attention and comfort.

So, what do you do? You keep trying. And you keep trying and trying and trying until you finally break through and get her attention. By this time, you are probably much more upset then you were at first and she's probably irritated because of how much you had to escalate to get her attention. The interaction between the two of you is unlikely to be ideal at this point, but despite that, it is better than no attention at all, so you get what you can by way of comfort and then try to get back to the business of being a kid. However, that business is hard to get back to because now you are also upset about the interaction you just had with your parent and you are also unsure whether continuing to curiously explore the world is even worth it, because the next time something goes wrong (which it inevitably will), you may have to go through the whole drama again and somehow it just seems easier to sit down and stay close to home.

Although a dramatization, this scenario captures in general what we believe life looks like for children who become anxiously attached. And notice what you would learn if this type of scenario played out regularly in your life. First, you would learn that getting the caring attention that you need means having to work very hard and having to make multiple, possibly escalating bids in order to get any attention at all. Second, you would learn that for some reason you don't appear to deserve immediate and caring attention from the people you love the most dearly and that you have to be demanding and possibly even irritating just to get a few scraps of attention thrown your way. It may begin to feel like you need others much more than they seem to care about you. Finally, you learn that the world is a scary place. You learn that the natural bumps and bruises (physical and emotional) that necessarily come with actively and curiously exploring the world of things and people are simply too high a price to pay because you can't count on help coming when you need it.

You learn not to be curious, not to be confident, and not to take chances. You learn instead to stay close to home, to keep a close eye on the people you count on for comfort, to cling tightly even when you don't need to. You also learn to put up with a lot of inattentiveness and maybe even punitiveness from your partner, if it means that at least every once and a while you might get some genuine soothing. Finally, and probably at a somewhat less obvious level, you begin to feel resentful that you've had to work so hard your whole life to get the caring attention you need.

What does this attachment style look like when the child grows into an adult and enters an intimate relationship? It appears to be characterized by just that ambivalence between feelings of desperate need for approval and attention and feelings of hurt and anger about never feeling quite full, never feeling like that other person cares as much as you need him or her to. The clinginess comes from feeling that our need for caring and security is rarely satisfied. So the anxious person stays on top of his partner, even when he doesn't really want to, just to guard against the nagging fear that that person will change her mind about him and wander away.

The anger comes from feeling hurt and rejected. We demand more attention, accuse our partners of selfishness and uncaring, and suppress some gnawing resentment about being ignored. Feeling a frustrated need for closeness is necessarily angering, as is any experience of having a cherished goal blocked. The tragedy for those of us who are anxiously attached is that it is difficult for even the best of partners to meet our heightened needs for reassurance and so we experience frustration more often than most.

CHALLENGES FOR THE ANXIOUSLY ATTACHED

The main challenge for the more anxiously attached is to take the type of interpersonal risks that allow us to learn that some partners are more reliable than others. We benefit from practicing standing more independently in the world. The goal is to allow ourselves to learn that we don't have to clutch tightly to a relationship in order for it to remain stable. Ultimately, we are after the adult equivalent of the child's wandering off to independently explore the world while gaining confidence that emotional support will be available to us if and when we need it. If we are willing to explore our worlds with an independent spirit, then we will learn whether or not our current partner will reliably show up for us when needed. We will be less likely to tolerate relationships that are unsupportive and more likely to foster relationships that genuinely meet our legitimate attachment needs.

Genuine intimacy requires that we neither reject our partners nor cling too tightly to them. Genuine intimacy requires that we simply join in being close to each other as whole and unique beings, neither defending against our openness and vulnerability nor seeking to have our partner rescue us from ourselves. The anxiously attached must practice toddling away from their partners to explore the world around them and allow for experience to teach them that more times than not, secure partners will respond to them when they reach out to be rebalanced. In fact, there is some evidence that securely attached partners only provide support when it is explicitly asked for and refrain from providing support otherwise. In other words, secure partners support our independence by allowing us to stand on our own two feet and only reliably step in to steady us when we explicitly reach out to them. It is only by wandering away from base that we are able to learn the base is solid and reliable.

What I mean by wandering or toddling away here is not necessarily literally spending more time away from your partner, although it does include that. It means learning to make decisions for yourself, despite your inclination to check all decisions first with your partner and to concede to your partner's wishes regardless of your own judgment and happiness.

The anxiously attached (and fearfully avoidant) often "go along to get along," readily giving away their own wants and desires in an effort to cling to the relationships. Something as simple as choosing which movie I would like to see can be difficult if somewhere inside I'm afraid that the choice I make has real implication for the stability of my relationship. The anxiously attached are often worried enough about losing their partners that they readily give in to their partners wishes over their own in both big and small ways at the cost of their own individuality and sense of self. In fact, many anxiously attached partners are not sure that they even know their own wants and needs, especially when other people are around.

The anxiously attached may only get a glimpse of their own hopes and dreams when they are alone and not under the influence of anyone else. I may feel like seeing the latest romantic comedy until my partner shows up wanting to see the latest action adventure. Then I'm no longer sure what I want or that what I want is worthwhile, so I just "go along to get along." I may suspect that I really want to be an architect or a nurse, until my partner voices his or her own innocent ideas about going into management or law. Then, again, I find myself unsure of what I really want or doubtful that what I want is worthwhile. I "go along to get along" hoping that at least I'll keep my partner happy, even if I have let myself down in some fundamental way.

USING AN ANXIOUS-AMBIVALENT STYLE TO FOSTER MARITAL HEALTH

So the anxiously attached must learn to listen and respond to their own instinct for trial and error, their own capacity to learn what they like and dislike, and their own power to move with confidence and grace. All this despite their nagging doubts and fears which, believe me, will not just go away. Those doubts and fears will have to be embraced and brought along for the ride. In turn, the partner of the anxiously attached must learn to be sensitive to this struggle and to give his or her partner the room that he or she needs to explore the world independently. We must also be attentive and ready for those moments when our anxious partner needs to be steadied, soothed, and set firmly back on her own two feet.

The key to fostering marital health for the anxiously attached is self-knowledge and self-awareness. The more clearly you recognize your own inclination to cling and demand reassurance, the better you will be at making healthier choices. One of the more helpful things we can do is to talk *about* our relationship patterns rather than simply acting them out. In the case of the more anxiously attached, we might talk to our partner about feeling clingy and demanding rather than simply being clingy and demanding. Sharing our challenges in this way creates an opportunity for genuine connection and understanding that simply being clingy and demanding doesn't do.

If you both know that this is an opportunity for growth in your relationship, then you will find its destructive potential significantly diminished. You will likely find yourself better able to ask for support in clear, unambiguous, and non-demanding ways. You will also likely find yourself better able to support your partner's autonomy in ways that actually strengthen your connection and the overall health of your marriage.

CHAPTER 12

THE FEARFULLY AVOIDANT ATTACHMENT STYLE

Attachment style #2 describes the "fearfully-avoidant" attachment style. Those of us with *fearful* attachment styles crave the affirmation and acceptance of others, but still avoid intimacy to avoid the possibility of being hurt. Thus, we are in the difficult position of both wanting real intimacy and avoiding the risks of being emotionally open to it.

It appears that fearful attachment forms in those families in which a child's bids for nurturance are more likely to result in active rejection rather than either nurturance or simple neglect. Leading attachment researcher Mary Ainsworth and her colleagues (1978) noted that, "a highly rejecting mother frequently feels angry and resentful toward her baby. She may grumble that he interferes unduly with her life, or she may show her rejection by constantly opposing his wishes or by a generally pervasive mood of scolding or irritation (p. 142)." Ainsworth's studies showed that these mothers demonstrated a strong aversion to physical contact with their babies, despite the fact that they tended to hold their babies just as much as other moms (usually taking care of them based more on the mother's schedule than the baby's). As Ainsworth continued to study the mothers of these infants, she noted that such mothers "provide their babies with unpleasant, even painful experiences associated with close bodily contact (p. 151)." Under such circumstances, children learn to avoid and escape from the closeness associated with relationships because they have learned that those relationships are frequently painful and scary.

When you think back on those times as a child that you were feeling off balance, you may remember feeling that you had to keep those feelings to yourself. You may have specific memories of being punished for crying or scolded for being scared or feeling awkward. You may have a sense that you rarely if ever went to either of your parents feeling vulnerable and seeking comforting. You may remember a sense of being scared of your parents, or at least generally uncomfortable around them, especially when you were feeling vulnerable. You might remember having to be fairly careful around one or both of your parents so as not to make them angry, and perhaps a general sense that making them angry was not hard to do.

If these examples fit for you, you likely learned that interpersonal vulnerability is scary; that you have to remain well defended and emotionally removed from others. At the same time, those of us raised in such circumstances still yearn for emotional closeness and comforting. We have simply given up on the hope that such things might really exist. The anxiety and discomfort that comes with emotional closeness may be simply too much to bear. So, when feeling sad, anxious, worried, lonely, or otherwise off balance, we have learned to either simply deny that we even have such feelings, or deny that those feelings are a "big deal." We may feel awkward or ashamed of ourselves when we feel unsettled. We often learn to take care of ourselves without burdening others with our pain. In fact, one of the most frequent things that I hear from partners with more fearful styles is that they don't like to burden other people with their problems.

Adults with a fearful avoidant attachment style are thought to think fairly poorly of themselves. Similar to the anxious style, adults with a fearful style tend to feel that they are "one-down" in a relationship and that perhaps they don't really deserve their partners' attention. Because they likely had to cope with a good deal of punitiveness as children, they are likely to tolerate being treated poorly or regularly rejected in their adult relationships. At the same time, adults with a fearful style tend to idealize others and feel that other people are better than they are, that other people have their lives more together, and the opinions of others are more trustworthy than their own. Unlike the anxiously attached, however, the fearfully attached withdraw in response to stress instead of approaching. They have learned that the world of close others is hurtful and predictably disappointing, so their response to stress is to avoid other people and try their best to cope on their own.

CHALLENGES FOR THE FEARFULLY AVOIDANT

As challenging as developing a more secure style is for the anxiously attached, it is even more challenging for the avoidantly attached. At the very least, the anxiously attached remain actively engaged in interacting with their partners around issues of closeness and intimacy, allowing them the ongoing and readily available opportunity to learn new lessons from those interactions. The avoidantly attached, however, since they are much less likely to reach out in moments of disequilibrium, can easily find themselves living with a perfectly dependable partner and never discover it.

The fearfully avoidant, although we may know that we are missing a sense of intimacy in our lives, are still not entirely comfortable seeking it or staying still for it. Our history has taught us that risking reaching out to others for support is too risky, too likely to lead to humiliation, disappointment, or regret.

The greatest challenge for the fearfully avoidant is taking the risk of actively reaching out for support when it is genuinely needed despite the gnawing fear we will be rebuffed, shamed, or somehow taken advantage of. We simply cannot know if our partner is a reliable source of comfort and support unless we take the risk of leaning on him or her. Of course, it's difficult to contend with the fear that risking and failing will be our ruin. Not wanting to burden others with our problems is a common refrain for the fearfully avoidant and the attendant fear is that if burdened even the tenuous and dissatisfying connection we have with our partners will turn painfully against us.

USING A FEARFULLY AVOIDANT STYLE TO FOSTER MARITAL HEALTH

To foster marital health, those of us who are more fearfully avoidant must develop some insight into our attachment style and use that knowledge to take chances we would otherwise avoid. If we notice that we are inclined to hide our worry or upset from our partners, then we can practice being more open and allowing our partners the opportunity to support us.

As with the anxiously attached, talking about the pattern instead of engaging in it can be a particularly powerful way of promoting healthy connection and attachment. If you can talk to your partner about feeling worried and wanting to keep it to yourself, then your partner learns something true about you. This in itself is practicing secure attachment and genuine intimacy. The key here is taking the chance to lean, to allow others to help us cope. The goal is to take advantage of the opportunity to learn that this relationship might be infinitely more supportive and reliable than the relationships you were raised in.

THE DISMISSIVE AVOIDANT ATTACHMENT STYLE

Attachment style #1 describes a *dismissive*-avoidant attachment style. The main difference between a dismissive-avoidant attachment style and a fearful-avoidant attachment style is that those of us with a more dismissive style *appear* to be less anxious or fearful about the approval of others, and instead seem to regard emotional closeness and emotional support as simply unnecessary and "beside the point."

A more dismissive style develops when children are simply unable to get their attachment needs met by their primary caretakers. Imagine a childhood in which most, if not all of your attempts to get your parents' comforting attention were simply ignored or dismissed. If most of your efforts to reach out for comfort failed, you would most likely learn that reaching out to others is pointless. You might learn that other people are good to have around for other reasons, but not for that reason, not to really pay attention to you when you most need it. Instead, you would learn that feelings of discomfort, unease, unhappiness, dissatisfaction, anxiety, worry, and sadness are best kept to yourself because other people don't really care about you in that way. In fact, you might come to think that other people are sort of useless when it comes to helping with such things, so what would be the point of sharing. At some level, the place inside you that needs comfort and caring simply goes numb. Instead, your world becomes about everything else *but* genuine intimacy. In fact, the words "genuine intimate partnership" may simply ring hollow or seem overly romantic or cloying.

Perhaps the saddest result of learning this type of lesson about life is that one of the most fundamental aspects of who we are as human beings, our need for intimate connection and our capacity to fully enter into genuine relationship with others, is so thoroughly stolen from us that we don't even know it's missing and we deny or denigrate any glimpses we get of open and authentic connection. At the same time, there may be a nagging sense that something vast is missing and we may spend our lives trying to fill that empty spot with other things. Some people fill that spot with anger and bitterness, others with alcohol and drugs, and some with achievement and recognition. But no substitute ever really works. The dismissively avoidant are ground down by loneliness while denying it at every turn.

CHALLENGES FOR THE DISMISSIVELY AVOIDANT

Perhaps the most challenging attachment style is the dismissively avoidant. In contrast to the fearfully avoidant, who tend to still want closeness even though pursuing it feels risky, those of us who are more *dismissively* avoidant tend to reject even the idea of wanting or needing closeness. Because our history has taught us that making bids for connection rarely if ever pays off, we are disinclined to even consider turning toward others for security and support. It is as though the desire to seek and make emotional connections with others has simply been extinguished by lack of attention.

Although they appear on the surface not to care, relationship scientists believe that the dismissively avoidant *do* still yearn for secure emotional relationships. They may not know that a lack of intimacy underlies their sense of "missing something" in their lives. They also may be at a complete loss when it comes to pursuing and fostering genuine intimacy. Nevertheless, the basic need remains.

USING A DISMISSIVE AVOIDANT STYLE TO FOSTER MARITAL HEALTH

The challenge for those of us who are more dismissively avoidant is to begin searching for something that we long ago came to believe simply doesn't exist, like Santa Claus or pots of gold at the end of rainbows. If you are someone with a more dismissively avoidant style, you probably long ago gave up on the seemingly childish belief that other people will be there for you when you need them. It becomes difficult to imagine that others might understand and accept you for who you are, even when you are at your most vulnerable. You stop even hoping that there might be people who can be trusted to make you feel lifted up and cared about when you are feeling out of balance and alone. The road forward for you means learning to ask for support when you need it. It means risking sharing with those you are closest to when you are feeling out of sorts and confused. It means risking being vulnerable and letting other people know you in your vulnerability.

It is probably wise for you and your partner to talk together about your attachment styles. Share with each other your histories of what it was like to seek support when you were a child. Talk to your partner about what it would be like to try to lean on each other for balance every now and again. Because learning to open up can be particularly challenging, this might also be a good time to consider hiring a well-trained couples therapist who can help you navigate the initially awkward stages of trying on a new way of being with each other. The upside is that once you get even a small taste of what it is like to be able to count on your partner's availability, you are likely to continue developing this area of your life despite the challenges involved.

If you scored highly on the dismissively avoidant scale, then reaching out for comfort and support may always be a particularly emotionally challenging aspect of your life. You may find that your first instinct is to avoid even when you know it is not in your best interest or in the best interest of your marriage. Accepting that your first impulse is to pull back may help you gain the perspective you need to "talk yourself into" reaching out. Although you may find that actively establishing and maintaining a secure adult attachment to your partner requires a certain emotional push on your part, you will also experience the benefits of doing so in terms of improved physical, mental, and marital health.

Fostering marital health means knowing that you have a more dismissive style and that working toward developing a more secure attachment in your marriage is essential to being as healthy and resilient as possible. Practicing sharing things about yourself and your life will get the ball rolling in the right direction. By getting more comfortable sharing the little things, you will also be getting more comfortable sharing the bigger things. If you can talk to your partner about the little day-to-day stresses of life, then when something really unsettling happens (and it will), you will already be more comfortable getting the support you need.

As the partner of someone with a more dismissively avoidant style, it is important to pay very close attention when he or she is sharing even the tedium of day-to-day life, and to respond with genuine love and attention. It's a bit like coaxing a very shy child out of a very dark place. If you are conscious that you are trying to gain the confidence of someone whose life has taught them to have confidence in no one, you may soon find that you have a partner who spontaneously wants to connect with you and is willing to rely on you in times of need. You may also find that you have a partner who you can more spontaneously connect with and rely on in your own times of need.

WHAT DO RELATIONSHIP SCIENTISTS KNOW THAT I SHOULD KNOW?

Relationship scientists have been studying attachment for decades. In fact, I believe it is fair to say that attachment has been one of the most intensively studied topics in all of relationship science. Scientists have studied attachment in primates, infants, children, adolescents, and adults. Each of these areas has produced scores of studies and all unite around a common theme. We need each other.

We are by nature interwoven, most obviously with those that we are closest to. The vicissitudes of life regularly throw each of us for a loop and we rely on the loving concern of others to steady and encourage us. Monkeys who are denied their attachment figures simply fail to thrive. They stop growing, they get sick and they are ultimately brutally rejected by their peers. The same holds true for human infants. When we do not have others attending to us in a concerned and responsive way, we cannot thrive.

This is as true for adults as it is for children. Studies have shown that insecure attachment styles in adults are associated with greater difficulties in relationships and in life in general. For example, recent research by Professor Glen Roisman of the University of Illinois has found that less securely attached adults experienced measurably greater degrees of physiological stress when discussing problems with their spouses than more securely attached adults. In other words, even the most basic types of intimate interactions are more painful for the less securely attached.

Our attachment styles affect other areas of our health as well. In a 1997 study, Dr. Kristin Mickelson of Harvard Medical School and her colleagues found evidence that insecure adult attachment styles predispose individuals to a range of disorders, including mood disorders such as depression, anxiety disorders including simple phobias, and even substance abuse disorders like alcoholism.

Relationship scientists have also found that the attachment styles that we develop as children tend to follow us into our adult relationships. Of course this makes sense. How could we fail to bring with us into our adult lives the lessons we learn about the world as children? At the same time, relationship scientists have also found that people who develop insecure attachment styles as children can, and often do, form secure attachment relationships as adults. In other words, our attachment history is not our destiny set in stone. Dr. Joanne Davila of the State University of New York at Stony Brook has found that partners tend to show increasingly stable attachment styles during the early years of marriage. She has also found that marital distress is associated with shifts toward more insecure styles. In other words, our attachment styles can shift in either positive or negative directions depending on the overall quality and trajectory of our marital health.

HOW WILL I KNOW WHEN TO SEEK HELP?

You may need to seek help from a relationship professional if you find that your own efforts are not leading to a greater sense of secure attachment. You may find that you are not entirely sure what style or combination of styles best captures your most common reactions. You may find that you doubt whether secure attachment is either attainable or important. You may find that despite knowing what you should be doing, you simply cannot talk yourself into doing it. You may find that you and your partner are simply out of step with each other and that it is too difficult to get on the same page at the same time. In such cases, it is no shame to seek out a brief stint of couple therapy. You might think of it as hiring a relationship coach, instructor, or trainer to help get you on course and gain the initial momentum you need for a healthy start.

HOW TO FIND A QUALIFIED THERAPIST

If you find yourselves getting stuck in your own efforts to improve the health of your marriage, seeing a qualified couples therapist could be beneficial. If you choose to do this, make sure you are seeing someone who has had specific training in working with couples. The research literature consistently suggests that therapy with someone who has had specific training significantly improves the odds that couples will move back into the maritally satisfied range and maintain those improvements over time. No treatment is guaranteed to work for everyone, but our best evidence suggests that couples that have become stuck in discomforting patterns, but that have not deteriorated to the point of severe distress, have a high likelihood of benefiting greatly from a short course of marital therapy. Too many times couples wait until their marriage has deteriorated beyond repair before they take advantage of the expertise of a trained marital health professional. The research, however, is consistent in finding that couples benefit the most from therapy when they are only experiencing some mild symptoms and before they are suffering from the full-blown marital disease.

How do you begin the search for a qualified marital health professional in your community? We usually recommend that couples either seek recommendation from family, friends, or clergy or conduct brief interviews with two or three different therapists in order to find one that they both feel they can work well with. If using the local yellow pages, look specifically for professionals who state explicitly that they work with couples and family issues. When interviewing these professionals, ask directly about their specific training in couples therapy and whether they consider it one of their specialties. You should look for the following characteristics when trying to choose a therapist: 1) a good couples therapist will not pit partners against one another; 2) a good couples therapist will not take sides, but instead, help each partner understand the other's viewpoint; 3) a good couples therapist is one with whom you can both feel honest and open.

You might also search the following directories for therapists in your area.

- The American Psychological Association: http://locator.apahelpcenter.org/index.cfm
- The American Association of Marriage and Family Therapists: http://www.aamft.org/index_nm.asp
- The Association of Behavioral and Cognitive Therapy: http://www.aabt.org/members/Directory/Find_A_Therapist.cfm

BIBLIOGRAPHY

Ainsworth, M. S., Blehar, M. C., Waters, E., & Wall, S. (1978). *Patterns of attachment: A psychological study of the strange situation.* Oxford, England: Lawrence Erlbaum.

Bishop, S. R., Lau, M., Shapiro, S., Carlson, L., Anderson, N., Carmody, J., et al. (2004). Mindfulness: A proposed operational definition. *Clinical Psychology: Science and Practice, 11*, 230–242.

Brown, K. W., & Ryan, R. M. (2003). The benefits of being present: Mindfulness and its role in psychological well-being. *Journal of Personality and Social Psychology, 84*, 822–848.

Caldera, Y. M., & Lindsey, E. W. (2006). Coparenting, mother-infant interaction, and infant-parent attachment relationships in two-parent families. *Journal of Family Psychology. 20*(2), 275–283.

Carson, J. W., Carson, K. M., Gil, K. M., & Baucom, D. H. (2004). Mindfulness-based relationship enhancement. *Behavior Therapy, 35*, 471–494.

Christensen, A. & Heavey, C. L. (1990). Gender and social structure in the demand/withdraw pattern of marital conflict. *Journal of Personality and Social Psychology, 59*, 73-81.

Clark, L. (2005). *SOS: Help for parents.* Berkeley, CA, Parents Press.

Collins, V. F., & Brown, S. B. (1998). *Couples and money: A couples' guide updated for the new millennium.* Sherman Oaks, CA, Gabriel Publications.

Cordova, J. V. (2001). Acceptance in behavior therapy: Understanding the process of change. *Behavior Analyst. 24*(2), 213–226.

Cordova, J. V., Gee, C. B., & Warren, L. Z. (2005). Emotional skillfulness in marriage: Intimacy as a mediator of the relationship between emotional skillfulness and marital satisfaction. *Journal of Social & Clinical Psychology. 24*(2), 218–235.

Cordova, J. V., Jacobson, N. S., & Christensen, A. (1998). Acceptance versus change interventions in behavioral couple therapy: Impact on couples' in-session communication. *Journal of Marital & Family Therapy. 24*(4), 437–455.

Cordova, J. V., Jacobson, N. S., Gottman, J. M., Rushe, R., & Cox, G. (1993). Negative reciprocity and communication in couples with a violent husband. *Journal of Abnormal Psychology. 102*(4), 559–564.

Cordova, J.V., & Mirgain, S.A. (2004). Problem-Solving Training for Couples (pp. 193–208). In, Chang, E.C, D'Zurilla, T.J., & Sanna, L.J. (Eds), *Social problem solving: Theory, research, and training.* Washington, DC, American Psychological Association.

Cordova, J. V., & Scott, R. L. (2001). Intimacy: A behavioral interpretation. *Behavior Analyst. 24*(1), 75–86.

Cordova, J. V., Scott, R. L., Dorian, M., Mirgain, S., Yaeger, D., & Groot, A. (2005). The Marriage Checkup: An indicated preventive intervention for treatment-avoidant couples at risk for marital deterioration. *Behavior Therapy. 36*(4), 301–309.

Cordova, J. V., Warren, L. Z., & Gee, C. B. (2001). Motivational interviewing as an intervention for at-risk couples. *Journal of Marital & Family Therapy. 27*(3), 315–326.

Davila, J., Karney, B. R., & Bradbury, T. N. (1999). Attachment change processes in the early years of marriage. *Journal of Personality and Social Psychology, 76*, 783–802

Davis, M. H. (1994). *Empathy: A social psychological approach.* Boulder, CO, US: Westview Press.

Doherty, W. J., Erickson, M. F., & LaRossa, R. (2006). An intervention to increase father involvement and skills with infants during the transition to parenthood. *Journal of Family Psychology. 20*(3), 438–447.

Eldridge, K. A., Sevier, M., Jones, J., Atkins, D. C., & Christensen, A. (2007). Demand-withdraw communication in severely distressed, moderately distressed, and nondistressed couples: Rigidity and polarity during relationship and personal problem discussions. *Journal of Family Psychology, 21*, 218–226.

Fincham, F. D. Beach, S.R.H. & Davila, J. (2004). Forgiveness and conflict resolution in marriage. *Journal of Family Psychology, 18*, 72–81.

Forehand, R. & Long, N. (2002). *Parenting the strong-willed child (2–6 year olds).* New York, NY, McGraw-Hill.

Gee, C. B., Scott, R. L., Castellani, A. M., & Cordova, J. V. (2002). Predicting 2-year marital satisfaction from partners' discussion of their marriage checkup. *Journal of Marital & Family Therapy. 28*(4), 399–407.

Gottman, J. M. (1999). *The marriage clinic: A scientifically based marital therapy.* New York, W. W. Norton & Company.

Gottman, J. M. (1993). *What predicts divorce?: The relationship between marital processes and marital outcomes.* New York, Lawrence Erlbaum.

Gottman, J.M., & DeClaire, J. (1998). *Raising an emotionally intelligent child.* New York, Simon & Shuster.

Jacobson, N. S., & Christensen, A. (1998). *Acceptance and change in couple therapy: A therapist's guide to transforming relationships.* New York, W. W. Norton & Company.

Jacobson, N. S., Christensen, A., Prince, S. E., Cordova, J., & Eldridge, K. (2000). Integrative behavioral couple therapy: An acceptance-based, promising new treatment for couple discord. *Journal of Consulting and Clinical Psychology.* *68*(2), 351–355.

Johnson, S. M., Makinen, J. A., & Millikin, J. W. (2001). Attachment injuries in couple relationships: A new perspective on impasses in couples therapy. *Journal of Marital & Family Therapy.* *27*(2), 145–155.

Jordan, J. V., Kaplan, A. G., Miller, J. B., Stiver, I. P., & Surrey, J. L. (1991). *Women's growth in connection: Writings from the Stone Center.* New York, NY, US: Guilford Press.

Kabat-Zinn, J. (1990). *Full Catastrophe Living: Using the wisdom of your body and mind to face stress, pain, and illness.* New York: Dell Publishing.

Kazdin, A. (2008). *Parent Management Training.* New York, NY, Oxford University Press.

Kiecolt-Glaser, J. K., Loving, T. J., Stowell, J. R., Malarkey, W. B., Lemeshow, S., Dickinson, S. L., & Glaser, R. (2005). Hostile marital interactions, proinflammatory cytokine production, and wound healing. *Archives of General Psychiatry.* *62*(12), 1377–1384.

Kiecolt-Glaser, J. K., & Newton, T. L. (2001). Marriage and health: His and hers. *Psychological Bulletin.* *127*(4), 472–503.

Latham, G. (1994). *The power of positive parenting.* Mumbai, India, P & T Ink.

Levenson, R. W., Carstensen, L. L., & Gottman, J. M. (1993). Long-term marriage: Age, gender, and satisfaction. *Psychology and Aging.* *8*(2), 301–313.

Linares, L. O., Montalto, D., Li, M., & Oza, V. S. (2006). A Promising parenting intervention in foster care. *Journal of Consulting and Clinical Psychology.* *74*(1), 32–41.

Mahoney, A., Pargament, K. I., Tarakeshwar, N., & Swank, A. B. (2001). Religion in the home in the 1980s and 1990s: A meta-analytic review and conceptual analysis of links between religion, marriage, and parenting. *Journal of Family Psychology.* *15*(4), 559–596.

Mahoney, A., Pargament, K. I., Jewell, T., Swank, A. B., Scott, E., Emery, E., & Rye, M. (1999). Marriage and the spiritual realm: The role of proximal and distal religious constructs in marital functioning. *Journal of Family Psychology*. *13*(3), 321–338.

Markman, H., Stanley, S., & Blumberg, S. (2001). *Fighting for your marriage: Positive steps for preventing divorce and preserving a lasting love*. New York: Jossey-Bass Inc.

McCarthy, B., & McCarthy, E. (2003). *Rekindling desire: A step-by-step program to help low-sex and no-sex marriages*. New York, NY, US: Brunner-Routledge.

McCarthy, B., & McCarthy, E. (2002). *Sexual awareness: Couple sexuality for the twenty-first century*. New York, NY, Da Capo Press.

McCullough, M. E., Worthington, E. L., Jr., & Rachal, K. C. (1997). Interpersonal forgiving in close relationships. *Journal of Personality and Social Psychology, 73*, 321–336.

McHale, J. (2007). *Charting the bumpy road of coparenthood*. Washington, D.C.: Zero to Three Press.

McHale, J. P., Kazali, C., Rotman, T., Talbot, J., Carleton, M., & Lieberson, R. (2004). The transition to coparenthood: Parents' prebirth expectations and early coparental adjustment at 3 months postpartum. *Development and Psychopathology*. *16*(3), 711–733.

McHale, J. P., Kuersten-Hogan, R., & Rao, N. (2004). Growing Points for Coparenting Theory and Research. *Journal of Adult Development*. *11*(3), 221–234.

McHale, J. P., & Rasmussen, J. L. (1998). Coparental and family group-level dynamics during infancy: Early family precursors of child and family functioning during preschool. *Development and Psychopathology*. *10*(1), 39–59.

Mickelson, K. D., Kessler, R. C., & Shaver, P. R. (1997). Adult attachment in a nationally representative sample. *Journal of Personality and Social Psychology, 73*, 1092–1106.

Miller, J. J., Fletcher, K., & Kabat-Zinn, J. (1995). Three-year follow-up and clinical implications of a mindfulness meditation-based stress reduction intervention in the treatment of anxiety disorders. *General Hospital Psychiatry*. *17*(3), 192–200.

Mirgain, S. A., & Cordova, J. V. (2007). Emotion skills and marital health: The association between observed and self-reported emotion skills, intimacy, and marital satisfaction. *Journal of Social & Clinical Psychology*. *26*(9), 983–1009.

Murray-Swank, N. A., Pargament, K. I., & Mahoney, A. (2005). At the crossroads of sexuality and spirituality: The sanctification of sex by college students. *International Journal for the Psychology of Religion*. *15*(3), 199–219.

Pargament, K. I., & Mahoney, A. (2005). Sacred matters: Sanctification as a vital topic for the psychology of religion. *International Journal for the Psychology of Religion*. *15*(3), 179–198.

Prochaska, J. O., DiClemente, C. C., & Norcross, J. C. (1992). In search of how people change: Applications to addictive behaviors. *American Psychologist*. *47*(9), 1102–1114.

Pybrum, S. (1996). *Money and marriage: Making it work together–a guide to smart money management and harmonious communications*. Exton, PA, Abundance Publishing.

Rich, J. (2003). *The couple's guide to love and money*. New York, NY, New Harbinger.

Robins, C. J., Schmidt, H., & Linehan, M.M. (2004). Dialectical behavior therapy: synthesizing radical acceptance with skillful means (pp. 30–44). In, Hayes, S.C., Follette, V.M.,; Linehan, M.M.(Eds)., *Mindfulness and acceptance: Expanding the cognitive-behavioral tradition*. New York, Guilford Press.

Roisman, G. I., (2007). The psychophysiology of adult attachment relationships: Autonomic reactivity in marital and premarital interactions. *Developmental Psychology, 43*, 39–53.

Rosenzweig, S., Reibel, D. K., Greeson, J. M., Brainard, G. C., & Hojat, M. (2003). Mindfulness-based stress reduction lowers psychological distress in medical students. *Teaching and Learning in Medicine. 15*(2), 88–92.

Saarni, C. (1999). *The development of emotional competence*. New York, The Guilford Press.

Sanford, K. (2006). Communication during marital conflict: When couples alter their appraisal, they change their behavior. *Journal of Family Psychology, 20*, 256–265.

Schilling, E. A., Baucom, D. H., Burnett, C. K., Allen, E. S., & Ragland, L. (2003). Altering the course of marriage: The effect of PREP communication skills acquisition on couples' risk of becoming maritally distressed. *Journal of Family Psychology, 17*, 41–53.

Schnarch, D. (2003). *Resurrecting sex: Solving sexual problems and revolutionizing your relationship*. New York, NY, Harper Press.

Scott, R. L., & Cordova, J. V. (2002). The influence of adult attachment styles on the association between marital adjustment and depressive symptoms. *Journal of Family Psychology. 16*(2), 199–208.

Shapiro, S. L., Schwartz, G. E., & Bonner, G. (1998). Effects of mindfulness-based stress reduction on medical and premedical students. *Journal of Behavioral Medicine. 21*(6), 581–599.

Snyder, D. K., Baucom, D. H., & Coop Gordon, K. (2007). *Getting Past the Affair: A Program to Help You Cope, Heal, and Move On–Together or Apart*. New York, The Guilford Press.

Sturge-Apple, M. L., Davies, P. T., & Cummings, E. M. (2006). Impact of hostility and withdrawal in interparental conflict on parental emotional unavailability and children's adjustment difficulties. *Child Development. 77*(6), 1623–1641.

Teasdale, J. D., Segal, Z. V., Williams, J. M. G., Ridgeway, V. A., Soulsby, J. M., & Lau, M. A. (2000). Prevention of relapse/recurrence in major depression by mindfulness-based cognitive therapy. *Journal of Consulting and Clinical Psychology. 68*(4), 615–623.

Wachs, K. S. & Cordova, J. V. (2007). Mindful relating: Exploring mindfulness and emotion repertoires in intimate relationships. *Journal of Marital and Family Therapy, 33*, 464–481.

Webster-Stratton, C. 1992. *The Incredible Years: A Trouble-Shooting Guide for Parents of Children Ages 3–8 Years.* Toronto, Canada: Umbrella Press.

Weiner-David, M. (2003). *The sex-starved marriage: A couple's guide to boosting their marriage libido.* New York, NY, Simon & Schuster.

INDEX

Acceptance Questionnaire, 94
Accepting Influence, 235–236
Active Listening, 54–58
Ainsworth, Mary, 256
Anger, 33–41, 90–92
Attachment Styles Questionnaire, 247–248

Baucom, Donald, 65, 132, 229
Beach, Steven, 132

Caldera, Yvonne, 2006
Children's health, xi
Christensen, Andrew, 36, 50, 232
Communication, 45–72; Communication Exercise, 69; Communication questionnaire, 47
Compassion: Mutual compassion, 32–33
Coop-Gordon, Kristina, 132
Coparenting Questionnaire, 202
Cummings, Mark, 216

Davila, Joanne, 132, 263
Davis, Mark, 88
Davies, Patrick, 216
Demand-Withdraw Pattern, 49–51
Defensiveness, 12
DiClemente, Carlo, 123
Doherty, William, 209

Eldridge, Kathleen, 51
Emotions: Dimensions, 23; Emotion Skills Questionnaire, *28*; Emotion Coaching, 29–30; Emotional Competence, 30
Empathy, 88

Fincham, Frank, 116
Forgiveness and Repair Questionnaire, 112

Gatekeeping, 210–212
Gottman, John, 17, 29, 39, 67, 141, 192, 234, 192, 234

Hurt, 6–9, 24–25, 30–32

Immune system functioning, x
Intimacy: Definition, 3; Questionnaire, 2; Vulnerability, 4–5; Not knowing, 14–15, 45
Invalidation, 236–237

Jacobson, Neil, 36

Kabat-Zin, John, 82
Kiecolt-Glaser, Janice, 231

Linares, Oriana, 209
Lindsey, Eric, 216
Love, 41–44

Mahoney, Annette, 138, 142, 144–146
Meade, Amy, 235
McCarthy, David and Emily, 174
McCullough, Michael, 114
McHale, James, 205–206, 217, 219
Mental health, x
Mickelson, Kristin, 262
Mindful Relating Questionnaire, 75
Mindfulness Exercises, 76, 78–79, 81, 84, 179
Mindreading, 51–52

Negative Escalation, 234

Paraphrasing, 58–61
Pargament, Kenneth, 145
Parroting, 61
Problem-solving questionnaire, 228
Prochaska, James, 123

Rasmussen, Jeffery, 217
Roisman, Glen, 262
Rosenzweig, Steven, 82

Saarni, Carolyn, 29
Sanford, Keith, 60
Schilling, Elizabeth, 65
Schnarch, David, 174–175, 179
Sexual Intimacy Questionnaire, 150
Shapiro, Shauna, 82
Snyder, Douglas, 132
Soft Startup, 234–234
Stages of Forgiveness, 122–127
The Stone Center, 141
Sturge-Apple, Melissa, 216

Teasdale, John, 82
Therapy; How to find a qualified couple therapist, 263–264

Unforgiveness, 113–114

Validating, 59–60

Wachs, Karen, 88
Weiner-Davis, Michelle, 174
Withdrawal, 10, 34–35, 237–238
Worthington, Everett, 114

ABOUT THE AUTHOR

James V. Córdova is associate professor of psychology and director of clinical training at Clark University. He has been conducting research in the area of couples therapy, intimacy, and the promotion of marital health for over a decade and is a leading figure in the field of couples research and therapy. He is the developer of the Marriage Checkup, a motivational interviewing approach to the promotion of marital health. He is the principal investigator of a National Institutes of Health grant investigating the efficacy of his Marriage Checkup as an intervention for maintaining marital health and preventing marital deterioration. Córdova received his PhD from the University of Washington in Seattle where he studied with leading couples researchers Neil Jacobson and John Gottman.

LaVergne, TN USA
17 March 2010
176387LV00002B/12/P

9 780765 706393